Wrestling Rewritten

Reimagining Professional Wrestling's Greatest Missteps and What-Ifs

BJ Pickard

Copyright © 2021 BJ Pickard

All rights reserved.

Printed in the United States of America

First edition, 2021

ISBN: 9798469704003

DEDICATION

For Isla

My favorite bruiserweight.

And Stella

Her trusty house wolf.

Without you, my life would be infinitely worse. Though I would have finished this book sooner.

CONTENTS

INTRODUCTION: FALLING IN LOVE	1
ONE: THE MONTREAL SCREWJOB	13
TWO: STARRCADE 1997	37
THREE: 173-1	55
FOUR: THE HIGHER POWER	73
FIVE: SURVIVOR SERIES WHODUNIT	97
SIX: THE BIG BANG	109
SEVEN: THE INVASION	133
EIGHT: THE REIGN OF TERROR	167
NINE: THE ALPHA MALE	183
TEN: THE NEW MONDAY NIGHT WARS	205
ELEVEN: NEXUS	225
TWELVE: BEST IN THE WORLD	241
THIRTEEN: FEAR MY NAME	269
FOURTEEN: LET HIM IN	285
FIFTEEN: THE "1" IN "21-1"	311
SIXTEEN: THE PHENOMENAL AEW	323

GLOSSARY

WRESTLING JARGON

"Don't work yourself into a shoot, brother."

* * *

Professional wrestling has a history and language all its own. As such, you may find the brief glossary of industry vernacular below helpful as you read this book.

Angle (n.)
  A fictional storyline.
Babyface (n.)
  A "good guy" wrestler; the protagonist of an angle. Sometimes shortened to "face."
Book (v.)
  To set up a match and/or write an angle. A "booker" is the person tasked with handling such responsibilities.
Bump (n.)
  The act of a wrestler's body hitting the mat.
Brother (n.)
  A generic term for fellow wrestlers; most notably, but not exclusively, used in promos by Hulk Hogan. The term has been utilized to underscore the level of familial intimacy traditionally held in an industry where one's health and safety is regularly entrusted to another.
Bury (v.)
  Refers to the intentional lowering of a wrestler's popularity or status in order to devalue the wrestler. The opposite of "push."
Buyrate (n.)
  The percentage of purchases for a specific pay-per-view relative to the total number of pay-per-views on the market.
Card (n.)
  The lineup of matches at a given event.
Champion's Advantage (n.)
  The rule that – in most circumstances – a championship cannot change hands as a result of a count-out or disqualification. A champion may lose a match by those means, but would (typically) retain their title unless pinned or submitted by the challenger.

Dark Match (n.)
    A non-televised match at a televised event.

Draw (n./v.)
    Someone or something fans are willing to pay money to see.

Feud (n.)
    A series of battles between specific wrestlers or stables; also referred to as a "program."

Finish (n.)
    The planned end of a match.

Finisher (n.)
    A wrestler's signature move that (usually) results in a finish.

Gaga (n./adj.)
    Pro wrestling "filler;" the extraneous, often gimmicky extras in a match.

Gate (n.)
    The sum of money received for ticket sales.

Get Over (v.)
    To become popular, despised, or credible in the eyes of fans.

Gimmick (n.)
    A wrestler's persona or character. In slang, it can also refer to a wrestler's unique personal items or merchandise.

Go Over (v.)
    To win a match.

Heel (n.)
    A "bad guy" wrestler; the antagonist of an angle.

Heat (n.)
    Discernable, often negative, reaction or crowd response.

Hotshot (v.)
    When a booker rushes an angle or feud for the sake of a short-term ratings boost or pop.

House Show (n.)
    A non-televised event.

Jobber (n.)
    A wrestler whose "job" is to lose. This terminology has become viewed as somewhat derogatory in recent years; the more socially accepted phrasing for such performers is "enhancement talent."

Kayfabe (n.)
    The presentation of fiction as if it were authentic. To "break kayfabe" would be akin to "breaking character" in acting. The origin of the word likely stems from professional wrestling's traveling carnival roots and was possibly derived from a Pig Latin scrambling of "fake" or "be fake."

Main Event (n.)
    The final and most consequential match on the card.

Mark (n.)
A fan unaware of or willfully ignoring the illegitimacy of professional wrestling as a competitive sport. A "smark" or "smart mark" is one who acknowledges pro wrestling's predetermined nature but speaks from a second-hand perspective, rather than experience from within the industry itself.

Overbook (v.)
The act of packing an overwhelming amount of nonessential variables into a match.

Pop (n./v.)
A sudden and significant crowd response.

Push (v.)
When a booker invests a series of wins and/or segments in a wrestler over a period of time. The opposite of "bury."

Sell (v.)
Reacting to a move or language as if it were authentic.

Shoot (n.)
Anything said or done that is real, authentic, or genuine.

Spot (n.)
A preplanned move.

Squash (n.)
A typically brief and one-sided match.

Stable (n.)
A group, alliance, or faction of wrestlers within a given company.

Structure (n.)
The formula for a standard pro wrestling match includes four primary elements: Shine, Heat, Comeback, and Finish. The babyface endears themselves to the crowd (shine); the heel does something dastardly to make the crowd feel sympathy for the babyface (heat); the babyface recovers and regains control (comeback); the match climaxes and concludes (finish).

Tag Team (n.)
Two wrestlers teaming together.

TitanTron (n.)
The video screen above the entrance ramp, named for the combination of "JumboTron" and "Titan Sports." The former was technology branded by Sony in the mid-1980s for arenas and stadiums. The latter served as the World Wrestling Federation's parent company in the 1990s.

Turn (v.)
When a wrestler switches from face-to-heel or vice versa. A "double-turn" is the rare circumstance when a babyface and heel switch roles during an angle or match.

Work (n.)
　　An event booked to happen. A "worker" is a synonym for "wrestler."

Worked-Shoot (n.)
　　A scripted segment that exposes elements of reality within a work in order to make audience believe the act is a shoot.

Workrate (n.)
　　An analysis of the moves and craftsmanship utilized in developing a wrestling match.

I

INTRODUCTION

FALLING IN LOVE

I'll never forget the night I first fell in love. The date was Monday, April 20, 1998. And, with all due respect to my wife, I was ten years old and the love I fell for was professional wrestling.

It happened – as these things often do – by accident. My best friend at the time had asked me to tape[1] that night's episode of *WCW Monday Nitro* for him, since he was going to be watching *WWF Monday Night Raw*. I was happy to help, even though I didn't quite understand his predicament at the time. But at 7:00 p.m. Central Time, I turned the television on to TNT,[2] threw a blank tape in the VCR,[3] hit record… and never left the room.

I don't know what other things ten-year-old me was planning to accomplish during that three-hour time period when the VCR was working its technological voodoo. In my defense, it was like a quarter-century ago and, again, I was ten. What I do know is that my

---

[1] As I will someday explain to my daughter, the verb "tape" in this instance meant "to record" and derived from the noun "videotape", which was a thing wrestling fans (and normal people, but mostly wrestling fans) used to trade in the 1990s.

[2] Channel 31 on our cable package at the time. The USA Network was Channel 32. This is important information.

[3] As I will someday explain to my daughter, the acronym "VCR" stood for "videocassette recorder" and referred to a magical device that recorded live television onto a physical cassette tape for on-demand replay at home. It was groundbreaking technology.

Monday nights would never, ever be the same.

How could they be? If I had not yet been sold by the very aggressive monologues provided by "Hollywood" Hulk Hogan and "Macho Man" Randy Savage, or the fast-paced, high-flying action in a match featuring Chris Jericho and Juventud Guerrera, it was over when a dude named Bill Goldberg physically ran through about five men, one after another, to win the WCW United States championship in less than five minutes. When he connected on his signature "Spear" maneuver, driving his shoulder into the abdomen of the defending champion, Raven, the crowd lost its collective mind. So did I. This was like nothing I'd ever seen before.

An hour or so later, Hogan defeated Savage to win the WCW World title in a match that I can comfortably conclude now was – as Michael Cole might say – "vintage" WCW. And by that I mean it was just *chaos*. The referee got knocked out. A bearded man known as "The Disciple" interfered on Hogan's behalf. A giant fellow named Kevin Nash came out to attack Hogan. A much smaller gentleman named Eric Bischoff started kicking Nash (which did not go well for Bischoff). Nash powerbombed Hogan and put Savage on top for the pinfall attempt, but before the referee could wake up, a new guy by the name of Bret Hart ran down to the ring and hit Nash with the championship belt before putting Hogan on top of Savage. Then one last guy, "Rowdy" Roddy Piper, came out to get in Hart's face and got dropped with a right fist. And with that, the show just... ended!

Long before I was introduced to terms like "heels" or "faces" or "overbooking," all I knew was that this – whatever *this* was – needed to be in my life.

When I went to school the next day at Immaculate Conception Elementary, I wrote about the main event I had just witnessed for Sister Marjorie's creative writing assignment. I don't believe the essay was well-received, but that didn't matter much to me. I was more interested to know what in the world my buddy could have possibly been watching *instead* of what I had just experienced. To learn there was *another* show – just like this one – on at the same time, on the same night ... well, let's just say that glorious piece of audio/visual equipment mastery we used to call a VCR got a whole lot of work at Stately Pickard Manor in the late 1990s.

Even from the beginning, I'm pretty sure I was always aware that what I was watching wasn't "real." I have a very distinct memory of staying up late with my dad a few months later in July and watching Goldberg defeat Hogan to win the WCW World championship on *Nitro*. I vividly remember saying, out loud, to my father, "They're not going to put the championship on him tonight, they have to wait till the pay-per-view. They won't give this match away for free!" Spoiler alert: they did. And we'll get there. But, again, *I was ten*.

But I also knew what I was watching wasn't "fake," either. Fiction, yes, but not "fake." If you're reading this book, there's a good chance you probably also don't use the "f-word" ("fake") to describe professional wrestling. I often concede that my favorite form of entertainment is choreographed violence with a predetermined outcome in a controlled environment. Which is admittedly a mouthful, but never the f-word.

Unless the f-word you're referring to is "fun," in which case pro wrestling is almost always that. When WWF and WCW exploded on cable in the late 1990s, smaller independent promotions started to pop up around the country to capitalize on the boom, including in my hometown of Eau Claire, Wis., where "Pillars of Power" Jim Gagnon launched All American Wrestling (AAW)[4] in 1998.

I have the great privilege of saying that AAW treated me to my first live wrestling event. You know the face Michael Scott makes in

---

[4] This AAW is not to be confused with the Chicago-based AAW, founded in 2004.

Season 3, Episode 7 of *The Office*? The "Branch Closing" episode? You know what I'm talking about. Yeah, it was like that. And yet, there was something incredibly endearing about this low-budget, civic center version of the sports entertainment phenomenon.

I can't put together the whole match card from memory anymore, but I do definitely recall there was a Hannibal. Also a Mannibal. And a Darkchild. And a Mad Wolverine. But I must confess the pièce de résistance was Mike "The Bull" Gueke, a 5-foot-10, 306-pound villain who would incapacitate his opponents with the help of a jockstrap he called "Mr. Jocko." Any resemblance to WWF superstar Mick Foley's slightly more successful sweat sock gimmick named "Mr. Socko" was purely coincidental, I'm sure.

Regardless, it was fascinating to subsequently discover that this jock-weaponizing deviant known as Mike "The Bull" had actually gone to high school with my mom. I had so many questions. I still do.

That wasn't the only brush with greatness my parents failed to disclose to me, though. George "Scrap Iron" Gadaski was an occasional school bus driver during my father's time as a youth in Amery, Wis. If you're not familiar with old "Scrap Iron," he wrestled for Verne Gagne's Minneapolis-based American Wrestling Association (AWA) in the 1960s and 70s, where he shared the ring with the royalty of wrestling's Golden Era. We're talking Harley Race, Larry "The Axe" Hennig, Killer Kowalski, Angelo Poffo, Red Bastien, "Cowboy" Bill Watts, "Mad Dog" Vachon, The Crusher, Dusty Rhodes, Nick Bockwinkel, Ray Stevens, Bobby Heenan, Pat Patterson – even Dennis "I'm Not Booked" Stamp![5] And, God bless him, Scrap Iron lost to every last one of them. My dad claims he saw Gadaski win once in a match at Amery High School, though the

---

[5] In the age of memes, Dennis Stamp has achieved immortality as a result of his repeated response of "I'm not booked," to explain why he would not attend one of Terry Funk's many retirement matches in the 1999 documentary *Beyond the Mat*.

internet has no memory of this.

But that was his job. (Scrap Iron's, not my dad's. Pronouns, pal.) He was there to make the other guy look like a star, no matter if his opponent already was one – like when he twice did the honors for then-eighteen-year veteran Killer Kowalski on AWA TV in 1966 – or if the man across the ring was having the very first match of his career, as was the case on December 10, 1972 in Rice Lake, Wis. when Gadaski carried a young man going by the name "Ric Flair" to a ten-minute draw. Nearly fifty years later, Flair was still showing up on *Monday Night Raw* and Gadaski became the answer to a pretty cool trivia question. The lesson of this aside is to say hello to your bus driver. You never know who they might have put over.

As I got older, most of my friends who watched when we were kids moved on from pro wrestling. I never did. I got busier with sports and girls – yes, many (not all, but many) pro wrestling fans do occasionally speak to women… several are even women themselves – but pro wrestling was always there. And whenever the circus came close to town, I tried to go. I took a road trip in college to see The Brothers of Destruction reunite on *WWE Smackdown!* in Des Moines, Iowa. I drove to Chicago to watch Sting win the Ten Pounds of Gold from Samoa Joe at *TNA Bound For Glory*. I even enjoyed multiple trips to non-televised Ring of Honor events at the Hopkins Community Center in the shadows of the Twin Cities, if for no other reason than to throw streamers into the ring.

Wrestling is just special. As comedian John Oliver (accurately) pointed out on a 2019 episode of HBO's *Last Week Tonight*, "Wrestling is better than the things you like." Whether people want to admit it or not, it's even woven into the fabric of our very being at this point. The New York Times actually published an editorial in 2016 entitled "Is Everything Wrestling?" to which the answer is both 'yes' and 'not nearly enough' because until everyone hears their music play when they enter a room, our work is not done.

Think about it, though. Sports? Obviously wrestling — entrances, introductions, celebrations: all wrestling. Back in my Arena Football days — which was basically pro wrestling unto itself — AFL super fan and current AEW super heavyweight Lance Archer tried to convince me that the competitive sports world could use more championship belts. I'm inclined to believe him. It's not like I'm going to disagree with a guy who calls himself the "Murderhawk Monster," though. In actuality, Archer was one of the first wrestlers I ever spoke with and he has continued to be nothing but awesome to me, further proving the long-held theory that those portraying bad guys in the ring are most often the best guys outside of it.

Reality television? Please. Wrestling was the original reality TV. And just about the only reality television program we haven't seen yet is a real-life Royal Rumble. Possibly at sea. I'm still working out the details.

Politics? Bro. American politics have very clearly been pro wrestling for some time — let's not even get into the fact that there was a WWE Hall of Famer in the White House for four years. The biggest problem with the politics-to-pro wrestling comparison is that we haven't quite transitioned from build to pay-off yet.

Consider this: when diplomacy fails in wrestling, we solve it with a steel cage match because it's the feud-ender.

When property is disputed in wrestling, we've got a solution there, too, and it's called a ladder match. The first one to the top gets all legal claims to the South China Sea. Something to look into, maybe.

I just think global conflict resolution might be better served to reevaluate the efficacy of one-on-one grudge matches. Powerbombs are better than nuclear bombs, folks. Every U.N. member will tell you that. And if all the pontification and posturing in Congress led to a Mitch McConnell versus Nancy Pelosi match, the numbers do not lie — put it on pay-per-view and we'd fix the national deficit in a day.

Of course, as evolved, rational people capable of critical thought, we know that violence doesn't solve anything.[6] *Choreographed* violence, though. That's the stuff. Because professional wrestling isn't about violence at all. It's about emotion. And a well-told wrestling story will take that emotion and manipulate it into money. Evil will evade justice over and over again until finally you are so fed up that you will fork over your hard-earned dollar bills to see the bad guy get what's coming to him.

At its best, professional wrestling is Shakespeare in spandex. I've often wondered how two sets of audiences could walk out of the Gershwin and Madison Square Garden at the same time, having both experienced drama and captivation in a state of suspended reality, but only one audience ever has to justify what they had just spent their time and money on. I know professional wrestling isn't really a full-fledged sport, though it is athletic and there is competition – albeit more behind the scenes than in front of the camera – but I would contend it is certainly an art form. And if you look beyond the pyro and baby oil, pro wrestling is just an overdramatized morality play told through the lens of physicality. I'll be the first to admit when pro wrestling is bad, there might not be anything worse. But when it's done right? Brother, there ain't nothing better.

Of course, there are a whole lot of those times when wrestling misses the mark. Which brings me to why I wrote this book. See, I find the most interesting question throughout wrestling history – or any history, for that matter – to be "what if?" That fascinating and frustrating conditional clause is inherent to what's known as "counterfactual history," or what former British Prime Minister Winston Churchill called "the terrible ifs" – those decisions that, if

---

[6] This claim is disputed by the victors of every war ever.

altered only slightly, might change the course of human history as we know it.

Counterfactual history and its natural successor, alternate history,[7] often explore relatively far-reaching "what if" questions as, "What if the Axis Powers won World War II?" or "What if John F. Kennedy had not been assassinated?"

The history of professional wrestling also has its share of counterfactual conundrums, though admittedly few of them lead to a level of dystopia quite on par with *The Man in the High Castle* or *11/22/63*. Still, wrestling fan forums are filled with discussion and debate about "what if Wrestler X had won the title?" or "what if Wrestler Y was still around?"

Of course, it would be impossible to establish, let alone answer, an exhaustive list of hypothetical questions surrounding seminal events in professional wrestling. Who has the time?! So to narrow our scope just a bit, here's a brief list of reasons why a question may not have made the cut for this book:

1. **The answer is too short.** Example: "What if Hogan wasn't the third man?" Answer: It wouldn't have worked. Actually, I guess we just did address that one. Good work, team!

2. **The answer exceeds the timeline of my fanhood.** Example: "What if Vince McMahon went to prison in 1994?"[8] Answer: These what-ifs are harder for me to address because I can't come at the question from the viewpoint of personal reflection. I can only base those

---

[7] Counterfactual history examines different possible outcomes of a historical event, while alternate history is the literary genre that presents a different historical outcome as if it had actually occurred.

[8] McMahon was indicted by a federal court for conspiracy to distribute steroids in 1993. He was acquitted by a jury the following summer.

answers on research and second-hand opinions, which would be fine, but not the book I wanted to write. I don't know what would have happened if Vince McMahon had gone to prison. Maybe Ted Turner would have bought the WWF. Maybe Linda McMahon would have never entered into politics. Maybe the world would have learned Jerry Jarrett's chicken salad recipe much, much sooner. Maybe nothing much would change at all. The possibilities are endless.

3. **The answer is subject to the societal climate of the era.** Example: "What if the 'Women's Revolution' would have come sooner?" Answer: Women's wrestling would be even healthier and more vibrant than it is today. It's no secret that the professional wrestling world has never been particularly star-spangled awesome for women. From being marginalized to over-sexualized, the days when female performers stood on equal footing as their male counterparts have historically been few and far between. But in whatever defense may be due to pro wrestling, the industry largely holds up a mirror to society. When equity and equality in gender, race, or orientation have come to the forefront in real life, pro wrestling has reflected that. Lingerie matches and pillow fights were routine for women's wrestlers in the 1990s and early 2000s because the pro wrestling fanbase cheered for them. Even when the product shifted to a TV-PG rating in 2008, WWE still maintained the edict that women shouldn't fight like men, and the marketplace didn't disagree. When society finally began to evolve beyond that philosophy, WWE listened. After just thirty seconds were allotted to the lone women's match on a three-hour episode of *Monday Night Raw* in 2015, internet fans launched the #GiveDivasAChance movement, which sparked massive – and relatively immediate – changes in how women's wrestling was

perceived by industry leaders and fans. As soon as society decided that women's wrestling needed to become a consistent priority, women's wrestling became a consistent draw. There's a pretty powerful lesson in that.

4. **The question disregards necessary developmental time in a given wrestler's career.** Example: "What if TNA had treated Kazuchika Okada like a star in 2011?" Answer: TNA likely would have had a better relationship with New Japan Pro Wrestling; however, Kazuchika Okada *wasn't* a star when he was in TNA.[9] In fact, it was Okada's experience in TNA that led to the creation of his "Rainmaker" gimmick and launched him to the top of the pro wrestling world. The Okada of 2011 was not the Okada of 2017 – a common hindsight error fans make when evaluating past talent rosters. Shawn Michaels wasn't "The Heartbreak Kid" in AWA; "Mean" Mark Callous wasn't The Undertaker in WCW; Generation Me weren't The Young Bucks in TNA; and Kenny Omega wasn't "The Cleaner" in WWE developmental. Not just in wrestling, but in life, it takes time for all of us to find our voice, so it's a little unfair to play the "what if" game in situations where talents were not yet ready to become the characters and performers they eventually became.

5. **The answer requires so many concessions that it pains me to think about.** Example: "What if Hogan versus Warrior II had been good?" Answer: I can't even wrap my brain around the circumstances necessary for this to have occurred.

---

[9] The portrayal of NJPW's future franchise player as a *Green Hornet* knockoff in TNA was reportedly a key factor in New Japan's disinterest in continuing business relations with TNA.

6. **The answer depends on matters of fate as opposed to creative decisions.** Example: "What if Wrestler X hadn't died?" Answer: The most heartbreaking examples of "what might have been" are also the ones we are least capable of answering because of the incredibly far-reaching ripple effects of an altered fate. I will say I would have loved to see Eddie Guerrero take on Shawn Michaels at *WrestleMania XXII*, or watched Owen Hart and Brodie Lee go on the world championship runs they deserved. I wonder if Brian Pillman might have joined Steve Austin and The Rock as the *three* biggest stars of the Attitude Era. Or how a healthy Paige might have altered the landscape of women's wrestling for years to come. In an industry where untimely deaths and career-altering injuries are unfortunately all too familiar, there is no shortage of fan fiction to be written on this topic alone. The "what ifs" in this book will focus (generally) on creative decisions as opposed to fate – though I will concede there are circumstances where one influences the other and vice versa.

For the questions that are answered in this book, we'll try to evaluate them based on what really happened, what could have happened, and what might have happened next. I am a firm believer that one should not complain about a problem without being able to offer a solution, so we need to address not just the mistakes, but how to correct them as well. Each incident is also unique unto itself, meaning the alternate timeline we go down in Chapter One has no bearing on the following chapters, and so on and so forth. The timeline effectively resets to reality at the end of each chapter. That's how time travel works, right?

Above all else, I hope this book conveys how much I love professional wrestling, and the people who have made it possible. Pro wrestling fans take this stuff seriously – maybe too seriously – because that's what you do when you love something. My intention in writing a book such as this is not to mock or "bury" anyone in the industry. In fairness to all creative staffs, writing for wrestling isn't easy and I'm no expert either; my booking experience prior to this venture was limited to childhood backyard wrestling.[10] This is simply a passion project focused on an art form I've loved since I was ten years old.

As Chris Jericho might say about some of the events in the chapters ahead, "it was a stupid idea from bad creative." For others, the phrase, "Plans change, pal," may be the best explanation. Then again, for a handful, there was never really a plan at all. And for a few, money or circumstances just got in the way of what would have been a better story. Whatever the case, the events, decisions, and characters detailed in the pages that follow were all pivotal in some way to creating the wrestling world we see before us today. Which means with a win here or a different guy there, we could have been looking at a vastly different landscape.

I hope you find the contents of this book informative, entertaining, and worthy of your time. And, who knows, maybe by the end you might even see pro wrestling a little more like I do: kind of silly, often illogical, even occasionally embarrassing… but when written well, absolutely beautiful, too. So, without further ado, ring the bell!

-BJ Pickard

---

[10] Our promotion was known as "IGWA." While WWE was offering its "In Your House pay-per-views, IGWA staged much more specific "In Your Basement" special events. This is a true story. Though the original meaning behind the acronym has sadly been lost to history, to those who lived it, "It's Great Wrestling, Always."

ONE

THE MONTREAL SCREWJOB

"Pick up the damn belt and get the hell out of here."

November 9, 1997
Moison Centre ● Montreal, Quebec, Canada
WWF Survivor Series

Shawn Michaels defeated Bret Hart (c) by submission for the WWF Championship (12:19).

* WHAT REALLY HAPPENED *

The single most significant event of professional wrestling's modern era occurred on Sunday, November 9, 1997 in Montreal, Quebec, Canada. The Moison Centre played host to the World Wrestling Federation's annual *Survivor Series* pay-per-view that night, which was headlined by WWF heavyweight champion Bret "Hitman" Hart defending his title against "The Heartbreak Kid" Shawn Michaels. What transpired at the end of the match would change the course of pro wrestling forever.

Before we get there, though, let's bring everybody up to speed on how we got to Montreal.

Bret Hart was Canadian wrestling royalty. Son of the legendary Stu Hart, Bret came to the WWF by way of his father's Stampede Wrestling promotion in 1984 and he had been a mainstay in the company ever since. The "Excellence of Execution" was a five-time WWF champion, two-time Intercontinental champion, two-time World Tag Team champion, two-time King of the Ring tournament winner, and was the co-winner of the 1994 Royal Rumble match.

Vince McMahon – owner and chairman of the WWF – built his wrestling empire on showmanship and larger-than-life characters. The WWF locker room in the 1990s included a number of men to whom wrestling provided – in kayfabe, of course – a secondary income. Such gimmicks included a garbage man, a tax collector, a prison guard, a plumber, and an undertaker. Some were more successful than others. And yet, in McMahon's world – or "Universe" to use his preferred branding – of giants, monsters, and blue-collar workers side-hustling as grapplers, Hart stood out for his work *in* the ring. A master technician between the ropes, Hart's classic matches with Mr. Perfect at *SummerSlam 1991*, his brother-in-law, The British Bulldog, at *SummerSlam 1992*, and his brother, Owen, at *WrestleMania X* and *SummerSlam 1994* remain mandatory viewing for any prospective pro wrestling fan.

But the performer Hart had perhaps the best chemistry with inside the ring was also the one with whom he shared the most animosity outside it: Shawn Michaels.

Michaels and Hart carved similar paths to success in the WWF. Both began as tag team specialists – Hart in tandem with another wrestling brother-in-law, Jim "The Anvil" Neidhart, as The Hart Foundation and Michaels with Marty Jannetty as The Rockers. The Hart Foundation and Rockers actually matched up more than a dozen times in 1989 and 1990 before Hart and Michaels broke out as stars in singles competition.

In 1992, the two moved on to feud over the WWF Intercontinental title, known at the time as the championship held by company workhorses and, more importantly, often a stepping stone to the coveted WWF Championship. Hart and Michaels made history on July 21 of that year, clashing at a taping of *WWF Wrestling Challenge* in the Federation's first-ever ladder match. When Hart won the WWF Championship from "Nature Boy" Ric Flair on October 12, his first pay-per-view title defense came against Michaels the following month at *Survivor Series 1992*.

Their rivalry reached new heights in 1996 when Hart defended the WWF title against Michaels in an epic Iron Man match at *WrestleMania XII*. In such a contest, the wrestler with the most pinfalls or submissions against the other in sixty minutes would be declared the winner. After an hour of action, the score was still 0-0, prompting WWF President Gorilla Monsoon to order the match to continue under sudden death overtime rules. Less than two minutes into the restart, Michaels connected with his Sweet Chin Music superkick to win the WWF championship for the first time in his career. The match is a masterpiece and still regarded by many as the greatest bout in *WrestleMania* history.[11]

With Michaels' reign on top underway, Hart took a break from the ring. His contract with the WWF was expiring and it was around this time that he was approached by World Championship Wrestling (WCW), the Atlanta-based wrestling promotion owned by television mogul Ted Turner which served as the primary – and increasingly aggressive – competitor to Vince McMahon's WWF.

WCW had long been viewed as "southern rasslin'" – a more traditional, sportsmanlike presentation of the pro wrestling artform and a stark contrast to McMahon's WWF. However, that mindset started to change in 1994 when Turner promoted Eric Bischoff to Senior Vice President of WCW. Bischoff had been an on-air interviewer for Verne Gagne's Minneapolis, Minn.-based American Wrestling Association (AWA) in the late 1980s before coming to WCW as an announcer in 1991. When "Cowboy" Bill Watts resigned his post as WCW Vice President of Wrestling Operations in 1993, Bischoff was elevated to Executive Producer and given the reins of

---

[11] Some would contend Hart's match with Stone Cold Steve Austin the following year, or Michaels' *WrestleMania XXV* bout with The Undertaker were better, and both have compelling arguments in their favor. The fact that Hart and Michaels each have multiple matches in the conversation for "greatest ever" at the Show of Shows should tell you just how good these two were.

the entire company the following year.

One of Bischoff's first orders of business in his new role was to move WCW production to Disney MGM-Studios in Orlando, Florida. That decision was quite strategic, as it not-so-coincidentally turned out that Hulk Hogan – wrestling's most well-known commodity then, and possibly ever – was filming a television series called *Thunder in Paradise* on the same lot. Hogan had left the WWF in June of 1993. By June of 1994, he was property of WCW. Bischoff brought in the other half of the WWF's famed "Mega Powers" later that year when "Macho Man" Randy Savage debuted on the December 3, 1994 episode of *WCW Saturday Night*.

When Turner decided to turn up the heat even more, WCW launched *Monday Nitro*, a weekly episodic television broadcast on the TNT channel in direct ratings competition with the WWF's flagship program, *Monday Night Raw*. Bischoff punctuated the program's pilot episode on September 4, 1995 by poaching another WWF star, Lex Luger. Luger's debut on *Nitro* – one night after wrestling for the WWF – was the first shot fired in the fabled "Monday Night Wars" for television ratings supremacy.

As the ratings war raged on, WCW continued to welcome WWF defections, none more significant or consequential than the signings of Scott Hall and Kevin Nash in the early summer of 1996. Hall and Nash – respectively known as "Razor Ramon" and "Diesel" – were two of the top stars during what the WWF called its "New Generation" era, the time period between Hulk Hogan's "Rock N' Wrestling Era" of the 1980s and what would become Stone Cold Steve Austin's "Attitude Era" of the late 1990s.

Bret Hart was, in many ways, the face of the New Generation, so it made sense that WCW would go after him hard as well, allegedly offering The Hitman a three-year contract worth up to nine million dollars. The WWF countered with an unprecedented twenty-year contract. Hart took the summer to weigh his options, but could not pass up the WWF's offer. He signed his new "lifetime" contract on October 21, 1996.

Unfortunately, that "lifetime" did not last long. Less than a year later, Hart had become increasingly disenchanted with the direction of WWF creative, and Vince McMahon – citing financial hardship – approached Hart about the possibility of breaking their deal. It is difficult to believe that so much had changed on both sides in the matter of just a few months and yet, it apparently had. In fairness to the WWF, this was around the time that McMahon began to get the ball rolling on making his Federation a publicly traded company, which would have necessitated the minimization of long-term financial investments. Still, it's a challenge to reconcile that such plans existed in 1997, but there was no forethought for them in 1996 when the agreement with Hart was reached. So. Financial peril? Perhaps. Buyer's remorse? Definitely.

It's also an interesting complication that 1997 Bret Hart may have been the best version of Bret Hart ever. His *WrestleMania XIII* submission match with Stone Cold Steve Austin was masterful, and the double-turn that resulted from it catapulted both men to new heights. Austin's refusal to submit, passing out in the Sharpshooter submission hold from a combination of pain and blood loss, made fans respect him as the top babyface in the game, while Hart's increasingly underhanded tactics and persecution complex made him a heel the likes of which he'd never played before.

Hart wasn't the only one with an attitude problem, though – Shawn Michaels had quickly become famous for his. Real-life immaturity and arrogance – along with his political sway with the boss as a member of "The Kliq" – caused Michaels to be unpopular among many backstage, including, and especially, Hart, though the two had largely kept their personal animosity in check when it came to matters of business up to that point.[12]

After winning the WWF championship for the second time in his career at the *Royal Rumble* in January 1997, Michaels dropped a bombshell on the February 13 special episode of *Thursday Raw Thursday*. What a name, right? Kind of makes you think about the good people who work in marketing. Anyway, due to a knee injury, Michaels said he would be forced to relinquish his championship.

"I know that over the last several months I've lost a lot of things and one of them has been my smile," Michaels tearfully said. "And I know it doesn't mean a whole lot to everybody else, but it means a lot to me. So I have to go back and fix myself, and take care of myself, and I have to go back and I have to find my smile because somewhere along the line I lost it."

How badly was Michaels' knee injured? That remains a matter of speculation to this day, and the answer depends on who you ask. According to Michaels, doctors told him it was career-threatening. Hart, on the other hand, believed the injury to be a charade for Michaels to avoid losing to Hart in a *WrestleMania* rematch, which was widely believed to be the plan following the success of their 1996 bout. The truth remains a matter of opinion, though Michaels was back in action by May, which does give some credence to Hart's theory. It's certainly possible that the initial medical assessment Michaels received was worse than the injury turned out to be; however, Michaels also legitimately forfeited WWF championships on six different occasions throughout the 1990s, which might be bad luck but also looks an awful lot like a pattern, so who knows?

---

[12] The Kliq was an off-screen collection of friends that came to possess a significant amount of backstage pull within the WWF in the mid-1990s. Members of the group included Shawn Michaels, Kevin Nash, Scott Hall, Triple H, and Sean Waltman. These men went on to comprise two of the biggest on-screen stables of the era in WCW's New World Order and WWF's D-Generation X.

What we do know is the heavyweight title was back up for grabs three days later at *WWF In Your House: Final Four*, and Bret Hart came away victorious. Hart's latest reign as champion was short-lived, however, as Steve Austin cost him the title in Hart's first defense against Sycho Sid the following night on *Raw*. Sid held the title for the next month before dropping it to The Undertaker at *WrestleMania*, two matches after the Hart-Austin classic.

While Taker occupied the heavyweight title scene for the next several months, Hart reunited with his old tag team partner, Jim Neidhart, and brought in Owen Hart, The British Bulldog, and Brian Pillman to form a newer, larger Hart Foundation, this time as a full-on heel stable.

Just as the Hart Foundation was gaining steam, Shawn Michaels came back into the picture, this time portraying on-screen the same brash and cocky persona that many had come to know in backstage interactions. The Michaels-Hart relationship crossed the point of no return on the May 19 episode of *Raw*, when, during a promo between the two, Michaels made a comment about Hart enjoying "Sunny days," implying that Hart – married and with children – was having an affair with Tammy Sytch, who portrayed WWF diva, Sunny. In reality, Michaels was the one who had engaged in a romantic entanglement with America Online's most downloaded celebrity of 1996, and there's no reason to believe anything more than close friendship existed between Hart and Sytch. Given the undue drama the comment caused in Hart's personal life, one can sympathize with his less-than-positive feelings towards Michaels at this time. The animosity boiled over several weeks later when Hart confronted Michaels about the comment, resulting in a real-life backstage brawl between the two men. Michaels was suspended for two months for his actions.

With Michaels again on the backburner, Hart seemed to transition from clear heel to more of a tweener character. While the Hart Foundation was generally booed in the United States for their anti-

American rhetoric, the group was treated to a hero's welcome north of the border. This was no more evident than at the July 6, 1997 *In Your House: Canadian Stampede* pay-per-view in Calgary, Alberta, Canada, where the five members of The Hart Foundation came away with a memorable victory in a ten-man tag-team main event match against Steve Austin, Goldust, Ken Shamrock, and the Legion of Doom. The pay-per-view as a whole has been increasingly celebrated over the years as one of the better events of its era, though the night's bittersweet final image of the Hart family in the ring together for what would turn out to be the last time is certainly sobering, in retrospect.[13]

In front of another favorable crowd in Edmonton, Alberta, Canada the next night on *Raw*, Bret Hart was announced as the No. 1 contender to The Undertaker's WWF Championship. Upping the ante, Hart promised that if he did not win the title at the August 3 *SummerSlam* pay-per-view, he would never wrestle on United States' soil again. In case the stakes weren't high enough, Shawn Michaels was then assigned to the match to serve as the special guest referee; however, a stipulation was added that would ban the San Antonio, Texas-native Michaels from wrestling in the United States as well if he did not remain impartial in his role.

The elements proved combustible when Hart spit in Michaels' face during the match, causing the Heartbreak Kid to retaliate with a steel chair. Unfortunately for Michaels, he missed Hart and connected with The Undertaker. Given the rules of the match, Michaels was forced to count the pinfall, awarding Hart with his fifth WWF championship.

Michaels returned to competition himself on the August 11 episode

---

[13] Brian Pillman passed away of a heart attack in October 1997. Owen Hart tragically fell to his death during a stunt on live pay-per-view in May 1999. A heart attack claimed the life of The British Bulldog in May of 2002, and Jim Neidhart succumbed to a head injury after what appeared to be a seizure-induced fall in August 2018.

of *Raw* for a match with Mankind. During the bout, Michaels' off-screen Kliq-mate, Hunter Hearst Helmsley (soon to become more casually known as "Triple H") and his bodyguard Chyna[14] interfered on Michaels' behalf, while a returning Rick Rude entered with a chair at the conclusion to ensure the HBK victory. By October, the collective would officially become known as "D-Generation X," playing off their membership to the Generation X demographic, as well as a promo in which Hart accused Michaels – whose crude and sophomoric on-screen behavior was bringing the WWF product to new levels of risqué every week – of being "nothing more than a degenerate."

Despite electing to put the company's top title on Hart a month earlier, by mid-September, Vince McMahon was having doubts about his current champion's future in the company. Concerned about his ability to continue to financially honor Hart's twenty-year contract, along with a feeling that the character had peaked, McMahon urged Hart to approach WCW about revisiting the contract offer from a year earlier.

Hart was reluctant to leave the WWF. After all, he had been a loyal soldier for the company since 1984. Still, there did not appear to be reciprocal interest in renegotiating Hart's deal on the WWF end. Hart may have been willing to stay, but he no longer seemed to fit into McMahon's vision for the company. Hart informed the WWF on November 1, 1997, that he would be leaving for WCW.

Though the WCW deal was done, Hart's pending departure was not to be made public until November 10, one day after the *Survivor Series* pay-per-view. He was still the champion heading into the event, and if word got out that he was leaving, it was believed that could hurt

---

[14] The "Ninth Wonder of the World" would go on to become the first woman ever to: main-event a primetime professional wrestling program; become No. 1 contender for the WWF championship; win the WWF Intercontinental championship; compete in a Royal Rumble match; and participate in the King of the Ring tournament. And it was all believable.

pay-per-view sales, as the outcome of the feature bout would become obvious. As it turned out, the opposite was true. News trickling out about the current champion leaving the territory only enhanced the intrigue of the match, as those in the know wondered how the WWF would handle the situation, and which of the match participants would acquiesce to doing the "job."

Under normal circumstances, the latter would not be a concern. However, since Shawn Michaels was involved, all bets were off. Michaels earned No. 1 contender privileges after defeating The Undertaker at October's *Badd Blood* pay-per-view in the first-ever – and possibly best-ever – "Hell in a Cell" match. The word "defeating" is used loosely here. Michaels was indeed the victor of the match, which earned a five-star rating from renowned wrestling journalist, Dave Meltzer. However, the majority of the bout involved a bloodied Michaels bumping all over the place for a dominating Undertaker. The match built to the debut of Kane, Undertaker's kayfabe brother, who was seemingly back from the dead and on a mission to bring vengeance upon his older brother. Kane made his shocking entrance with Paul Bearer, Undertaker's former ring manager, by ripping the cell door off its hinges and executing his version of Taker's signature Tombstone Piledriver on "The Deadman." Michaels crawled over to make the cover for the win.

While Hart and Michaels had agreed to set aside their personal differences for the good of the business after their throw down in June, that proved impossible. Hart recalled in his autobiography, *Hitman*, that when discussions began with Michaels about how to transition the championship off Hart, the challenger's attitude did not impress the champion.

> "I added, 'I also want you to know that I have no problem dropping the belt to you if that's what Vince wants.' He glared back at me. 'I appreciate that, but I want you to know that I'm not willing to do the same for you.'"

From that point on, Hart was adamant about two things: he would not be dropping the title to Michaels and he would not be ending his WWF career with a loss in his home country of Canada.

That posed a real conundrum for the WWF, which needed to get the belt off of Hart so he – or, more likely, Eric Bischoff – wouldn't take it to the competitor's television show. Bischoff had done this once already when he scooped up reigning WWF women's champion Alundra Blayze and had her literally dump the title in a garbage can on national television. However, he has since claimed the WWF was in no real danger of that scenario happening with Hart, as Turner Network's legal team had advised him not to push the envelope any further, as they were already fighting legal battles with the WWF over the similarities between the portrayals of Scott Hall to Razor Ramon and Kevin Nash to Diesel on WCW television. Also, the McMahon's hands were not necessarily super clean on this front either, as Ric Flair famously brought WCW's "Big Gold Belt" with him when he came to the WWF in 1991, claiming to be the "Real World Champion." In his and the WWF's defense, Flair himself owned the belt; however, this illustrates how valuable one company's championship can be in the hands of another. So, with your champion refusing to lose to your challenger and your competitor potentially plotting to embarrass your biggest championship on national television if given the chance, what's a promoter to do?

Well, if you're Vince McMahon, you call for a double-cross. McMahon assembled a small circle of confidants to walk through the plan. Late in the match, Michaels would wrap Hart in The Hitman's own finishing maneuver, the Sharpshooter. Once locked in, McMahon would instruct referee Earl Hebner – who was told of the plan just moments before heading out for the match – to ring the bell when told and award the bout to Michaels by way of submission.

And that's exactly how it went down. Despite allegedly being concerned about a screwjob finish, Hart believed he and McMahon had agreed that Hart would win the match by reversing Michaels' Sharpshooter into one of his own, and the champion would subsequently relinquish the title the next night on *Raw* or lose it a few weeks later before leaving for WCW. Instead, McMahon orchestrated a shoot screwjob to take the title off Hart without the champion's prior knowledge or consent as fans and the former champion looked on with disbelief.

Before things got out of hand, McMahon ordered Michaels to "pick up the damn belt and get the hell out of here." Members of the Hart Foundation made their way out to ringside in an attempt to restrain Hart, but their success was limited. Enraged by the betrayal, Hart spit in McMahon's face, destroyed ringside equipment, and traced the letters 'W-C-W' in the air. When he arrived backstage, he gave McMahon a literal parting shot, punching the Chairman in the face before leaving the venue, and the WWF.

Jim Neidhart, The British Bulldog, and Rick Rude – disgusted by what had transpired – each asked for and were issued their releases from the WWF and joined Hart in WCW after the incident. Bret's brother, Owen, requested his release as well but it was not granted. Vince McMahon, meanwhile, quickly became the biggest and best on-screen bad guy in the business, despite his insistence that "Bret screwed Bret." It's interesting to note that while McMahon's subsequent feud with Stone Cold Steve Austin (the man who would eventually take the WWF title from Shawn Michaels) was the program that turned the Monday Night Wars' momentum in the WWF's favor in 1998, McMahon genuinely did not intend to play the heel. According to longtime manager, booker, and general wrestling historian Jim Cornette, McMahon actually thought fans would side with him over Hart. ...They did not... As soon as McMahon realized he was the baddie, we were off to the races.

While McMahon settled into life as wrestling's biggest villain over the next several years, things did not go so well for the two men who shared the ring that night in Montreal. After injuring his back in a title defense against The Undertaker at *Royal Rumble 1998*, Shawn Michaels did the honors for Austin at *WrestleMania XIV*, and then went on injured reserve for the next four years. Hart would go on to win the WCW World Heavyweight championship twice and the United States championship four times over the next two years of in-ring action but was forced into early retirement in 2000 after suffering a severe concussion in a WCW title defense against Goldberg at *Starrcade 1999*.

Before moving on to discuss what might have happened if things shook out a little bit differently, it's worth noting that there are some who would have you believe the "Montreal Screwjob" – as it came to be known – wasn't actually a screwjob at all.

"To me, I feel the same way now seeing it back as I did the first time I saw it," Scott Hall said on VICE's *Dark Side of the Ring* in 2019. "It's a total work."

He's not alone in thinking that. Many within the industry have shared similar sentiments over the years.

I will say this: if it was a work, 1) it would be the greatest work in the history of works, and 2) that would mean Hart was in on it. This seems unlikely given how much time has passed and considering everything that's happened to Hart, Michaels, and wrestling since.

Still, the theory does have some compelling points, specifically the decision to televise Hart's post-match tirade. The lack of a camera cutaway when Hart made his W-C-W gestures does raise an eyebrow. It's also curious that Hart would be naive enough to go along with Michaels using Hart's own finisher against him and not think something was up. For someone who was said to be paranoid about the prospects of a screwjob already, that seems a strange position to put yourself in, even with his immense trust in Earl Hebner as the official of record. Then there's the added wrinkle that Hart was in the middle of filming his *Wrestling with Shadows* documentary at the time. It's a little shocking that McMahon would allow Hart's cameras backstage to document the aftermath if the situation were truly a shoot. And we've already talked about how so many of the WWF decisions surrounding Bret Hart in 1996 and 1997 made very little sense. So the conspiracy theory is not meritless, even if it may not be true either.

Regardless of who knew what and when, the Montreal Screwjob has remained one of the most discussed, debated, and, for better or worse, imitated events in modern pro wrestling history. But the thing is… it didn't have to go down like that.

* WHAT COULD HAVE HAPPENED *

The most frustrating aspect of the Montreal Screwjob is that it was entirely preventable at so many points along the way.

For starters, if Bret Hart didn't figure into the long-term WWF plans in 1996, why re-sign him to a twenty-year contract? And, once it was clear that Hart was headed to WCW, what was WWF doing putting him in the title picture? If anything, wouldn't it make sense to *devalue* him before the guy departs to the competition? WCW was already regularly beating the WWF in the ratings war by this point – why in the world would McMahon continue to play with fire by not only keeping Hart in the main event picture, but sending him off to another company with more controversy and attention being paid to him than any talent before or since? The moment Vince McMahon decided to tell Bret Hart to go fishing for offers from WCW, Bret Hart should have been removed from the title scene, end of story.

Another option available to the WWF would have been for Hart to drop the belt on the November 3 episode of *Raw*. Hart's fourth WWF championship ended on *Raw* back in February, and major title changes on free TV were a fairly regular occurrence during the Monday Night Wars, as both WWF and WCW pulled out all the stops to ensure fans knew anything could happen on either *Raw* or

Nitro. There was also a house show on November 8 in Detroit that could have served as a title change opportunity. Hart did not appear on that pre-*Survivor Series* go-home episode and was reportedly against losing the title the week prior to the event because they had already promoted the match with Michaels for the pay-per-view and he didn't want to let down his Canadian fans.

So, to recap, he didn't want to lose to Michaels, didn't want to lose in Canada, and didn't want to lose before the pay-per-view. I don't feel bad for Vince because he created this mess, but I do understand how we got what we got.

With Hart being hellbent on entering *Survivor Series* with the belt around his waist, the *best* – and possibly *only* other – option under those circumstances would have been to go with the original plan Hart and McMahon supposedly arranged on the day of the event. The match would end in a disqualification around the seventeen-minute mark and Hart would forfeit the title the next night on *Raw*, where he could address the fans and say goodbye to the WWF on his terms.

Hart had floated the idea of continuing to work with the WWF into December, despite his WCW contract officially beginning on December 1, and Bischoff was receptive to the idea; however, he was only obligated to keep the news of Hart's signing a secret until after *Survivor Series*. Would anyone realistically expect Bischoff not to say anything about the WWF's current and active champion leaving that company for his, just out of the goodness of his heart? And could anyone reasonably blame him for doing otherwise? This would not be a viable option.

BUT – what if we could avoid this mess of Hart leaving altogether? What if, on November 1, instead of choosing WCW, Hart and the WWF came to an agreement for him to stay? In that case, it would seem all options would be back on the table for *Survivor Series*. Hart's objections to losing to Michaels and losing in Canada were predicated on his leaving the Federation. With Hart no longer leaving, he would, presumably, be open to dropping the title to Michaels in Montreal, given that he would have the opportunity to get the win back down the road, and would be returning to Canada in the future as a member of the WWF roster. Hart and the WWF still had a Shawn Michaels problem – which was summarized by HBK himself when he proclaimed, "The Heartbreak Kid lays down for absolutely NOBODY!" – but Michaels did put Austin over with a win at *WrestleMania XIV*, so perhaps if tensions were allowed to cool a bit, things could have worked out in a more positive way between the two most successful performers of "The New Generation."

* WHAT WOULD HAVE HAPPENED NEXT *

What would happen next in the Hart/Michaels saga would depend on which of the Choose Your Own Adventure scenarios you want to adopt.

If we took the simplest path and removed Hart from the title picture as soon as he was told to explore his options with WCW (because, honestly…), Hart would still end up in WCW but without the main event send-off. The Shawn Michaels/Undertaker feud extended to *Royal Rumble 1998* anyway, so it would have been easy enough to keep the title between the two of them once Hart's departure was imminent. Beyond that, nothing much would have changed for the WWF. For the competition, WCW would have had to find a different way to screw up the main event of their biggest pay-per-view ever, *Starrcade 1997*, but we'll get there in the next chapter.

If Hart were to drop the title prior to *Survivor Series*, who would he drop it to? The Undertaker would seem the most reasonable answer, having been the champion before Hart and the top contender at the *Royal Rumble* after Michaels took the belt. Also, if the desired outcome of *Survivor Series* was for Michaels to leave with the championship, the introduction of Kane to the storyline in October would provide an easy-out to protect The Undertaker by way of outside interference in another losing effort against Michaels. Hart, meanwhile, could have his farewell tour where he could speak his truth and exit the WWF gracefully. And, again, WCW would have had to find a different way to screw up the main event of their biggest pay-per-view ever.

If Hart and Michaels fought to a DQ finish, as planned, and Hart forfeited the title the following night on *Raw*, Hart would get the sendoff he wanted, but things would be more interesting for the WWF championship plans. Since the Federation was already embarking on a tournament for the Light Heavyweight championship the following month, it's unlikely that the company would have booked a second tournament at the same time. Instead, another version of February's *Final Four* pay-per-view scenario would seem to be in the cards. Shawn Michaels and Ken Shamrock could certainly go one-on-one for the title at *D-Generation X: In Your House* (as they did in reality), but that feels less intriguing than if it were a multi-man match in this situation. The Undertaker, again, would seem like a natural fit as a third man, and if it were another four-way bout, Vader didn't have much else on his schedule. Considering how dominant Vader was in WCW and New Japan, it's baffling how WWF couldn't get even a fraction of that out of him during his 1996-98 run with the company. Regardless, at the end of this scenario, I think Michaels would still end up with the belt, nothing much else would change for WWF heading into 1998, and WCW would still have to find a different way to screw up the main event of their biggest pay-per-view ever.

The most interesting – and unpredictable – timeline is if Hart and the WWF managed to patch things up and he remained with the company for at least the next handful of years. The issue with that scenario is threefold: 1) the WWF was *really* well-booked in 1998; 2) Bret Hart really *didn't* fit into the WWF's plans, which means he no longer would have been a perennial main event player; and 3) while Hart staying in the WWF may have changed some things for the better, it would also have far-reaching ripple effects that would negatively impact others. We'll call this the "Back to the Future 2 Principle."

Think about it this way – in 1998, Stone Cold and The Rock were elevated to the WWF championship scene, The Undertaker and Kane was a main event feud, Mankind became a world title contender, and Triple H took over Shawn Michaels' spot as not just the leader of D-X, but as a bona fide singles draw. Moreover, perhaps the greatest heel character in the history of the business was born out of the Montreal Screwjob: Mr. McMahon. McMahon's defiant "Bret screwed Bret" mantra was the catalyst for the evil boss authority figure that served not just as the primary antagonist for the hottest wrestling star in the industry, but also created the archetype that has plagued nearly every other white meat babyface champion for the last two decades.[15] What I'm saying is Bret Hart may have been a top-of-the-card talent, but the top of the card was full and whatever we do with our revisionist history plot here needs to protect each of those men above so their stories get told the right way.

To illustrate this point a little further, let's just run through the first scenario that comes to everyone's mind real quick. What if Bret retained at *Survivor Series* so he could go on to defend against Austin at *WrestleMania*? No one is going to complain about another Austin-Hart match; however, we need to consider what happens to Shawn Michaels in this timeline. In reality, Michaels injured his back in the casket match he had with The Undertaker at *Royal Rumble 1998* defending the WWF championship. That injury ended up putting Michaels on the shelf for four years from 1998-2002. If Michaels didn't get injured, he wouldn't retire, Triple H wouldn't take over D-

---

[15] Eric Bischoff should get credit for doing it first, but even he would agree that nobody has played the role of corrupt boss better than Vince McMahon. Unfortunately, we've had plenty of bad-guy authority figures to compare them both to since 1998.

X, and Michaels wouldn't get the life reset he needed from 1998-2002 and I fear for his health and safety if that didn't happen. In addition, the outcome of the casket match – wherein Kane sets the casket on fire with The Undertaker inside – is a huge development in the Brothers of Destruction storyline, and we don't want to lose that either. Theoretically, HBK and Taker could still have the casket match at the *Rumble* without the WWF championship being involved, since there's no shortage of bad blood[16] between the two, but I don't know if there's enough motivation there to warrant such a stipulation… but maybe.

A more likely approach would be for Michaels to take the title from Hart at *Survivor Series* in Montreal. Hart's biggest issue with Montreal seemed to be the fact that it was his last pay-per-view in the WWF. He wanted to go out as a hero for his Canadian fans and, if he were to lose, lose to someone he respected. Well, if he were no longer leaving, none of that should have been a problem anymore. Bret could drop the title to Michaels, which is what the WWF wanted anyway, and then he could take the next two months to not only recharge, but still potentially feed the rumor mill about what his next move would be. Could he wind up in WCW after all? Call the hotline now to find out! (Kids, get your parents' permission to dial.)

So let's fast-forward to January of 1998. Bret Hart would have been off WWF television since *Survivor Series* in November. Everyone loves a good surprise entrant at the *Royal Rumble* so we'd slot Bret in as one of the 30 competitors in the battle royale – maybe give him Tom Brandi's spot (sorry, Salvatore), but instead of entering at No. 3, we'd give him No. 30 so he would come out last. The anticipation for 'who will be No. 30' is more of a recent phenomenon, but wrestling fans have always loved a good surprise.

---

[16] Not to be confused with the October In-Your-House pay-per-view, *Badd Blood*.

We know that Steve Austin and The Rock were the future cornerstones of the company, so we would keep them in the ring as the final two competitors. We would also want to keep Faarooq in as one of the final four, because the friction with The Rock is integral to Rocky's story arc. The fourth of the final four competitors should stay the same, too: Dude Love. He would be the man to eliminate Hart.

The latest iteration of the Bret Hart character would be a paragon of virtue. He wouldn't necessarily be a heel, but – true to life – he'd take pro wrestling *real* seriously and conduct his business "by the book." He wouldn't be compelled by that "shades of grey" nonsense – in Hart's mind, the world would exist in black and white. There would be right and there would be wrong and at this time, Hart would see a whole lot of wrong going on in the WWF.

When Bret got eliminated by Dude Love, he'd lose it. Bret's no dummy. He would know that Dude Love was just Mick Foley dressed up like a goof. Which would have been fine, but Foley also entered the Rumble match as both Cactus Jack *and* Mankind. How does one guy get three entries into one match? That's not fair! That's not right! ~~Karen~~ Bret would want to speak to the manager. We could use this moment to bring Vince McMahon back as the on-screen authority figure and keep him on track to become the "Mr. McMahon" character.

In a backstage segment on *Raw,* Hart could air his grievances to McMahon, who would say he understood and sympathized, but would tell Bret there's nothing he could do about it now. What was done would be done, and (after his victory at the *Rumble*) Shawn Michaels would defend the WWF Championship against Steve Austin at *WrestleMania* in March. Still, in recognition of Bret's tenure and track record, McMahon would say he'd see about lining Hart up with a title shot after *WrestleMania*. In exchange for the favor, though, McMahon would direct Hart to do something about Jeff Jarrett, who had begun appearing on WWF television wearing the

NWA North American championship.

"What would your dad do if a man showed up to a Stampede Wrestling event wearing the championship of someone else's company?" Vince might ask rhetorically. "Can you imagine? They'd still be untying that poor fool from the pretzel Stu would have wrapped him into! I've got a few other things on my plate tonight – how's about you go remind Mr. Jarrett how we do things here in the World Wrestling Federation. Then I'll see what I can do about getting that WWF championship back around your waist."

As the self-appointed guardian of professional wrestling's unwritten rules, Hart would agree, and since the success rate for talking things out in the WWF is basically zero, Hart would attempt to teach Jarrett a lesson in respect at February's *No Way Out* pay-per-view. That match would get spoiled, though, when the NWA tag champs, The Rock 'n' Roll Express, would make a run-in on Jarrett's behalf. Fortunately for Hart, that would also usher in the returns of Jim Neidhart and The British Bulldog and suddenly we'd have a full-blown donnybrook. With Owen Hart occupied with Hunter Hearst Helmsley in the European title scene for the moment, this would set up a six-man tag team match at *WrestleMania*, The Hart Foundation versus the NWA.

Once the Harts dispatched of the NWA, McMahon would be a man of his word and deliver on making Hart the No. 1 contender for Steve Austin's newly-won WWF championship. As McMahon cut his famous "we can do this the easy way or we can do this the hard way" promo for Austin on the *Raw* after *WrestleMania*, he would cite Hart as a prime example of how a champion is supposed to conduct himself, challenging Austin to live up to that standard. We all know how this would turn out.[17]

Over the next two months, Bret Hart would play the role Dude Love

---

[17] Bird, kick, stunner, repeat.

occupied in the real-life storyline. Mick Foley's rise would still take place from June on; he just wouldn't work Austin right away after *WrestleMania*, and you wouldn't really miss that anyway. Austin and Hart would main event *Unforgiven* in a match that would end in disqualification. At *Over the Edge* in May, Austin would defeat Hart clean, forcing the Hitman to begrudgingly acknowledge he may no longer be "the best there is" ... at least not right now. Maybe he would need to take a break to get his mind right. Get back to basics.

When the *SummerSlam* event opened in our alternate timeline on August 30, 1998, the first thing we would hear after the signature, pyro, and ballyhoo[18] would be the familiar guitar riff of The Hitman's entrance theme. Bret Hart would make his way down to the commentary table to watch the first match of the evening, as D'Lo Brown defended the European Championship against Val Venis. Despite being one of the most decorated champions in WWF history, the European title is the one championship that eluded the "Excellence of Execution."

Hart would be impressed with the in-ring abilities of both competitors, but less enamored with their temperaments. Over the next several weeks, Hart would mix it up with the likes of Mark Henry, Droz, and Jeff Jarrett, while D'Lo Brown and X-Pac would trade the European championship back and forth. Hart and D'Lo would match up at the September *Breakdown: In Your House* event to vie for the No. 1 contender spot. The veteran would edge the promising upstart in a quality undercard performance. As Bully Ray might say, "Bret Hart went over, but D'Lo Brown[19] got over." The

---

[18] WWF run-sheets began with the words "Signature/Pyro/Ballyhoo" atop the page before launching into the script for the night, referencing the logo sequence, fireworks display, and crowd shots that would open each show.

[19] The career of D'Lo Brown is something of a "what if" in and of itself. While it's possible that his career had already reached its pinnacle, Brown was never the same wrestler after a botched running powerbomb in a 1999 match left Darren Drozdov – Brown's opponent in the match – a

next month at *Judgement Day: In Your House*, Hart and X-Pac would put on a clinic with the Kid pulling off a major upset to deny Hart from becoming the WWF's second-ever Grand Slam champion.[20]

The next month at *Survivor Series*, Hart would draw Edge in the first round of the "Deadly Games" fourteen-man tournament to crown a new WWF champion (slotted in the spot Steven Regal and X-Pac occupied in the real timeline); however, the match would never take place. Instead, The Brood would seize the opportunity to brutalize Hart, putting him on the shelf for the rest of the year. Meanwhile, Vince Russo's masterpiece would still get to play out at *Survivor Series*, with all the cards seemingly stacked in Mankind's favor but The Rock ending up being the "corporate champion" all along. Who knows, maybe without the Screwjob finish the previous year, this swerve would be an even bigger hit than it already was.

Upon Hart's return in January of 1999, a *Royal Rumble* matchup with Edge would have show-stealing potential. After that, it would have been great to see Bret reunite with his brother, Owen, for a tag team run. It hurts to even think about, but the elephant in the room is what would have happened to Owen if Bret never left for WCW. One would imagine, with Bret still in the picture, we would have never gotten the Blue Blazer angle and Owen wouldn't have fallen to his death at *Over the Edge 1999*. That alone is enough to want to change the timeline. As we imagine what else might be altered, consider that Chris Jericho and Kurt Angle would make their WWF

---

quadriplegic. Brown was the first wrestler to hold both the European and Intercontinental titles simultaneously, a feat only replicated by three other men: Jeff Jarrett, Kurt Angle, and Rob Van Dam – each of whom went on to become world champions. Brown never did.

[20] A Grand Slam champion is the winner of the company's four major titles: WWF, Intercontinental, European, and Tag Team. Shawn Michaels became the first Grand Slam champ when he won the European title on September 21, 1997. The next Grand Slam champion wasn't crowned until Triple H won a share of the tag team titles with Steve Austin on April 29, 2001.

debuts in 1999, and Eddie Guerrero, Chris Benoit, Dean Malenko, and Perry Saturn would arrive by the end of January 2000. Just think about the programs either Bret or Owen could have had with any and all of those men.

The ripple effects of a changed Montreal timeline are both incredible to consider and impossible to project. The matches that might have happened, the career – even life – trajectories that could have changed – it's fascinating and exciting and heartbreaking to think about. And yet, it seems the only thing we really know for certain is that if Bret Hart could have avoided the Montreal Screwjob altogether, WCW still would have needed to find a different way to screw up the main event of their biggest pay-per-view ever. But God bless 'em, they would have.

TWO

STARRCADE 1997

"I'm just not feeling it. I don't think it's the right time."

December 28, 1997
MCI Center ⦿ Washington, D.C.
WCW Starrcade

Sting defeated Hollywood Hulk Hogan (c) by submission for the WCW World Heavyweight Championship (12:53).

* WHAT REALLY HAPPENED *

Perhaps the greatest slow-burn build in the history of professional wrestling, the World Heavyweight Championship match between Hollywood Hulk Hogan and Sting at World Championship Wrestling's annual *Starrcade* event in December of 1997 was a showdown nearly two years in the making.

The story really began on May 27, 1996 when Scott Hall – known at the time to wrestling fans as the World Wrestling Federation's "Razor Ramon" – made his way through the crowd at the Macon Coliseum in Macon, Georgia to interrupt an exhibition match between Steve Doll and The Mauler on *WCW Monday Nitro*. WCW announcers Tony Schiavone and Larry Zbyszko were dumbfounded as the six-foot-seven, denim-clad Hall climbed over the guardrail with his signature toothpick in his mouth, demanding a microphone.

"You people, you know who I am," Hall said in Razor Ramon's 'Scarface' accent that would cause WCW legal headaches in the coming months. "But you don't know why I'm here."

To the average WCW fan, it felt like *Monday Nitro* had just been invaded by one of the WWF's top superstars. After all, Hall came to the ring through the crowd, unnamed and unannounced, and went on to call out Ted Turner (owner of WCW and the whole network), WCW Executive Vice President Eric Bischoff, lead interviewer (and WCW hotline scoop man) Gene Okerlund, and the WCW locker room, finishing his promo with, "You want a war? You're gonna get one."

Two weeks later on June 10, 1996, Hall was joined on the stage by another familiar face, Kevin Nash – previously known as the WWF's Diesel, a one-time WWF champion and 1995's top singles wrestler of the year in Pro Wrestling Illustrated's annual *PWI 500* publication. Nash reiterated Hall's threats towards WCW, albeit with some confusion between verbs and adjectives as they related to being "Where the Big Boys Play."

Hall and Nash were henceforth dubbed "The Outsiders," a moniker that didn't do a whole lot of heavy lifting in dispelling the notion that Razor Ramon and Diesel were sent from the WWF to destroy the competition in WCW. Bischoff (in his EVP role) would contend that Hall and Nash weren't coming to WCW as WWF wrestlers, but rather as former WCW wrestlers (which they were), who weren't treated well in WCW (which they weren't), who went to WWF to become stars (which they did), and who had now returned to WCW to wreak havoc on the company that overlooked them (which is preposterous).

"In my head, the way I looked at it, Vince [McMahon] had sent us here to take over," Hall said of The Outsiders' WCW debut on the *83 Weeks* podcast in 2021.

In any case, The Outsiders challenged Bischoff (at this time portraying his on-screen television character, a fictional version of his role as real-life EVP of the company) to assemble a team of three top WCW wrestlers to face Hall, Nash, and a mystery partner of their choosing at the upcoming July pay-per-view event, *Bash at the Beach*. On the *Nitro* following June's *Great American Bash* event, a "random" drawing determined that "Macho Man" Randy Savage, Lex Luger, and Sting would represent WCW against The Outsiders.

The "Hostile Takeover" match had started to look like WCW's trio would take on The Outsiders in a 3-on-2 format, with the mystery third man nowhere to be found. The odds were even when Luger was knocked out and taken to the back after being caught in the middle of friendly fire from his teammates' high-impact maneuvers. Sting and Savage battled, but Hall and Nash pulled out every dirty trick in the book, punctuated by a low blow by Nash on Macho Man with the referee distracted. That's when Hulk Hogan marched down the aisle. Hall and Nash booked it to the outside, obviously wanting no part of what wrestling's greatest good guy was about to dish out to them. And then it happened. Hogan landed his patented atomic leg drop on Savage, not once but twice! Hogan – "Say Your Prayers, Eat Your Vitamins" Hogan – was The Outsiders' third man. He joined hands with Hall and Nash as fans pelted the ring with garbage. He christened the group as the "New World Order of wrestling, brother."

Indeed it was.

To be certain, Hogan was the only reasonable choice to be the third man. It had to be him. If WCW would have been able to pry Bret Hart away from the WWF in 1996, the concept might have worked, but it would have been a very different New World Order. Sting – the purported backup plan – wasn't right for the job and the rumors of ex-WWF talents such as Mabel or Crush were just nonsense.

Hogan went on to win the WCW World Heavyweight Championship by defeating The Giant at *Hog Wild* in August, and the nWo ran roughshod over WCW for the better part of the next 18 months. The story took a key turn on the September 9 episode of *Nitro*, however, when rogue referee Nick Patrick lured Lex Luger outside to the nWo limousine where it then appeared that "Sting" attacked his tag team partner. This was not the "real" Sting, but rather an nWo version of the face-painted babyface portrayed by Jeff Farmer... but fans – and more importantly, Luger – didn't know that at the time.

The following Sunday *Fall Brawl*, Team WCW – which consisted of Luger, Arn Anderson, and Ric Flair – questioned the loyalty of the squad's proposed fourth member for the annual War Games cage match, despite Sting's insistence that he did not attack Luger on *Nitro*. Team nWo took advantage of the dissension in the WCW ranks, locking in Farmer (Fake Sting) as the faction's fourth member, alongside Hall, Nash, and Hogan. The ruse didn't last too long, as the real Sting made his entrance in the match as WCW's fourth member and dispatched of the nWo himself. The real Sting then exited the ring, shouting back at his Team WCW comrades, "Now do you believe me?"

After Sting left, the nWo recovered and defeated Team WCW to win the War Games match. But the story was just beginning.

The following night on *Nitro*, Sting – with his back to the camera – cut a scathing promo on all those who doubted his allegiances.

> "I want a chance to explain something that happened last Monday night at *Nitro*. Last Monday night, I was on an airplane flying from L.A. to Atlanta. When I got to Atlanta, I tuned the TV to *Nitro*. And I thought I was watching a rerun! It was a very convincing film. Often imitated, but never duplicated, though. And what else did I see? I saw people, I saw wrestlers, I saw commentators, and I saw best friends DOUBT the Stinger. That's right, doubted the Stinger! So I heard Lex Luger say, 'I know where he lives, I know where he works out, I'm gonna go get him.' So I said to myself, I'll just go into seclusion. I'll wait and see what happens on *Saturday Night*, and I tuned in Saturday night,

and what'd I see? More of the same... more DOUBT. Which brings me to *Fall Brawl*. I knew I had to get to Fall Brawl and get face to face with the Total Package to let him know that it wasn't me. And what I got out of that was, 'No Sting... I DON'T BELIEVE YOU STING!' Well, all I gotta say is I have been mediator, I have been babysitter for Lex Luger, and I've given him the benefit of the doubt about a thousand times in the last twelve months. And I've carried the WCW banner, and I have given my blood, my sweat, and my tears for WCW! So for all of those fans out there, and all those wrestlers, and people that never doubted the Stinger, I'll stand by you, if you stand by me. But for all of the people, all of the commentators, all of the wrestlers, and all of the best friends who did doubt me, you can stick it! From now on, I consider myself a free agent, but that doesn't mean that you won't see the Stinger; from time to time, I'm gonna pop-in when you least expect it."

Sting stayed off television until the October 21, 1996 episode of *Nitro*, when he returned to attack Fake Sting as the nWo watched. Attempting to seize on Sting's continued anger at WCW, the nWo offered Sting a spot in the faction.

"The *real* Sting may... or may not ... be in your price range," Sting responded. "The only thing that's for sure about Sting is that nothing's for sure."

Sting would not pick up a microphone again until January 8, 1998.

During that time, the nWo's size and power grew, while Sting's look and demeanor changed. The bleached blonde buzz cut and colorful face paint were long gone, replaced by a much darker, more menacing appearance. Sting wore a black trench coat and carried a black baseball bat. He grew out his hair – long and black – and painted his face a ghostly white with black streaks, a look inspired by Brandon Lee's 1994 film *The Crow*, a movie about a supernatural avenger, not too unlike the vigilante character Sting would soon become.

Sting lurked in the rafters of the arena throughout 1997, silently watching as the nWo wreaked havoc on WCW. Despite initial fears that the "free agent" may still align himself with the villainous nWo, Sting made his allegiance known at *Uncensored* in March of 1997, descending from the rafters to attack Hall, Nash, and the group's most recent turncoat, Randy Savage. As he turned towards the entrance ramp, Sting left no doubt about what his endgame might be. He pointed his baseball bat directly at the man responsible for what Sting had become, Hollywood Hulk Hogan.

As the year progressed, Sting made it a habit to rappel from the ceiling to attack nWo members or protect trusted WCW wrestlers from harm at the hands of Hogan's cronies. With Sting clearly itching for a fight, WCW on-screen Commissioner J.J. Dillon looked to sign the vigilante up for a match against someone from the New World Order. Apparently not a fan of the television product himself, Dillon offered up Curt Hennig and Syxx as potential opponents. Sting ripped up the contracts in front of Dillon. Poor J.J. could just as well have quoted Forrest Gump and told the audience, "I am not a smart man." He was not booked to be one during this storyline.

Everyone knew who Sting wanted. Mostly because he told us at *Uncensored* and in every action he took over the following six months. The incompetence of WCW's on-screen management was one of the exceptionally few upsetting parts of the entire build. The Commish caught up with the rest of us on the August 18 episode of *Nitro* after Sting literally grabbed him by the tie, pointed to a fan's sign that said "HEY J.J., STING WANTS HOGAN!" as the crowd chanted, "Hogan, Hogan, Hogan!" And when that apparently *still* didn't take, Sting brought a sign into the ring that said "Hulk vs. Sting", causing the place to come unglued.

Sting continued to unleash vengeance upon the nWo in the months leading up to *Starrcade 1997*, with the lone exception coming on the November 10 episode of *Nitro*, when Hogan somehow dropped him with one punch and the rest of the gang joined in on the beatdown. This was an upsetting moment as well, not necessarily because Hogan got his hands on Sting, but because A) Sting threw his baseball bat to the side in a showdown with a gang; and B) sold Hogan's grazing punch to the back of the head as if he'd been hit with said baseball bat.

Earlier in that episode of *Nitro*, Bischoff, now a full-fledged on-screen heel and member of the nWo himself, announced to the world that Bret Hart – victim of the previous evening's Montreal Screwjob at *WWF Survivor Series* – was on his way to World Championship Wrestling … and the five-time WWF champ would be joining the nWo.[21] Hart had a non-compete clause in his WWF contract, so he wouldn't be wrestling anytime soon; however, his first appearance as a member of the WCW roster came on the December 15 episode of *Nitro*. He was named the special guest referee for Bischoff's upcoming Starrcade match against Larry Zbyszko for control of *WCW Monday Nitro* and seemed likely to play some role in the event's highly-anticipated bout between Hogan and Sting.

The wrestling world was ready for the payoff of WCW's longest and most well-crafted storyline, when Sting would finally defeat Hogan once and for all, reclaiming the world championship and saving WCW from being overtaken by the nWo. All the pieces were in place to give fans the expected – but oh, so satisfying – conclusion to this beautifully told story.

And then game day arrived.

---

[21] This was wishful thinking only by Bischoff's on-screen character. Hart did not actually join the nWo upon his arrival to WCW, though he would the following year.

On the day of the event, Bischoff (as WCW's actual EVP, not the on-screen character) met with Sting and Hogan in his office to go over details before the match. When Sting walked in, Bischoff and Hogan were immediately unimpressed. Bischoff recalled Sting looked noticeably smaller than before, as if he hadn't been in the gym for some time. He hadn't bothered to tan – which, admittedly is part of the typical presentation process for most wrestlers who are out performing in what basically amounts to underwear, but frankly seems less important for a guy who's spent the last year-and-a-half wearing trench coats and corpse paint[22] while hanging out in the rafters of arenas with turkey vultures, but I digress. Most significantly, in Bischoff's eyes, Sting seemed disinterested in what was to be the culmination of nearly two years-worth of work.

"When you've got a talent that shows up and is totally not prepared or engaged, has had twelve or sixteen months to get ready for this moment where we're going to make this huge, huge change in the direction of the company, and the guy shows up like he just heard about the match forty-five minutes ago, it tends to make you rethink your position," Bischoff told Conrad Thompson on the December 18, 2018 episode of the pair's podcast, *83 Weeks*.

Bischoff acknowledged that Steve Borden – the man behind the face paint – had been embroiled in a series of personal issues at home, which likely informed much of his disposition; however, after the meeting in Bischoff's office, Hogan no longer felt comfortable with his dance partner for the evening.

"We had one plan and that afternoon," Bischoff recalled on Christy Olson's *After 83 Weeks* recap show in 2018. "[Hogan] changed his mind and said, 'I'm just not feeling it. I don't think it's the right time.'

---

[22] When she was four, my daughter had a Sting action figure that she called "Skeleton Boy." I loved everything about that. Now, every time she sees The Stinger, she exclaims, "It's Sting!" in her best Tony Schiavone voice. I love everything about that, too.

And we went a different direction."

The "different direction" turned out to be a play-off of WWF's *Survivor Series* main event from seven weeks earlier. As Hogan attempted a pinfall on Sting, Nick Patrick – a referee known to be in the pocket of the nWo – would execute a fast count, slapping his hand to the mat three times at a faster rate than usual before Sting had the opportunity to kick out, effectively cheating him out of the championship. Seeing this grave injustice, Bret Hart, a beacon of light in these dark times, would make his way out to the ring to "stop the steal," as it were, and restart the match, after which time Sting would mount his comeback, defeat Hogan fairly, take back the WCW championship, and there would be much rejoicing.

And that's how it happened. Except for one small detail. NICK PATRICK DIDN'T ACTUALLY COUNT FAST! And because he didn't count fast, it appeared to anyone with functioning eyes (despite insistence from the announce team – and God bless them for their efforts) that there was no controversy – Hogan just beat Sting. And *that*, boys and girls, is why we have to go back in time to fix *Starrcade 1997*. It is true that Sting left with the belt at the end of the night, but it didn't grant fans the masterpiece-closing resolution they – and the story – deserved. Instead, whether due to miscommunication (Nick Patrick apologists might argue the referee was not given clear instructions by the agent or talent ahead of the match) or conspiracy (wrestling conspiracy theorists might argue Nick Patrick was explicitly told to count to three at normal speed), the finish was botched.

The convoluted ending gave Hogan reason to petition for a rematch the following night on *Nitro*. Naturally, the match ran over *Nitro*'s allotted time slot – an issue very much on-brand for WCW,[23] though this one was intentional. Footage of the finish premiered on the

---

[23] See: *Halloween Havoc* 1998.

debut episode of WCW's new Thursday night program, *Thunder*, on January 8. Obviously, we got resolution after that, right? Obviously, you're not familiar with WCW.

No, the rematch was chock-full of shenanigans. The final scene before Nitro went off the air was referee Randy Anderson getting pulled into and knocked out by a Stinger Splash. With Anderson rendered unconscious, Nick Patrick ran in to take over officiating duties. How noble of him. Hogan went on to roll up Sting with both a fistful of tights and Sting's legs in the ropes, but Patrick counted to three anyway because he's on the nWo payroll. Just to be clear, Hogan PINNED Sting. AGAIN.

Sting shared his feelings on Patrick's lack of objectivity by clotheslining the dirty ref out of the ring. He subsequently put Hogan in the Scorpion Death Lock, just in time for original referee Randy Anderson to wake up and call for the bell. In the end, we have two referees with differing opinions. What's a Commissioner to do?

Well, if you're J.J. Dillon, you vacate the championship. In fairness to J.J., he was only playing a character here. It's not his fault that the character of Commissioner J.J. Dillon was just the worst. Regardless, Sting threw the championship belt at Dillon's feet and grabbed a microphone for the first time since October of 1996.

"You got no guts," Sting said, pointing his baseball bat at Dillon. "And you," he continued, turning to press the bat to Hogan's throat. "You're a dead man."

I will concede that this was indeed a moment. However, it only serves to reinforce the fact that Sting *was* the guy to take down Hogan all along. And in the end, Sting went over Hogan at *SuperBrawl* in February to win back the vacant title. So what was the point in cooling off the feud with controversy and convolution at Starrcade? Whatever the justification, it's not good enough.

* WHAT COULD HAVE HAPPENED *

After perhaps the most patient and nearly-perfect build in pro wrestling history, at *Starrcade 1997*, Sting needed to win and Sting needed to win *clean*.

No shenanigans. No controversy. No not-actually-fast fast counts. No re-enacting Montreal just because it was topical.

Good had to conquer evil. Decisively and definitively. That's what needed to happen.

The match did not need to be a Seven-Stars-In-The-Tokyo-Dome mat classic.[24] The story didn't call for that and that's not really who Sting nor Hogan were, and that's okay. The seven-star match was the friends we made along the way, specifically the eighteen-month story arc that got us to the title bout; *Starrcade 1997* was merely the coronation. In fact, the simple solution that would solve all of this and send the fans home happy would be a quick-and-easy Goldberg-style squash match, but my guess is, "That doesn't work for me, brother."[25]

It's been more than two decades since this debacle and there is no shortage of hindsight or rebooking theories out there about what

---

[24] Critics of his five-star match ratings system often mock Dave Meltzer about a perceived bias towards Japanese-style wrestling by claiming a given match "would have been seven stars in the Tokyo Dome!" Fun fact, though: the match Meltzer actually awarded seven out of five stars to – Kenny Omega versus Kazuchika Okada at NJPW *Dominion 2018* – took place at Osaka-jō Hall, not the Tokyo Dome. So. Take that, haters.

[25] Hogan had a creative control clause in his WCW contract that effectively granted veto powers over storyline directions he did not like. Hogan may not have used this memorable six-word response as often as he's accused of; however, *Starrcade '97* appears to have been one occasion when Hogan did use his contractual privileges to alter a match.

should have happened instead. Here's my take on it:

If we couldn't have Sting run through Hogan in three minutes or less like he really should have, then we could have turned to WCW's newest free agent acquisition. Bret Hart could have – and should have– debuted at *Starrcade 1997*, but not in the roles he did. His WCW debut should not have been as a special guest referee in the Eric Bischoff versus Larry Zbyszko semi-main event match. Nor should he have been the special enforcer for the Sting versus Hogan bout. In fact, if I had the pencil, I wouldn't have advertised him ahead of time as having a prescribed role at all. Instead, I'd have spent the weeks leading up to the event priming fans to wonder what, if any, role Hart would play at *Starrcade*.

There would be no sign of Hart by the time the main event rolled around. Hogan would enter first and with him would be Scott Hall and Kevin Nash, the two other founding members of the New World Order to properly close this storyline – and spin off into the next. These two would be needed nearby but not literally at ringside. Considering the occasion, maybe Bischoff would have sprung for a makeshift nWo "suite" towards the commentary area off to the side of the entry ramp. Sting, meanwhile, would still enter with his big laser show and iconic music, complete with the haunting child voiceover and everything.

The match would get underway, with Hogan gaining the upper hand early. Sting hadn't wrestled in more than a year and would have to overcome ring rust in addition to the villainous champion. As the match progressed, the tide would start to turn, likely a result of Hogan's own hubris, creating an opportunity for the challenger to mount a comeback. With momentum no longer on his side, Hogan would need help.

The nWo music could hit, causing Sting to prepare for a 3-on-1 attack. But before The Outsiders could make it too far from their off-ramp viewing area, they'd be cut off by none other than the debuting Bret Hart, who would make it clear that if they want to interfere in the championship match, they'll have to go through The Hitman to do it. Despite Hogan's pleas, Hall and Nash would be hesitant to engage. That hesitation would prove costly, as one by one, members of the WCW locker room would begin to emerge. Diamond Dallas Page, Lex Luger, and The Giant would join Hart in standing between The Outsiders and the ring. Neither Hart nor the WCW talents would interfere in the match itself. They wouldn't even need to get physical. Hart could have made his debut by proactively preventing interference because this match should have ended cleanly.

The Outsiders, having realized the numbers were no longer in their favor, would look at Hogan and retreat, abandoning the champion. Hogan would be all alone and know what was about to happen. He would stare into the steely eyes of the challenger and accept his fate, as Sting unleashed a furious attack, a beating eighteen months in the making. He would hit the Stinger Splash, lay Hogan out with a Scorpion Death Drop, and apply the Scorpion Death Lock in the dead center of the ring, forcing Hogan to submit, thus reclaiming the Big Gold Belt for WCW in this alternate timeline.

The ring would fill with WCW competitors, celebrating good's ultimate victory over evil. The last man to enter the ring would be Bret Hart. A path would clear and Hart and Sting would go face to face. No words would be said. No words would be needed. Hart would first looks Sting in the eyes, then at the belt draped over his shoulder. He would give the title a pat, look back up at Sting, and the new champion would watch as Hart left the ring and made his way up the ramp, bringing Sting's epic battle with the nWo to a close and beginning a new, uncertain chapter with WCW's newest acquisition.

* WHAT WOULD HAVE HAPPENED NEXT *

The revised ending would immediately establish Bret Hart as a main event level talent with eyes on the WCW championship. It would also lay the seeds for a potential Sting versus Hart feud in 1998. More importantly, it would give a clean end to the WCW/nWo storyline and set the stage for an nWo implosion in 1998. Hall and Nash left Hogan for dead, and he watched them do it. This would lead to a split between Hollywood and the Wolfpac, with Hogan and his loyalists representing the Black and White and The Outsiders leading the Red and Black.

It's also important to remember that 1998 was going to be the year of Bill Goldberg. So how would the *Starrcade* change impact Goldberg's rise? Wouldn't he need Hogan to pass the torch? And if Hogan got the belt back would that undo what we just fixed at *Starrcade 1997*? There's a lot to unpack there, and we'll dig into some of it later on; however, let's first establish that most good stories have definitive conclusions. The Sting versus nWo story was completed at *Starrcade*. We may revisit those characters in similar circumstances again down the road and evil is most certainly going to rise to power again in the future.

Think about how many times Batman faces off with the Joker. It's a lot more than once, and, despite the Caped Crusader coming out on top in every encounter, he never really vanquishes his foe for good. It's one of the pitfalls of maintaining a deontological philosophy.[26] Batman also isn't the only hero Joker messes with, nor is Joker the only villain occupying Batman's free time. Wrestling is no different. When story arcs are resolved, new stories begin. Sometimes they repeat, sometimes they rhyme, but the circumstances change to make the past into prologue for a new feud.

Sting's victory at *Starrcade* would not be undone, nor would WCW be set back, by Hogan reclaiming the championship months later,

---

[26] Deontologists judge the morality of an act on the act itself, regardless of consequences. Therefore, if killing is always wrong, one should never kill, even if ending one life would save many more. It's a real Trolley Problem.

especially if Sting lost the belt to a transitional champion – as he did in reality when Randy Savage took the title at *Spring Stampede 1998* – or if he lost it through unscrupulous means. Sting's story of vindication would have been completed at *Starrcade* and that arc would have been closed. Moving forward (with the benefit of hindsight, of course), we know Bill Goldberg is the next "guy" and we know Hogan – because of all he represents in the greater pro wrestling landscape – would be the best one to anoint him, which means Hogan would need the title back. So how might we get there?

The answer is maybe not too far off from where things really did go, with a few different wrinkles along the way. Goldberg would still need time to build, so the actual timeline of a midsummer championship coronation would still work well. And honestly, I'm not as opposed to the title match taking place on free TV instead of pay-per-view, but we'll tackle that in a bit. For now, let's just pencil in Goldberg's title victory coming, as it did, on Monday, July 6, 1998.

With that as our end date, let's go back to the aftermath of *Starrcade*. Sting would be champion, the nWo would be in shambles, Hogan would be off television, and Bret Hart would be a new top level babyface. It would make sense for Hart to begin a meta-feud with The Outsiders, known besties of Hart's greatest rival, Shawn Michaels. Perhaps Hart and Sting would team up to take on The Outsiders at *Souled Out* in January with singles programs against both Hall and Nash coming for Hart in the months that followed.

For Sting, the next several months would provide an opportunity to reestablish the World Heavyweight championship as a WCW title after so many months of nWo domination. A babyface versus babyface match between Sting and Lex Luger might headline *SuperBrawl VIIII* in February. At *Uncensored* in March, the newly rebranded "Big Poppa Pump" Scott Steiner might get a shot at the Big Gold Belt.

Sting's reign would come to an end at *Spring Stampede* against Randy

Savage, just as it did in reality. However, the circumstances surrounding the match might have been a little different. Before the event, Bret Hart and Randy Savage would battle to become the No. 1 contender. Savage would win the match after a man in a black trench coat wielding a baseball bat took a swing at Hart's knee. *What have you done, Sting?!*

Of course, for anyone familiar with the previous two years of WCW television, this wouldn't smell right. But Bret Hart wasn't around for the previous two years and he wouldn't want to hear any of it either. To Hart, the 'eye in the sky don't lie' and that mysterious man in black sure looked like Sting. At *Spring Stampede*, Hart would bring a baseball bat of his own and, when the moment was right, he would even the score with the Stinger, costing him the championship and putting the belt around the waist of the Macho Man.

The following night on *Nitro*, Hollywood Hogan would return, challenge Savage, and reclaim the title for himself when the nWo's old deus ex machina, Jeff Farmer, revealed himself as the mysterious assailant by attacking Savage during the main event. A feud with The Outsiders would be inevitable for Hogan, and a few months of the fractured nWo choosing sides and alliances would be a fun side story to tell. This would also bring about a summer program between Sting and Hart, a feud that actually took place later in the year over the United States championship.

The table would also be set for Goldberg's run to the World title. On Monday, April 20, 1998, Goldberg would take out Raven (and the entire Flock) to claim the United States championship. On Monday, July 6, 1998, he'd be hoisting up both the U.S. and World title belts. In between, he'd just keep smashing opponents and stacking wins.

After toppling challengers at May's *Slamboree* and June's *Great American Bash* pay-per-views, Goldberg would look like the clear top contender for the world title. Conventional wrestling wisdom would say it would be better to book the championship match for *Bash at the Beach* in July in order to rake in the pay-pay-view money instead of just popping a cable rating; however, with Hogan and Dennis Rodman already teaming up to fight Diamond Dallas Page and Karl Malone in a matchup that delivered on mainstream appeal, *Bash at the Beach* wasn't the spot for the Goldberg bout. *The Great American Bash* might have worked fine for a Goldberg versus Hogan match, but I really don't have a problem standing by WCW's decision to give the match away on *Nitro*; it was an incredible moment. What I would change is the build.

Instead of announcing such a huge contest on *Thunder* four days before the bell rings, WCW should have spent the time after *The Great American Bash* building towards a special episode of *Nitro* on July 6 from the Georgia Dome in Atlanta. If they were going to establish Goldberg as the unquestioned No. 1 contender, they should have gone all in on it. Hype it for weeks as the former Georgia Bulldog and Atlanta Falcon defensive lineman's homecoming. With forty-thousand-plus in attendance – quadruple the number of fans who would be in the stands at the upcoming *Bash at the Beach* pay-per-view – this was already going to be a special event, so why not market it that way? Years later, All Elite Wrestling and NXT were both successful in elevating otherwise regular weekly television episodes into something more simply by branding them with creative themes like *Winter is Coming* or *New Year's Evil*.[27] WCW could have easily done the same, and it wouldn't have even required much work, as their tried and true *Clash of the Champions* moniker had

---

[27] Fun fact: Before it became an NXT television special in 2021, *New Year's Evil* was the name of proposed WCW pay-per-view event co-branded with the rock band *KISS* and scheduled for December 31, 1999 at Sun Devil Stadium in Tempe, Ariz. The plan was for the half-concert, half-wrestling show to climax at exactly midnight local time to welcome in the year 2000 (and whatever mischief Y2K might bring with it). Plans ultimately fell through, but WCW didn't let the quality show title go to waste. The company ended up using *New Year's Evil* as the moniker for the final *Nitro* of the century on December 27, 1999.

served as a go-to for television specials dating back to the NWA and Jim Crockett Promotions days.

With a big stadium venue, creative marketing behind the event, and a month to build, Goldberg's championship victory could have been even more historic and memorable – without being compromised by correcting the errors of *Starrcade 1997*. Now, the errors of *Starrcade 1998*? We might as well go there now.

THREE

173-1

"We've killed the golden goose."

December 27, 1998
MCI Center ◉ *Washington, D.C.*
WCW Starrcade

Kevin Nash defeated Goldberg (c) by pinfall for the WCW World Heavyweight Championship (11:20).

* WHAT REALLY HAPPENED *

Bill Goldberg made his television debut as a professional wrestler on September 22, 1997. Sporting black trunks and black boots, Goldberg defeated Hugh Morrus in two minutes and forty-three seconds on *WCW Monday Nitro* and mouthed to the camera, "That's number one."

Another 172 victories would follow, as September 22, 1997 became the first of 462 consecutive days that Bill Goldberg was unbeatable in World Championship Wrestling.

The Goldberg match formula was not particularly complicated. As Eric Bischoff put it: "He'd step into the ring, he'd hit you, he'd hit you again, he'd spear you, he'd jackhammer you, he'd be in the locker room seven minutes later, and the crowd was going nuts."

Goldberg's iconic, security-led walk from his private locker room to the ring usually lasted longer than the subsequent match did. And, just to clear up a common misconception: the security team wasn't there for Goldberg's protection; it was there to protect everybody else from Goldberg. The more you know, right? Billed at six-foot-four and 285 pounds, Goldberg was a short-burst, high-impact monster who came to professional wrestling by way of the National Football League after the Carolina Panthers made him the first player released in the history of the franchise.

In truth, WCW did not plan an undefeated streak for this former defensive lineman who made his television debut with just six documented professional wrestling matches under his belt. It just kind of happened. He was the perfect guy at the perfect time. He rarely spoke, his skillset was relatively limited, and his ring attire was as basic as it could possibly be, and yet in 1998, Goldberg possessed a je ne sais quoi that fans could not resist.

WCW knew it had something special by the end of 1997 but it wasn't really until the following spring that people started to notice that Goldberg had never lost a match. Well, at least not on television. In a bit of trivia that will someday win you big money on *Jeopardy!*, a fellow by the name of Chad Fortune actually handed Goldberg his first loss in a *WCW Saturday Night* dark match on July 24, 1997 – Goldberg's last contest prior to debuting on *Nitro* that September. Regardless, after his U.S. championship title victory over Raven on the April 20, 1998 episode of *Nitro*, Goldberg's "official" record stood at 75-0.

There has always been some debate about number inflation when it comes to Goldberg's record. Early on, the number was factual, but at some point it started to grow exponentially. However, it should also be recognized that, despite the number being overstated, it did remain both mathematically and theoretically possible. The pace was less than three matches a week and a typical Goldberg match lasted all of about three minutes, so it could have been done. Plus, friendly reminder to everyone reading that this is pro wrestling. Everything is embellished, including the heights, weights, and actual fighting ability of every wrestler ever. That's showbiz, baby. But if you really want to get bent out of shape about the accuracy of Goldberg's win total, you do you, brother.

The new – and apt – catchphrase of "Who's next?" began to circulate over the summer of 1998 as Goldberg continued to rack up victories. His most significant win came on July 6, 1998 when he defeated Hollywood Hogan to become the WCW World Heavyweight champion in front of more than 40,000 fans at the Georgia Dome in Atlanta. Perhaps his greatest match came later in October when he defeated Diamond Dallas Page, occasionally known simply by the initials "DDP," to retain the title at *Halloween Havoc*.

His match against Page was also the first time Goldberg appeared vulnerable. Not only did he miss his first spear attempt on DDP, instead hitting the ring post with his shoulder, but he legitimately knocked himself out on a second spear attempt when he accidentally drove his head into the mat while finishing the tackle. When Goldberg tried to lift Page up for the Jackhammer, for the first time ever, he couldn't muster the strength. When he tried again, Page countered with his own finishing move, the Diamond Cutter.

Years before Randy Orton rebranded the maneuver as the RKO, Page's Diamond Cutter was arguably the most "over" move in the industry. Any time DDP hit the Diamond Cutter, the crowd erupted. When he hit it on Goldberg, the reaction was deafening. Page couldn't capitalize, though, as Goldberg was able to recover, hit the Jackhammer, and cover DDP for the 1-2-3.

The *Halloween Havoc* match removed any doubts about Page's status in the main event scene. It was also the first real crack in Goldberg's armor, and while fans weren't turning on him quite yet, it certainly showed they were open to the possibility of another babyface usurping the world title.

That's where Kevin Nash came back into the picture. The co-founder of the New World Order two years earlier, "Big Sexy" broke up the band into two factions on April 20, 1998 – the same night that Goldberg won the U.S. title. Hollywood Hogan remained a villain and led the nWo Hollywood faction, while Nash created the fan-favorite nWo Wolfpac.

Nash was already a well-established main event player; prior to coming to WCW, he had held the WWF championship for nearly a full calendar year while wrestling as "Diesel." His nWo run made him a "cool" heel and his popularity reached an all-time high with his turn to the Wolfpac. In short, there's no good argument why Kevin Nash *shouldn't* have been in the WCW World Heavyweight title picture by the end of 1998.

At the November *World War 3* pay-per-view, Nash came out the victor in a three-ring, sixty-man battle royale match to name the No. 1 contender for Goldberg's championship. It was around this general timeframe that Nash joined the WCW creative team – a group of wrestling minds charged with developing storylines and results for the product. It was also around this general timeframe that the WCW creative team began to feel that the Goldberg storyline had gone as far as it could and his winning streak needed to end.

Now, Nash didn't actually start booking matches – at least not in an official capacity – until February of 1999, so the notion that he "booked himself to beat Goldberg" is false. Did he have enough influence to put himself in position to do it? Sure. But, as Nash has accurately pointed out, "At 6-10, 300 pounds, you walk into a room anywhere and you've got stroke." Political influence in wrestling is not inconsequential, but at the end of the day, Eric Bischoff made the decision to end the streak at *Starrcade*, not Kevin Nash.

Bischoff's decision is certainly debatable, but the streak did have to end at some point, so, for the moment, let's say *Starrcade* was the right spot to end it. Was Kevin Nash the right choice to do it? At that time, it would have been difficult to say he wasn't. If Goldberg was the most popular act in the company, Nash was an exceptionally close second. The crowd reactions alone as the two men were introduced at *Starrcade* would illustrate that. But if you don't trust your eyes or ears, take a look at the stats: while the Sting-versus-Hogan-headlined *Starrcade 1997* netted a WCW-record 700,000 pay-per-view buys, no pay-per-view in company history had a larger gate than the $584,236 that Goldberg and Nash delivered at *Starrcade 1998*. Moreover, the best overall gate in WCW history – $930,735 – came eight days later when the rematch between the two was supposed to main-event *Nitro*. The numbers do not lie: people wanted to see this match.

The bulk of their *Starrcade* tussle was pretty solid, too. It wasn't a five-star mat classic by any means, but it absolutely had a "big fight feel" and was everything one might hope for or expect from two men of their size and stature. There was even some sneaky-good athleticism on display. Goldberg utilized his impressive strength to powerslam the super-heavyweight with ease and Nash dug deep into his arsenal to pull off a falling arm bar submission maneuver, albeit it briefly, due to Goldberg pulling his arm out seconds later.

"I had this piece of wrestling art that I was going to hang and all of a sudden Jackson Pollock threw up on the corner of my canvas," Nash lamented about the short-lived mat wrestling exchange in 2020.

The effort both men had put into the match to that point was all really good. As was so often the case, it was the finish where they went and WCW-ed it up. After Goldberg hit Nash with a spinning heel kick, Disco Inferno – who, if you are not familiar with his work, was everything you might think he would be – took advantage of the no-disqualification stipulation by attacking the champion, though he was quickly speared for his efforts. Then, Bam Bam Bigelow – a recent defection from ECW who had his sights set on Goldberg since debuting in WCW a few weeks earlier – came out and got a few punches in before being clotheslined out of the ring. Finally, to put the cherry on top of the overbooking sundae, Scott Hall showed up disguised in a yellow "Event Staff" polo and zapped Goldberg with a cattle prod. Rationale being – one assumes – if it works on a

2,000-pound bull, it ought to take down a 285-pound Goldberg. Goldberg allegedly wanted to use an actual taser for this spot, but WCW officials realized this was objectively insane, so instead they duct taped a stun gun and instructed their champion to convulse all over the ring when it started clicking. I'm genuinely not sure which idea was worse.

Regardless, Kevin Nash was still incapacitated from what must have been just one hell of a spinning heel kick, so he didn't see any of the interference, which protected his babyface status for the time being. When he came to, Nash picked up Goldberg for the Jackknife Powerbomb. The crowd went wild as the referee counted to three, giving Nash the WCW World Heavyweight championship and Goldberg a record of 173-1.

The streak was over. Later that night, WCW commentator Bobby Heenan told his colleagues prophetically, "We've killed the golden goose." They didn't call him "The Brain" for nothing. Beating Goldberg was one thing, but even Heenan had no idea just how bad it was about to get. Goldberg, Nash, and Bischoff have all conceded the ending to *Starrcade 1998* was not good; however, the story could have been salvaged. It – and arguably WCW – reached the point of no return eight days later.

After reviewing the tape and seeing the interference for the first time, Nash offered Goldberg a rematch for the championship to take place on the January 4, 1999 episode of *Nitro*. Unfortunately, Goldberg was kayfabe arrested for "aggravated stalking" of Miss Elizabeth during the show. Good-guy Goldberg did not commit any wrongdoings, of course; it was just a ploy to keep him out of the arena and he was released to return to the building when police found Liz's story "inconsistent and unbelievable." Fans, meanwhile, found the angle as a whole to be more abhorrent than suspect. In any case, with Goldberg in custody and Nash in need of an opponent, none other than Hollywood Hogan returned to save the day as the fill-in challenger.

After a lengthy standoff in the ring, Hogan looked to throw the first punch, but stopped to instead poke Nash in the chest with his index finger. And, God bless him, Nash took what might have been the biggest bump of his career, selling the poke like he'd just taken a bullet. Hogan covered him for the three count to reclaim the world championship. Hogan, Nash, Hall, and Scott Steiner celebrated in the ring together, having successfully pulled the wool over everyone's eyes. The nWo was officially whole again and WCW had officially jumped the shark.

When Goldberg arrived at the arena moments later, he sprinted down to the ring and took out the four men in succession. Then Lex Luger showed up presumably to give Goldberg backup, but as soon as Goldberg turned to lift Hogan up for a Jackhammer, Luger hit him from behind with a double-ax handle smash. The nWo then beat Goldberg down some more, handcuffed him to the ropes, and spray painted his back with the letters "nWo." The incident has come to be known as the "Fingerpoke of Doom."

This alone would have been enough to do WCW in, but the self-immolation for the night did not end there. This was also the same night that, on the "other" channel, Mick Foley would defeat The Rock to win the WWF championship. As was relatively common practice for WCW – whose *Nitro* was live while WWF's Raw was often taped – WCW told viewers what was going to happen… and the viewers left to watch it. *Raw* also wrapped up before *Nitro* that night, so when channel-changers came back to *Nitro*, they got to see WCW's cluster in all its glory, or lack thereof. For many, it would be the last time they came back at all.

In hindsight, the whole thing remains both shocking and unsurprising. Shocking, simply because watching an entire company figuratively nosedive in real-time is just a shocking experience in general. But it was also unsurprising, because this is what WCW did, over and over and over again. Finishes were perpetually overbooked and planning was consistently short-sighted, but the issue most damning, in the end, was that WCW could not – or would not – escape the allure of the nWo. From the original trio, to massive expansion, to knock-off creations, to the Wolfpac, to nWo 2000 – listen, if people recycled metals the way WCW recycled the nWo storyline, there would be no energy crisis. The nWo was an incredible idea that made a ton of t-shirt money and should have died in 1997. Full stop.

But it didn't. Instead, WCW managed to swiftly and soundly kill off the momentum of its two most popular performers just so Hulk Hogan could get his win back. Hogan didn't get to be the one to end the streak, but he was the *only* one who benefited from the streak ending. Eight days after *Starrcade 1998*, Hogan was once again WCW champion and leading a fully rebuilt nWo.

Goldberg would never again hold the WCW World Heavyweight championship. Despite becoming arguably the biggest mainstream star the company ever created – he was on the cover of *TV Guide* in December of 1998, which, in 1998 was a real BFD – Goldberg had just one world title reign that lasted all of 174 days.

Nash's title victory at *Starrcade 1998* was the first of his WCW career. He went on to win it four more times, but because of how he won (and lost) the title, no reign would ever be more consequential than his first. And while criticism for his brief initial title run is well-deserved, that criticism has probably been misdirected over the years.

"I beat Goldberg to turn around and lay down for Hogan – what did I get for all that?" Nash asked Jim Ross rhetorically on an episode of *The Ross Report* in 2017. "...If Kevin Nash was booking that, Kevin Nash would be getting the run of a lifetime."

That certainly would have been a better option than the one we got.

* WHAT COULD HAVE HAPPENED *

The interesting thing about *Starrcade 1998* is that WCW hadn't actually booked themselves into a corner. There were several options the company could have pursued to either end the streak *or* effectively alter the Goldberg storyline in a positive way.

The first – and simplest – option would be to keep the main event matchup as it was but instead of overbooking the finish with run-ins and non-lethal force, Nash could have just beaten Goldberg clean. Here's the thing about Nash – he was a *huge* star and when he did pin Goldberg at *Starrcade 1998*, the crowd wasn't mad about it. Not only was it believable for him to be able to threaten Goldberg physically, but by December of 1998, he had the presence and popularity to be "the guy" for WCW.

Longtime WCW booker Kevin Sullivan pitched a finish for the Nash/Goldberg match similar to the sequence Goldberg had with Diamond Dallas Page at *Halloween Havoc*: Goldberg could have gone for a spear, missed, and hit the ring post. Instead of falling to the outside, Goldberg would stay within the ropes, turn back to the center of the ring, and fall victim to either a Big Boot or Jackknife Powerbomb from Nash, resulting in a fluke pin with Goldberg perhaps kicking out just after the referee's hand hit the mat for three.

If Nash *wasn't* the guy to end the streak, then Diamond Dallas Page was. Page gave Goldberg the best match of his career at *Halloween Havoc*, so a return match at *Starrcade* would have done big business as well. Getting there would have been easy too, since the *World War 3* pay-per-view in November had the No. 1 Contender stipulation attached to the sixty-man battle royale. Instead of going into a program with Bret Hart for the United States championship, Page could have stayed in the World title picture and gone over in the battle royale to set up the rematch with Goldberg at *Starrcade*.

Page had Goldberg beat after hitting the Diamond Cutter back at

Halloween Havoc, but he couldn't muster the strength to pin the champion. Goldberg got the time he needed to recover and from there it was spear, Jackhammer, lights out. The rematch at *Starrcade* would focus on that. Page would know he could defeat Goldberg; he would have studied game tape and had always been resourceful – long before the "RKO Outta Nowhere" meme, the Diamond Cutter could come anytime, anywhere. All Goldberg seemingly had at his disposal were the spear and the Jackhammer, so if Page were to "simply" avoid those two moves, the Big Gold Belt could have been his. This kind of build would also challenge Goldberg to expand his repertoire a bit with a couple unexpected maneuvers, showing that he too would have learned from their previous matchup.

Towards the end of the match, Page could have hit the Diamond Cutter out of desperation – perhaps by countering a running powerslam or something like that – but once again he would have lacked the wherewithal to cover the champion. As both men would struggle to get up, Goldberg would have found his bearings first and connected on the spear. Still shaking off the effects of the Diamond Cutter, Goldberg, slower than usual to get back to his feet, could have set up for the Jackhammer. When he finally got Page in position, DDP would have floated over to attempt another Diamond Cutter just like he did at *Halloween Havoc*, but this time Goldberg would block it and push Page face-first into the corner where he would crumple to the canvas. Goldberg would shake off the cobwebs and set up again for the spear. His sprint would begin when Page got back to his feet. As Goldberg approached, DDP would instinctively counter the spear into the Diamond Cutter and fall on top of Goldberg for the 1-2-3. The streak would be over and though Goldberg would lose clean, he would lose clean to a worthy opponent, and after being hit twice with the most "over" move on the planet.

Or, what if *Starrcade* would have been the *first* singles matchup between Goldberg and Page? What if Goldberg had fought someone else at *Halloween Havoc*? Shortly after winning the WCW Television championship in August of 1998, "Lionheart" Chris Jericho began calling out the undefeated World Heavyweight champion. Jericho went on to defeat a Goldberg impersonator at *Fall Brawl* in September and even recruited a toothless trucker by the name of Ralphus to serve as his personal security escort, mocking Goldberg's famed entrance. This was all done in an effort to set up what Jericho hoped would be the "greatest squash match of all-time." That match never came to fruition, though, as Goldberg – in real life – was not amused by Jericho's antics and got the angle killed in a non-match segment on *Nitro*. This was bad business. But what if Goldberg and WCW had done *good* business and granted Jericho his match with Goldberg at *Halloween Havoc* in October?

The WCW title match wouldn't have closed the show; Hollywood Hogan versus The Warrior would have – which is a whole different conversation that is probably best left tabled forever. No amount of revisionist history could fix that train wreck so let's not even try. But if Goldberg defended against Jericho, the latter would have made the former look like a million bucks and saved the DDP match for the biggest pay-per-view of the year in December.

Another option would be to keep the title on Goldberg at *Starrcade 1998*. Although Goldberg's winning streak may have seemed excessive, his time as champion was actually quite limited at just 174 days. During that time, he also only successfully defended the title against three real main event players: The Giant, Sting, and Diamond Dallas Page, and of those three, only the Page match was on pay-per-view. A hard-fought, clean victory over someone of main event stature at *Starrcade* would have lent even more credibility to Goldberg's run on top of WCW.

There would have been one other way to keep the streak alive and the title on Goldberg. That would have been to lean into the supposed boos he had begun to receive and turn Goldberg heel. WCW creative may have been correct in its assertion that Goldberg's streak had gone as far as it could, but only because they saw him strictly as a *babyface*. If Goldberg would have let the hate flow through him and turned to the dark side, the streak could have taken on a whole new life as he transitioned from conquering hero to unstoppable villain.

Goldberg matches were famously formulaic. All that would have been necessary to turn him heel would be to change the formula from doing only what he *needed* to do, to doing everything he *wanted* to do. Instead of taking care of business in three minutes or less, he could have toyed with opponents and resorted to underhanded, unnecessary tactics whenever he could. Against a top babyface like Nash at *Starrcade*, it would be easy to attack a knee early on, but use the no disqualification stipulation to go well beyond respectable measures, shifting his focus from winning the match to injuring his opponent.

Any of these options would have been better than the overbooked train wreck we saw at the actual *Starrcade 1998*. More importantly, each would have (hopefully) prevented the "Fingerpoke of Doom" eight days later, possibly saving, but certainly slowing down WCW's eventual demise.

* WHAT WOULD HAVE HAPPENED NEXT *

In the immortal words of a musically-inclined King George III, "What comes next?"

Let's start with the scenario wherein Kevin Nash defeated Goldberg at *Starrcade*. In truth, even if we kept all the shenanigans from the real timeline, all that would be needed to salvage this scenario would be to avoid the "Fingerpoke of Doom." Nash could have had a real run with the belt, and the rematch with Goldberg could have headlined the next big pay-per-view, *SuperBrawl*, in February.

If Nash were to stay a babyface, a matchup with former partner Scott Hall could have been the main event for January's *Souled Out*, with the storyline focused on Nash not needing or wanting Hall's help to win the big one.

If Nash were booked for a heel run, the proposed rematch with Goldberg could have still happened on the January 4, 1999 episode of *Nitro*, where Hall would again involve himself in the match, this time with Nash's demeanor shifting from shocked Pikachu face to Cheshire Cat grin. The ensuing beat down from The Outsiders – not the full-blown Hogan-led nWo – could keep Goldberg out of action for several weeks, leading to a dramatic return in time for *SuperBrawl*.

The buy rates and gate for the *Starrcade* match and proposed *Nitro* rematch respectively show that there was money and interest in a feud between Goldberg and Nash, so a late winter/early spring program between the two – spanning at least through *Uncensored* and *Spring Stampede* – would have made a lot of sense.

The scenario where Diamond Dallas Page ends the streak at *Starrcade* in a rematch from *Halloween Havoc* would seem to easily lend itself right into the Page heel turn we actually saw in the spring of 1999. Beating the unbeatable Goldberg at the WCW's biggest pay-per-view would have gone straight to DDP's head and provided Page with lifelong bragging rights to annoy fans with, similar to what Chris Jericho received by defeating Steve Austin and The Rock in the same night to become the first WWF Undisputed Champion. Page was an outstanding blue-collar babyface, but he could also play an insufferable heel. This feather in his cap would have given him the cachet to portray the latter to the fullest at a time when WCW desperately needed a new baddie on top for the babyface(s) to chase in a post-nWo world. Plus, this could have given the company its own version of a Rock/Austin rivalry, with Goldberg and DDP capitalizing on their undeniable in-ring chemistry by headlining multiple pay-per-views together over the next several years.

If Goldberg didn't lose at *Starrcade 1998*, the question then becomes when would be the right time to snap the streak? WCW erred in not publicly maintaining the accurate victory total, and in that way, they were somewhat backed into a corner to end the streak sooner than later. It's difficult to imagine the same fan excitement being generated once Goldberg's win total would have surpassed 200, for example. When the babyface ceases to be the protagonist of the story, and the conversation shifts from 'who's next' to 'who's left,' then we've got a problem. Maybe by win No. 173 we had already reached that point.

But, for the sake of argument, let's say Goldberg beat Kevin Nash at *Starrcade*. Where would he go from there? The answer is probably a lengthy title run. It *is* truly shocking that a performer viewed so synonymously with both WCW and the World Heavyweight championship decades later only held the title one time for about a six-month period in actuality. That's it. For the kind of build the streak storyline got, one would have imagined his reign would have lasted at least twice as long as it really had. But, just like one of his matches, Goldberg's run was a hard-hitting spectacle that was over before you knew it.

With WCW's big-money pay-per-views – *Starrcade* (December), *Halloween Havoc* (October), *Bash at the Beach* (July) – all occurring in the second-half of the year, it stands to reason that Goldberg's run as champion, had he not lost in 1998, would have continued until one of those events later in 1999. Until that time, he would have upgraded the level of his pay-per-view opponents to include established main event players – the likes of Nash, Hall, Sting, Page, Flair, and Savage. Simultaneously, WCW would take that six-to-eight month period to build up its next homegrown star. Considering some of the WCW talent that would headline pay-per-views for the WWF over the next several years – Chris Jericho, Eddie Guerrero, Chris Benoit, Booker T – options were certainly available.

And what about the scenario where Goldberg turns heel? That's an interesting one. We do know that the man Bill Goldberg did not like his character being portrayed as anything short of a superhero. To his credit, he has leveraged that to do a lot of good in the world and

I'm not going to be critical of the guy for using a fictional persona to make a very real difference in the lives of kids who need it. Goldberg deserves all the admiration in the world for being a first-class human being. All that said, in this particular pro wrestling storyline, we'd need to adopt Harvey Dent's life philosophy that, "You either die a hero or you live long enough to see yourself become the villain."

Bad guy Goldberg wouldn't necessarily be a "bad guy" … he'd mostly just be bored and not finding the kind of competition he'd be looking for. He'd be Brock Lesnar before there was Brock Lesnar. This version of Goldberg probably wouldn't care much about Heath Slater's kids either.[28] He would just be a ruthless beast, running through anything and everything in his path. If a cruiserweight match was taking place when Goldberg wanted the ring, said cruiserweights might land in the third row. His matches wouldn't be "hardcore," but they would appear increasingly and unnecessarily more violent. The caliber of his pay-per-view opponents in this scenario would again be a step up from his previous foes, as the spotlight would turn away from Goldberg and onto WCW's top-tier performers who would be working to chase and defeat the monster for the title.

So who then would be the right choice to end the streak and save WCW from the wrath of Goldberg? Well, both Nash and Page would remain credible candidates to play the role of savior. Then again, they also each would have already had their shots and wouldn't have gotten the job done. Sting was always good for a top babyface run and actually had a pair of pay-per-view singles matches against Goldberg in 1999 at *Slamboree* and *Halloween Havoc*. However, Sting

---

[28] While campaigning for a (kayfabe) contract on the August 15, 2016 episode of *WWE Monday Night Raw*, Heath Slater explained to Brock Lesnar that he needed his job because he had kids. For a brief moment, fans saw an empathetic side to the Beast Incarnate. "I got kids, too, man," Lesnar said. "Come on in here. I feel you. Let's talk about your kids." Then Lesnar leaned in close to inform Slater, "I don't give a shit about your kids," before beating the tar out of the One Man Band. Tremendous television.

already played out his "purveyor of good" storyline with the nWo in 1997. Sid Vicious came to WCW in June of 1999 and was actually in a storyline with Goldberg by September. He was another guy with main event credibility who would have been a legitimate physical challenger to Goldberg. To that end, if we want to talk about physical presence, no one could match the muscles on Big Poppa Pump, so rising singles star Scott Steiner could make some sense. And it certainly would have elevated somebody like Chris Jericho to be the one to upset the champion. Jericho debuted in the WWF in the summer of 1999, but the promise of an actual program with Goldberg might have kept him around WCW for a little while longer. Plus at least then we would have gotten some measure of payoff for Jericho's outstanding promo work against a disinterested Goldberg in the fall of 1998.

But I think we all know the correct answer – the only answer – for who should have been the man to end a heel Goldberg's undefeated streak. That's right, brother. He's got the Red, White, and Blue flowing through his veins. He was born and made in the U-S-of-A. Say your prayers and eat your vitamins because what's Goldberg gonna do when Hulkamania runs wild on him?! Back in his babyface red-and-yellow gear from the days of yore, Hulk Hogan would return to get his win – and title – back from Goldberg! Goldberg would issue an open challenge to anyone who wanted to show up for a fight at *Bash at the Beach*. WCW would hype the match – and mystery opponent – for weeks. And then, three years to the day since he turned his back on WCW, the Hulkster would return to be the hero the company needs – nay, deserves! Damnit, people – that's long-term booking right there!

Would it help build new stars? No. Would it benefit Goldberg in any significant way? Not really. But would it pop you? Absolutely it would. And short of knocking down a grown man with an index finger to symbolize the peaceful transition of power, isn't this the most WCW option available to us?

Less facetiously, though, it does at least provide a redemption arc for the most famous wrestler of all-time and *doesn't* rehash the New World Order storyline. A good Hogan run at this stage might even function similar to how John Cena's United States championship run was handled in 2015. Hogan wouldn't necessarily need a weekly open challenge format to defend the title, but a reformed Hulkster might take the opportunity to avoid there being another heel stranglehold on the WCW title for a little while, welcoming new challengers, and letting the many quality young workers that WCW employed at the time get the rub by sharing the ring with Hogan, while ultimately losing to him.[29]

After his loss, Goldberg would take some well-deserved time off and return later in 1999, still a monster, but perhaps a humbler one. As a fan-favorite again, he would be able to take advantage of feuds against the likes of Scott Steiner and Sid Vicious, and, who knows? Maybe he could make his way back into the main event of *Starrcade* one more time. Perhaps not against Bret Hart, though.[30]

Goldberg's winning streak should not have been an albatross for WCW – it should have been an opportunity. And so long as creative could have avoided anything involving finger-poking, there were plenty of quality storyline options available for Goldberg to keep the product both exciting and interesting for some time to come.

---

[29] He'd be reformed, not stupid.

[30] Hart suffered what would be a career-ending concussion in the World championship match against Goldberg at *Starrcade 1999*.

FOUR

THE HIGHER POWER

"It was me, Austin! It was me all along!"

June 7, 1999
Fleet Center ◉ *Boston Massachusetts*
WWF Monday Night Raw

* WHAT REALLY HAPPENED *

The night after *Judgment Day 1998*, The Undertaker found himself in the middle of a WWF ring playing a surprisingly unfamiliar role: a heel.

Despite being known by such monikers as "The Lord of Darkness," "The Demon of Death Valley," and "The Reaper of Wayward Souls," The Undertaker actually spent a shockingly small amount of time doing the devil's bidding. Over the course of an incredible three-decade-long WWE career, Taker spent more than twenty-five years as a babyface, and his turn at *Judgment Day* in October of 1998 launched his first heel run in nearly seven full years.

But one thing you could always say about The Deadman: when he went to the Dark Side, he went hard. With the assistance of what he called his "Ministry of Darkness," The Undertaker promised to unleash a plague upon the World Wrestling Federation. Unfortunately, that plague turned into one of the most convoluted, nonsensical, and downright disturbing storylines in WWF history.

To assemble his Ministry, The Undertaker enlisted the services of the most despicable man he knew, the appropriately named Paul Bearer, who just one night earlier betrayed his own son – The Undertaker's half-brother, Kane.

Before we go any further, it's important for you, dear reader, to understand that as far as pro wrestling storylines go, not a one has ever been more soap-opera-fantastic than that of The Undertaker and Kane. Let me explain. ... No, there is too much. Let me sum up:

The Undertaker was born into a family of morticians. With a name like "The Undertaker," how could he not be, right? Well, he was. He also had a younger brother named Kane. Undertaker was a bit of a pyromaniac as a youth, and one time while playing with matches, he burned down his family's funeral home by accident (or was it?), killing his parents and, *presumably*, his brother. Now, Paul Bearer - a fellow mortician at the funeral home[31] - survived the fire and went on to forge a managerial partnership with The Undertaker upon arriving in the World Wrestling Federation in 1991. However, fans knew nothing of The Undertaker's tragic past until Bearer confessed it to the world following his blackmailing and betrayal of his protégé in 1997. But that wasn't all Bearer revealed. Kane was alive! Bearer rescued The Undertaker's little brother from the fire and hid him for years in an asylum. Why, you ask? Well, it turned out - as these things often do - that Bearer had an affair with The Undertaker's mother and Kane was actually Bearer's biological son. Physically and emotionally scarred, Kane would soon come to the WWF himself to unleash the literal fires of hell upon The Undertaker. What tangled webs we weave... If I missed anything, don't worry, it will all be explored in full this fall on Peacock's new hit comedy, *Young Taker*.[32]

Anyway. Bearer's masked monster first debuted at *Badd Blood* in October 1997 by tearing the door off a steel cell to assault The Undertaker and cost him the WWF championship against Shawn

---

[31] Fun fact: Bill Moody, who portrayed Paul Bearer, actually had a degree in mortuary science and was a certified embalmer and mortician in real life.

[32] This is not factual; however, should it ever come to be, please pass along my interest in an Executive Producer credit to NBCUniversal.

Michaels in the first-ever Hell in a Cell match. At *Royal Rumble* in January 1998, Kane attacked his brother again, this time dumping The Undertaker in a casket, padlocking it shut, and setting it on fire. Born of fire and whatnot, Kane was a little on the obsessive side when it came to torching co-workers, especially his brother. Two months later, The Undertaker re-emerged from the Great Beyond to tell Kane he had gone away to "soothe the souls" of his deceased parents, as he would need to break the promise he made to them that he would never fight his own brother.

"I will walk straight through the fires of hell to face you, Kane," the risen Undertaker exclaimed on the March 3, 1998 episode of *Raw*. "And when you look into the eyes of your older brother, you will understand why I am the most feared entity in the World Wrestling Federation. You will understand why I am the Reaper of Wayward Souls. And you will understand why I am the Lord of Darkness."

It should be noted that The Undertaker is still the good guy at this point. As if that wasn't clear before, he buttoned up his pre-*WrestleMania* promo with a line that every older brother has lovingly shared with his younger brother at one time or another: "May the hounds of hell eat your rotting soul." Classic brother stuff.

In hindsight, this may be the promo that actually launched The Undertaker's descent into darkness because in the months that followed, a much more malevolent and sadistic Undertaker emerged. In April, he set his brother ablaze in the first-ever "Inferno Match." Fortunately for Kane, he fared slightly better in that bout (only burning an arm) than Bray Wyatt did in the 2020 concept redux.[33]

---

[33] The 2020 *TLC* pay-per-view event ended with the morbid but entertaining spectacle of "The Fiend" being fully engulfed in flames at the hands of Randy Orton. Wyatt remained off television for the next three months until returning as an extra crispy undead demon at *Fastlane* in March of 2021.

Two months later, The Undertaker's hand was raised following one of the most incredible spectacles in pro wrestling history. The June 1998 *King of the Ring* pay-per-view became instantly legendary due to the amount of punishment (both planned and unplanned) that Mick Foley endured over the course of seventeen unforgettable minutes in (and out of) the ring with "The Phenom." This included The Undertaker hurling Foley from the top of the twenty-two-foot "Hell in a Cell" structure through the Spanish announce table at ringside *to start* the match, then chokeslamming Foley through a panel on top of the cage (which was not supposed to break), and subsequently turning Foley into a human pincushion when he chokeslammed the near 290-pound man onto a pile of thumbtacks.[34] After the first two massive bumps, the camera panned to a now iconic shot of Foley appearing to smile, with a tooth hanging beneath his nose after it had been knocked out and up through his lip. Foley left the match with a concussion, dislocated jaw and shoulder, bruised ribs, and with fewer teeth than he had when he started. That match - whether intentionally or inadvertently - succeeded in turning Mick Foley into one of the most respected performers the industry has ever seen[35] as well as showcasing the kind of violence and destruction The Undertaker was capable of inflicting upon even the most courageous and capable of WWF performers.

The increase in aggression would boost The Undertaker into the WWF championship scene throughout the summer and into the fall. For a while, it even appeared that he and his brother had made amends and were working together for one of them to win the WWF

---

[34] "Oh, glitter!" This was the reaction my wife had upon first seeing Mankind dump out a bag of what was very much not glitter across the canvas.

[35] In his New York Times' best-selling book, *Have a Nice Day!: A Tale of Blood and Sweatsocks*, Foley recalled Vince McMahon telling him after the match, "You have no idea how much I appreciate what you have just done for this company, but I never want to see anything like that again."

title. That came to a screeching halt at *Judgment Day* in October when the main event pitted The Undertaker against Kane for the vacant WWF championship, with former champion Stone Cold Steve Austin tasked with officiating the match. Though Austin would ultimately refuse to crown a new champion during the contest, Paul Bearer emerged with a steel chair in hand towards the end of the match. But instead of striking The Undertaker - the man whom he had been tormenting for more than a year - Bearer swung the weapon at his own son, Kane.

This brings us back to October 19, 1998 - the day after *Judgment Day*, when Bearer stood alongside The Undertaker for the first time in more than a year. Bearer justified his actions by calling Kane "stupid" and "weak" and claimed The Big Red Machine was incapable of understanding the darkness, which prompted play-by-play man Jim Ross to interject, "He's your son for God's sakes, you rotund demon," which is objectively one of the greatest lines ever uttered on cable television.

The Undertaker and Kane continued to have a Ross-and-Rachel sort of relationship for the better part of the next twelve years. That is to say, if Ross and Rachel were undead wizard brothers who occasionally agreed to coexist in between extended periods of literal attempted murder. By the end of November 1998, also like Ross and Rachel, The Undertaker and Kane were on a break and at least one of them was interested in assaulting other people.[36] For The Undertaker, that other person was Stone Cold Steve Austin.

On the November 16, 1998 episode of *Raw*, just as it appeared Austin was poised to reclaim the WWF championship from The Rock - who won the title one night earlier at *Survivor Series* - The Undertaker marched down to the ring ... with a shovel ... and did his best Mark McGwire impersonation with Austin playing the part

---

[36] This is a *Friends*-themed paragraph.

of a Steve Traschel fastball.[37] A week later, The Undertaker went from sadism to Satanism, attacking and abducting Austin from a "local medical facility."[38] He and Paul Bearer then drove Austin to a funeral home where they intended to embalm him alive. Fortunately for Austin, Kane showed up just as The Undertaker raised a trocar above Austin's lifeless body while speaking in tongues. So that was a disturbing thing that happened.

The angle went from emotionally distressing to ecumenically offensive on the December 7, 1998 episode of *Raw*, when an Austin promo was interrupted by the Undertaker's "symbol" spontaneously bursting into flames at the top of the stage. It was very important to the WWF to use the word "symbol" because if it were to be called a "cross," this would have been in extremely bad taste… not just because of the whole burning cross connotation (which is pretty freaking bad just on its own), but also because the show ended with The Undertaker literally crucifying Austin on the cro- … "symbol." So there was that. The Undertaker's solo segment of the feud ended at *Rock Bottom* six days later on December 13 when Austin - with help from Kane - defeated The Undertaker in a "Buried Alive" match.

A few weeks after The Undertaker was buried alive - because, of course, that's how a "Buried Alive" match ends… with someone being hurled into an open crypt and covered in dirt - a midcard wrestler by the name of Dennis Knight was abducted and

---

[37] This was the year that Michael Jordan and the Bulls were enjoying their "Last Dance," Mark McGwire and Sammy Sosa were racing to sixty-two home runs, and the Monday Night Wars were at their peak. Few summers have ever produced better television.

[38] The word "hospital" has long been on Vince McMahon's list of banned words. The alleged reason is to prevent overzealous fans from bombarding local hospitals with phone calls and visits inquiring about the status of injured wrestlers. I genuinely don't know what's crazier: Vince's linguistic policies, or the fact that he might actually be wise to maintain them.

imprisoned by Bradshaw and Faarooq. Bradshaw and Faarooq had come together in November to form a hard-hitting tag team called "The Acolytes" under the guidance of The Jackyl, a cult leader sort of character portrayed by Don Callis. However, when Callis was released from his contract the following month, management of The Acolytes was transferred to an unknown new leader.

On the January 11, 1999 episode of *Raw*, that leader was revealed to be none other than The Undertaker, when he arrived to ritualistically "sacrifice" Knight. As he recited an incantation, The Undertaker - now sporting a black robe and hood - took a dagger to his wrist and funneled the blood into a chalice for Knight to drink. It may be difficult to remember, but this was, at one point, a professional wrestling program. Nevertheless, The Undertaker went on to carve his "symbol" (again, not a cross) into Knight's chest, rechristening his newest disciple as "Mideon." It was all deeply troubling.

The Undertaker promised that "the next sacrificial lamb will be led to slaughter" at the *Royal Rumble* on January 24. That lamb weighed 485 pounds and went by the name of Mabel, though he would soon be reborn as "Viscera." The Undertaker confronted Mabel during the Rumble match and strongly encouraged him to "accept the Lord of Darkness as your savior." The Acolytes and Mideon then proceeded to assault Mabel and - you guessed it - abduct him.[39] Mabel may not have worked out to be the nWo's third man, but he was about to become the fourth disciple of The Deadman.[40] But just like the nWo, when you're Ministry of Darkness, you're Ministry of Darkness 4-Life. (Because you have to give The Undertaker your

---

[39] The WWF had a real abduction problem in the late 1990s.

[40] When Eric Bischoff, Scott Hall, and Kevin Nash were debating on who should be the third man for the debuting New World Order at *WCW Bash at the Beach 1996*, the Wrestling Observer Newsletter reported at one point that Mabel was the top candidate. This was not true, of course. Hulk Hogan was revealed as the third man and the rest is history. As a result, we will all forever wonder what might have been...

soul and what not.)

As WWF morale did not improve, the beatings continued. On February 1, the Ministry initiated The Brood[41] - the vampiric trio of Gangrel, Edge, and Christian - into the group by beating down Edge and Christian and hanging Gangrel. And by "hanging Gangrel," I mean they fashioned a literal noose around the man's neck and hung him over the ring ropes. The segment closed with Michael Cole asking, "Is this some sort of ritual? This is highly unusual." The words that came out of Michael Cole's mouth during this angle were not great.

The first mention of "The Higher Power" came on the February 15, 1999 episode of *Raw*, one night removed from the *St. Valentine's Day Massacre* when the Ministry of Darkness beat down and abducted Mr. McMahon's personal enforcer, the Big Boss Man. Though McMahon was still fully entrenched in a feud with his longtime nemesis, Stone Cold Steve Austin, The Undertaker and his minions made their way to the ring with a message for the Chairman.

> While you were preoccupied with your petty obsessions, I have amassed an army - an army that will destroy you and your corporation. Each soul that we take, we take in the name of a far greater Power than even myself. And in that Power's name, in Its grandest vision, in Its grandest dream, and in my Ministry's destiny, I will own the World Wrestling

---

[41] Despite being together for all of about eight months, The Brood remains one of the very best and most enduring creations of the Attitude Era. The trio made its entrance by rising up from a ring of fire on the stage. Gangrel had fangs and drank a "red substance" from a goblet, which he then spat all over himself and the crowd. The group's entrance music was haunting and incredible, too. Fun fact: you know the whispering vocals on The Brood's theme? If you play the song backwards, the voice just repeats, "I buried Paul," a reference to the longstanding Beatles' urban legend of Paul McCartney's alleged demise. Everything about The Brood was tremendous.

Federation.

These are the sorts of things that happen when you don't offer stock options or health insurance to your employees.

Nevertheless, in kayfabe or reality, Vince McMahon has never responded well to threats. The following week, McMahon declared The Undertaker would compete in an Inferno match against his brother, Kane, in hopes that Kane would rid him of this turbulent dark priest. During the contest, Paul Bearer delivered a box to Mr. McMahon, who had joined Jerry Lawler and Michael Cole at the commentary desk. The box contained a stuffed teddy bear, which distressed McMahon greatly. The Undertaker won the match by setting Kane's boot on fire, then brought McMahon to his knees by lighting the bear ablaze as well. "A bear in flames, Mr. McMahon lying on the ramp, what does this all mean?" Michael Cole shouted as *Raw* went off the air.

It would be some time before Cole and the rest of the world would know the answer to that question. That said, The Undertaker soon began to clue the audience in on his plan by claiming to hold the key to McMahon's heart and soul and warning that soon there would be nothing between The Deadman and "her." While fans waited for this apparent mystery woman's identity to be revealed, McMahon booked The Undertaker to meet the Big Boss Man at *WrestleMania XV* in a Hell in a Cell match. The Undertaker responded by setting his "symbol" (still not a cross, no matter how much it absolutely looked like or was used as one) on fire on McMahon's front lawn. I'm sure the neighbors were thrilled.

The Undertaker went on to defeat Boss Man at *WrestleMania* in a match that was, at best, rough. However, what fans remember most is not the match itself, but what happened after. Following The Undertaker's victory, The Brood rappelled down from the rafters and landed on top of the cage. They then ripped open one of the center panels of the cage and lowered down a noose. The Undertaker placed the noose around Boss Man's neck (with a harness attached on the back since they thankfully didn't actually want to murder a man live on pay-per-view) as Paul Bearer used a remote control to lift the cell off the ground.

"This was horrible," longtime producer Bruce Prichard acknowledged in 2017. "This was embarrassing. This was bad. I felt so bad for The Undertaker and Boss Man, everybody involved in this. I felt bad for me. It sucked… and on top of it, the next night, Boss Man just goes out and works a match."

Fans in the arena didn't quite know how to respond to a man being hung in front of them, but at least they were spared from the horrific post-match commentary.

"Could this be symbolic?!" was a thing Michael Cole actually said. Four. Effing. Times.

Listen. It's not a secret that WWF/E announcers are *heavily* produced, so it's not fair to blame Michael Cole for saying outrageously stupid things on commentary when he's being screamed at in his headset to say outrageously stupid things on commentary. But holy Lord of Darkness, that might be the dumbest line by a play-by-play man in professional wrestling history.

The night after *WrestleMania*, Mr. McMahon's "heart and soul" and the object of The Undertaker's threats was revealed to be McMahon's twenty-two-year-old daughter, Stephanie. It turned out that the stuffed teddy bear The Undertaker lit on fire several weeks earlier had been Stephanie's favorite childhood toy. McMahon attempted to keep Stephanie safe from The Undertaker - who had demonstrated himself to be a boundaryless psychopath with no depths to his depravity - by bringing her to the arena. Of course, this did not work and she was, of course, abducted. Thankfully, McMahon ally Ken Shamrock was able to torture her whereabouts out of The Brood's Christian and rescue Stephanie from the boiler room of the arena.

The Undertaker was none too pleased with his evil plans going awry, so he got his revenge on "The World's Most Dangerous Man" the following week by abducting Shamrock's sister, Ryan, and suspending her above the stage on top of The Undertaker's "symbol." Taker slipped up by actually calling it a cross a week later when he was attempting to sacrifice Ken Shamrock. Whoops.

The feud with Shamrock ran through *Backlash* in April, when The Undertaker earned a one-on-one pinfall victory before refocusing his attention to the McMahons. As the pay-per-view closed, Stephanie McMahon was shown waiting alone in her father's limousine when the privacy partition rolled down to reveal The Undertaker as the vehicle's driver. And thus, the "Where to, Stephanie?" meme was born.

The next night on *Raw*, the Ministry carried Stephanie out to the ring tied to The Undertaker's "symbol" for a union of unholy matrimony. Before the ceremony was complete, Stone Cold Steve Austin made the save, taking out the Ministry with Stunners and steel chairs to save the innocent daughter of his greatest rival from the clutches of evil.

While the storyline up to this point had drifted into bad taste on occasion (or possibly on a regular basis, depending on your views about abduction, cultism, and pseudo-crucifixion), it was still fairly compelling, and certainly memorable, television. The "Black Wedding," as Jim Ross referred to it on *Raw*, was likely the moment the angle jumped the shark, though. The Undertaker even confessed in 2020 that his method of choice for corporate extortion in 1999 was probably the most bizarre incident of his thirty-year career. But at least it made logical sense, even if it wasn't totally believable. I mean, a wrestler trying to gain controlling interest in the company by marrying the boss' daughter? Like that would ever happen. But the story made sense, which is more than can be said for what happened next.

Three days after Austin saved Stephanie from becoming Mrs. Undertaker, the WWF debuted a new television program called, *Smackdown!* on UPN. It was on the pilot episode of *Smackdown!* that Shane McMahon merged his Corporation stable with the Undertaker's Ministry of Darkness to form… The Corporate Ministry! This is where the wheels fell off the wagon, and not just because having Big Boss Man join forces with The Undertaker a literal month after The Undertaker put a noose around Big Boss Man's neck and hung him from a steel cage was completely illogical… but that definitely set the tone for the nonsense fans were about to endure.

On the May 3 episode of *Raw*, Shane revealed that he had long been The Undertaker's inside man, facilitating The Undertaker's invasion of the McMahon family home and enabling the abduction of his sister in order to siphon power away from his father. Quite frankly, it would have been easier to just take a hit out on his dad like a normal person, but much like Washington Sentinels interim head coach Jimmy McGinty, Shane McMahon is anything but conventional.

The Undertaker soon after again began referencing the "Higher Power" he answered to. During the main event of the May 31 episode of *Raw*, The Higher Power made its physical debut when The Ministry tied Steve Austin up in the ring ropes and fell to their knees as a hooded figure emerged from the entryway. The Higher Power lifted his hood to reveal himself only to Austin, who was none too pleased to learn the truth.

The following week, the rest of the audience joined Austin in being none too pleased to learn the truth. With the entire Corporate Ministry gathered in the ring, Shane McMahon was set to unmask The Higher Power, but wanted his father present to witness it. Mr. McMahon then appeared on the TitanTron, claiming to be "close enough" right where he was.

"I say the evil, demonic S.O.B. show his face to the world now," Vince shouted at the figure in the ring.

And so, The Higher Power took off his hood and revealed himself to be... Vince McMahon.

"It was me, Austin! It was me all along!" McMahon yelled with glee.

J.R. spoke for all of us when he reacted with an exasperated, "Aw, son of a bitch..." on commentary.

The WWF did succeed here in pulling off a shocking reveal. Mostly because it didn't make any goddamn sense.

"If [Vince] Russo was managing the local Pizza Hut," author R.D. Reynolds once said of the WWF's lead writer, "you'd order a pizza and they'd deliver a newspaper. Sure it was a surprise, but it didn't make much sense, nor did you want to order from them again. But it sure fooled you, didn't it?"

McMahon went on to explain that he orchestrated the whole plan to teach Stone Cold Steve Austin a lesson that he would never forget. "I know how to get back at Austin for winning the title at *WrestleMania* - I'll arrange for my daughter to be kidnapped! That'll show him!" Airtight logic, if you ask me.

The "best" part of this payoff is that it was overshadowed by a new storyline almost immediately. Seconds after the reveal, Stephanie and her mother, Linda, appeared at the top of the stage to inform Mr. McMahon that Linda had stepped down as CEO of the World Wrestling Federation and she and Stephanie transferred their combined fifty-percent ownership in the company to Linda's hand-picked successor, Steve Austin.[42] The Undertaker hitched his wagon

---

[42] And then Austin only lasted about three weeks as CEO because he conceded power right back to the McMahons in a ladder match at *King of*

to a real winner with this Higher Power.

With the McMahon family drama now the primary focus of the angle, the Corporate Ministry soon dissolved and The Undertaker's run as the top heel in the company came to a close. The WWF then settled back into the familiar Austin versus McMahon feud for the remainder of the year, which begs the question Denny Crane insisted one should never ask: what's the point? In the end, there wasn't one; but in the WWF's defense, two things appear very likely to be true. First, Mr. McMahon as The Higher Power was not the original plan; and second, the WWF knew the payoff would be a flop so they moved on from it literally as soon as possible.

Eric Bischoff has long espoused a storytelling formula called "SARSA," which stands for "Story, Anticipation, Reality, Surprise, Action.

"When all five are there in a big way, we can live off that idea for two or three years," Bischoff said in his 2006 book, *Controversy Creates Cash*. "If a story doesn't have at least three of the SARSA elements… I don't want to hear it."

The Higher Power angle had a story that was twisted and disturbing, anticipation that built up for weeks, characters that were real and compelling, and it certainly climaxed in a surprise – albeit a lousy one. So as far as the SARSA concept for successful storytelling is concerned, the angle misfired on surprise and dropped the ball entirely on the action. But as glaring as the payoff problem was, we can take some solace in knowing that at least that's a pretty straightforward issue to correct.

* WHAT COULD HAVE HAPPENED *

So who should have been The Higher Power? It depends on who

---

the Ring on June 27. What a journey.

you ask.

Bruce Prichard has said the original plan was for The Higher Power to be revealed as Christopher Daniels, who was working in WWF Developmental at the time. But as soon as Vince McMahon saw him, McMahon said "absolutely not" due to Daniels' height, which was billed at six-feet-even. With all due respect to Daniels - who is an incredible performer with a Hall of Fame resume - this was probably the right call. Now, Daniels did have success in storylines of tangential nature in Ring of Honor as the leader of The Prophecy, as well as in TNA and on the independents with his "Fallen Angel" gimmick, so it is entirely possible that he could have made The Higher Power work to some degree in the WWF, simply because of how good of a performer he was. However, the reveal would have absolutely flopped because Daniels was unknown to a national television audience and wasn't physically imposing enough or verbally skilled enough at the time to be a believable master to someone of The Undertaker's stature.

Interestingly enough, Daniels was (briefly) part of a very similar storyline in WCW one year after The Higher Power angle. As Vampiro and Sting engaged in a pseudo-supernatural blood feud, Daniels was cast in the role of "Syndrome," Vampiro's mysterious hooded superior. The Emperor Palpatine/Darth Vader relationship angle was quickly scrapped but should this piece of trivia ever be on *Jeopardy!*, now you know.

Another potential option for The Higher Power would have been the "rotund demon" himself, Paul Bearer. However, the storyline would have needed to be altered a bit to make it work. Bearer would have needed to disappear from television after betraying Kane instead of immediately joining forces again with The Undertaker. Had Kane dispatched of his father in October and Bearer hadn't been seen on television since their falling out, then Bearer's reunion with The Undertaker would have had enough shock value and storyline cohesion to get over.

Shane McMahon made some sense and was even Jim Ross' kayfabe pick leading into the reveal. The Corporate Ministry was not great... but, it at least followed *some* logic. Not so much the Boss Man aligning with the man who hung him part, but I can at least in concept buy Shane as The Undertaker's inside man; the dots can be connected there. That said, I still don't buy Shane as a true "Higher Power." It would seem to me that The Undertaker would still be the one *really* calling the shots, and he'd just be leveraging Shane as an angry, ambitious young man who made a deal with the devil.

Since Russo-era booking was always good for a swerve, what if the name outside The Higher Power's office did in fact read "McMahon" ... but instead of Vince or Shane, it was Stephanie? This angle would have had some legs because Stephanie orchestrating her own abduction in order to destroy her absentee father both personally and professionally is a logically-sound, believable, and compelling story. It's also one we know that Stephanie would have told well because she did betray her father out of vengeance by aligning with top bad guy and future husband, Triple H, six months later at *Armageddon* in December. Exceptionally few men possessed the credibility to appear as The Undertaker's master. But Stephanie, I'd buy.

Other names bandied about over the years have included Ted DiBiase, Jake Roberts, and Mick Foley. DiBiase would have been an interesting callback, as he was the man who (kayfabe) brought The Undertaker to the WWF in 1990, *and* introduced WWF fans to "The Ringmaster" - Steve Austin's original WWF gimmick in 1996. DiBiase served as Austin's manager from January through the end of May when, due to pre-match stipulations, DiBiase was forced to leave the WWF after Austin lost to Savio Vega in a Caribbean Strap Match at *In Your House: Beware of Dog*. Austin later confessed in that he lost the match on purpose in order to get rid of DiBiase (who in actuality was departing the WWF for WCW). So DiBiase would have had a storyline motive to get back at Austin, as well as a prior positive relationship with The Undertaker for their union to make sense. It's even reasonable to imagine the "Million Dollar Man" as The Higher Power because what's more powerful than the almighty dollar? "Everybody's got a price…" That said, as a Christian minister in real life, the whole Satanism thing likely would not have jived well with DiBiase's personal convictions. Not everybody is cool with ritualistic sacrifice and abduction, and while I can't speak for DiBiase personally, as a fan, I just don't see it working.

The Jake Roberts rumors were just that - rumors. He was never seriously considered for the role, though a sober Jake "The Snake" in control of The Undertaker and his minions would have certainly made for interesting television. Plus, Taker and Roberts had history - they worked together to take down the Ultimate Warrior in the summer of 1991 and fought against each other at *WrestleMania VIII* the following April. Roberts had a well-documented history with Steve Austin, too. After winning the 1996 King of the Ring Tournament by defeating a "born-again" Roberts in the finale, Austin cut the promo that elevated him to superstardom:

> The first thing I want to be done is to get that piece of crap out of my ring. Don't just get him out of the ring, get him out of the WWF because I've proved, son, without a shadow of a doubt, you ain't got what it takes anymore! You sit there and you thump your Bible, and you say your prayers, and it didn't get you anywhere. Talk about your psalms, talk about John 3:16… Austin 3:16 says I just whipped your ass!

Almost overnight, "Austin 3:16" became the biggest catchphrase in professional wrestling. But it came at Jake Roberts' expense. Perhaps that embarrassment would have been the catalyst for Roberts to re-engage with the dark side, so that three years later he could have his revenge. Plus, all those ritualistic sacrifices would have the added creep factor of Jake's python (not a euphemism, an actual serpent) slithering over top of the victim's body. I won't lie - this option is very appealing to me, even if it was never really on the table.

Mick Foley is among the most intriguing names rumored to be considered for the role. According to the Wrestling Observer Newsletter, the WWF was interested in turning a major babyface heel to portray The Higher Power and Foley was pegged as the man for the job. However, Foley did not believe his body was in good enough shape for what would lead to a premiere match with Austin, so he rejected the offer. If the reporting is true, it's difficult to accept Foley's justification of a broken down body being the reason it didn't work out, since he would go on to win the WWF championship in the main event of *SummerSlam* against Austin and Triple H two-and-a-half months after The Higher Power was revealed.

The harder sell for me, though, is picturing the guy who spent much of 1998 pulling a sweatsock named "Mr. Socko" from his tights as the mastermind of the Ministry of Darkness in 1999. In fairness to Foley, he did create three very distinct characters in Dude Love, Cactus Jack, and Mankind, with (at least) two of the three being deeply disturbed individuals. However, what made them compelling was the physical violence and brutality they were able to dish out and endure. The Higher Power character was far more cerebral and, dare I say, demonic. There would also have to be some reason for Foley to align with The Undertaker - historically his greatest rival - and battle against Austin. All that said, I'm not going to be the guy to bet against Mick Foley. If he would have been interested, Old St. Mick probably could have found a way to make it work, somehow.

There's also the theory that there should not have been a Higher Power at all, or that The Higher Power should have existed only in the deluded mind of The Undertaker. Not having an actual Higher Power may have been a better option than what we got, mostly because The Undertaker was doing outstanding promo work on his own and never had a need to answer to anyone else anyway.

There is one other logical name to consider for the role of The Higher Power, though, and that is Don Callis. Callis debuted as "The Jackyl" on WWF television in September 1997, portraying a character that Jim Ross referred to as the "David Koresh of the World Wrestling Federation." A smooth-talking dude with a messianic complex would seem to be the perfect fit to be The Higher Power. He would have been an easy insertion into the role as well, since he laid the groundwork for such a reveal on multiple occasions in 1998. During his time managing the seven-foot Kurrgan on an episode of *WWF Shotgun Saturday Night* in April, Callis proclaimed: "I am putting the World Wrestling Federation and Vince McMahon on notice that I will take over the WWF. The 'Revolution of The Jackyl' is coming." Several months later, Callis aligned The Acolytes - Bradshaw and Faarooq - to usher in what he called an "age of tribulation."

When Callis was released from his contract in December of 1998, his plans for revolution were never fulfilled. Had he remained with the company and been revealed as The Undertaker's Higher Power, that story would have had a conclusion and Callis would have earned a huge boost in legitimacy as a result of wooing The Undertaker, of all people, to *The Jackyl's* Ministry of Darkness.

Now, his Jackyl character wasn't perfect, especially towards the end of his WWF run. Had Callis been tabbed to be The Higher Power from the beginning, a few minor tweaks would have been needed to better position his character with the rest of the Ministry of Darkness. For starters, no bubblegum - Satanic cult leaders can't chew gum. I don't make the rules. The Jackyl could still take pleasure in the violence carried out by his Acolytes - actual jackals do "laugh," after all - but his verbiage and disposition would have needed to take a much different, darker tone. Lastly, The Jackyl claimed The Acolytes were committing "violence for the sake of violence." That doesn't work for me, brother. The vast majority of pro wrestling is violence for the sake of violence. No, The Higher Power would want violence for the sake of the "greater good." He could want to purify the World Wrestling Federation through suffering and target those who needed to "atone for their sins." It's not like the WWF was shy about leaning into religion since they were having crucified people on national television and whatnot, so why not make The Higher Power an agent of the apocalypse, hellbent on unleashing his own Book of Revelation upon the WWF?

Given the names listed above, the WWF did have more than a few reasonable options that would have been shocking, compelling, and coherent with the story being told. The Higher Power reveal as it was did become iconic, but for all the wrong reasons. If the role were recast, perhaps it could have achieved that status for all the right reasons instead.

* WHAT WOULD HAVE HAPPENED NEXT *

One unavoidable issue for whoever would have been selected to portray The Higher Power was that their protégé would only be around through September. The Undertaker suffered a shoot torn groin shortly after *SummerSlam* in August and then tore his pectoral in December, keeping him off television until the following May when he returned dressed in biker gear as "The American Badass." According to Kevin Nash, there is a fascinating reason for why The Undertaker was no longer dressing like the devil.

"[WCW] had 'Taker close," Nash recalled in 2015, referencing the fact that The Undertaker's WWF contract was expiring in 2000 and WCW was very interested in acquiring his services. "All of a sudden he wasn't 'The Deadman.' He became the American Badass for a reason. He would have been the biker character and gone by [his legal name] Mark Calaway."

So The Undertaker's injuries likely gave an expiration date to the Ministry of Darkness, and it's very interesting to consider how close they came to ending his tenure in the WWF altogether. Knowing that the angle - at least in its planned incarnation - had an end date, how might the storyline have progressed if someone other than Mr. McMahon was chosen as The Higher Power?

Well, the truth with this angle is that it really didn't matter that much who ended up being The Higher Power as long as it made logical sense. Mr. McMahon did not make logical sense, which is why the choice for him to be The Higher Power failed and the angle died shortly thereafter. If The Higher Power had been someone else - Jake Roberts, Paul Bearer, Don Callis, et cetera - the angle could have continued on until at least The Undertaker's leave in the fall. Certainly each of those potential nominees would have brought their own flavor to the character, but in the end, regardless of who it was - as long as it wasn't Mr. McMahon - the selection would have stayed true to the original intent of the angle: a hostile, demonic takeover of the World Wrestling Federation by The Undertaker and his disciples.

Regardless of who The Higher Power was, the reveal should have come much sooner than it did. The Undertaker began teasing the character in February, but it wasn't paid off until June. Instead of putting that part of the story on the backburner for four months, the reveal should have been out of the way either by *WrestleMania* or at the *Raw* after.

From there, it should have been full steam ahead at Mr. McMahon and his Corporation. If The Rock retained the WWF championship against Stone Cold Steve Austin at *WrestleMania*, it would have made sense for him to go straight into a feud with The Undertaker as Mr. McMahon's defending corporate champion. Obviously, we already know from the real timeline that the inverse of that would have worked just fine as well. The Rock's alliance with McMahon just makes for a cleaner story in respect to The Undertaker's original motives.

Post-*WrestleMania*, the WWF title shouldn't have been the only championship the Ministry was focused on either. If The Undertaker truly sought control of the World Wrestling Federation, he would have employed professional wrestling's Golden Rule: he who has the gold makes the rules, so the Ministry should have been targeting *all* the gold. That also would have helped to elevate The Undertaker's minions beyond their underling status, which wasn't done particularly well during the angle. The Undertaker should have been on top, but if The Acolytes also took the tag titles, Mideon claimed the European belt, and Viscera became the Intercontinental champion, all at the same time, suddenly the faction would appear not just scary, but unbeatable in the ring as well. With a Ministry member in just about every segment of the show, the group really would have been taking over the WWF.

As for The Higher Power? Take your pick. To me, the Jake Roberts path is the most interesting one because of the possibility of a blow-off match against The Undertaker once things went south later in the year. Whether by simple battle plan disagreement or The Undertaker ceasing to remain the biggest, baddest dog in the yard, once Roberts and The Undertaker no longer saw eye-to-eye, the two would have to get physical. A one-on-one crazy gimmick match - I'm thinking a *Raiders of the Lost Ark*-themed Snake Pit Match - where The Undertaker could dispose of Roberts once and for all would have been a fitting way for the feud to end.

Another route to go with it - and the route likely needed if Bearer or Callis were chosen – would be to have The Higher Power begin to favor a new main event muscle to do his bidding. My pick for this player would be Big Show. Formerly known as WCW's "Giant," Big Show arrived in the WWF in dramatic fashion by tearing through the bottom of the ring to disrupt a steel cage match between Steve Austin and Vince McMahon at the *St. Valentine's Day Massacre* event in February. He won his first WWF championship at *Survivor Series* in November but often felt a bit directionless in between those two seminal points (and, frankly, for most of the rest of his two-decade-long WWE career). Stepping right into a feud with The Undertaker after his *WrestleMania XV* face turn would have been a big deal for Big Show. It would have been equally big, then, for The Undertaker to convert his former rival over to the dark side to form The Unholy Alliance. Big Show wouldn't have been just a tag team partner, but a monster henchman for The Deadman until The Higher Power recognized that perhaps The Undertaker was getting in the way of just how dominant Big Show could become... *or* Big Show would come to that conclusion on his own, breaking free from the Ministry and vowing to conquer the dark side en route to his own WWF title crusade later in the year. Either way, Show's booking would have been purposeful and main event-level throughout his first year with the company. Or, instead of having a Higher Power at all, Undertaker could have just debuted Big Show himself, call him "Armageddon" or something, and run roughshod over the Federation together for six months or so.

And if Stephanie were The Higher Power? What a different world we might be living in... The Undertaker might be holding down EVP and COO positions in WWE right now! Probably not, though – and to be clear, Triple H earned the career he had. He was a star and a champion long before he and Stephanie got together. Still, if Stephanie had been paired up on-screen with The Undertaker instead of The Game, would NXT exist today? Would Chyna's career (or life) had turned out any differently? The ripple effects of Stephanie guiding the Ministry of Darkness on their path of destruction are exponential, both in and out of the ring.

But instead of any of that, we got the reveal of Mr. McMahon as The Higher Power, which was certainly shocking... but it was a surprise for the sake of a surprise. We didn't know it yet, but we had been hoping for *The Good Place* and instead we got *How I Met Your Mother*.[43] The story was fun along the way, but in the end, Vince was the one Ted Mosby wanted all along and we in the audience were left feeling lied to and wondering where nine years of our lives went. Or something like that.

Regardless, had the WWF committed to the original intent of the Ministry of Darkness angle, the end result would have been a much

---

[43] Or as I like to call it, *How I Met and Promptly Moved On From Your Mother.*

more cohesive storyline that still would have offered an unexpected reveal… just one that made logical sense, too. There were options available and if the WWF had gone out on a limb for one of them, my guess is The Higher Power would still be talked about today and our memory of the angle would be much more positive than it is. Instead, all we have are memes and what might have been. But at least we've got memes.

FIVE

SURVIVOR SERIES WHODUNIT

"There was no plan."

November 14, 1999
Joe Louis Arena ◉ *Detroit, Michigan*
WWF Survivor Series 1999

* WHAT REALLY HAPPENED *

The landscape of professional wrestling was changed significantly on August 3, 1997. In fact, the entire trajectory of the sport came within a few centimeters of being altered perhaps beyond recognition.

Stone Cold Steve Austin, on the verge of superstardom as the hottest solo act in the business, was embroiled in a feud with Owen Hart over the WWF Intercontinental championship. Late in their match at that August's *SummerSlam* pay-per-view, Hart attempted a sit-out Tombstone piledriver maneuver on Austin. As Hart reversed Austin's own piledriver attempt, Austin's head slipped down further than it should have, resulting in his skull being forcefully driven directly into the mat. The sudden impact aggravated a bone spur on Austin's C4 vertebra, resulting in a bruised spinal column and temporary paralysis.

"As soon as my head hit that mat, I was thinking Christopher Reeve," Austin recalled in 2011. "'Cause I knew I was never gonna walk again, ever. I couldn't feel anything from my neck down."

Fortunately, Austin's paralysis was only temporary. Despite being visibly injured, Austin was able to summon the strength to roll Hart up for the pin before being helped backstage by several WWF referees. The injury kept Austin out of the ring for the next three months and would eventually cost him his career, as he was forced into early retirement at age 38 in 2003.

Still, it appeared Austin's bad neck did little to hinder his climb to the top of the WWF mountain. He remained a regular on television throughout most of the next two years, winning the 1998 *Royal Rumble* in January and claiming his first WWF championship at *WrestleMania XIV* in March. Behind the scenes, though, both the WWF and Austin himself had to adjust their game plans significantly as a direct result of the injury. Only nine of the thirty-five televised matches Austin was a part of in 1998 were singles bouts that ended with a traditional and decisive pinfall or submission victory. Fourteen matches ended in disqualification or as no contests; another fourteen were multi-man contests; and nine of the thirty-five had unique gimmicks or stipulations attached to them.

Austin also transitioned his in-ring style from a technician to a brawler during this time, and the WWF continued to find creative ways to make him a part of the program without requiring him to take bumps night-in and night-out. This in turn led to many iconic *Monday Night Raw* moments that extended beyond the bell-to-bell action, including the December 8, 1997 episode where Austin hurled The Rock's recently acquired Intercontinental title into the Piscataqua River, the January 19, 1998 episode where Austin went face-to-face with the "Baddest Man on the Planet" Mike Tyson, and the infamous March 22, 1999 episode where Austin drove a Coors Light beer truck down the ramp and flooded the ring – and Vince McMahon's Corporation stable – with the perfect shot of refreshment.

The smoke and mirrors made it possible for Austin to remain not just actively engaged, but in the company's premier spot for the better part of two years. By the fall of 1999, though, the effects of going so hard for so long while coping with such a significant injury were becoming evident. The New York Post reported that Austin underwent a myelogram ahead of that November's *Survivor Series* pay-per-view. The medical test involved injecting iodine-based dye into the spine in order to see the extent of any vertebrae damage on an X-ray. The results showed significant pressure on Austin's spinal cord and there was no getting around it this time: he needed neck surgery.

This was not particularly good news for anyone. Not only was the WWF's cash cow going to be out of action for at least the next nine months, but there was no guarantee he would ever be back in the ring at all. Complicating matters, the four-time former WWF champion was currently being advertised to compete against The Rock and Triple H in a triple threat match for the WWF title at *Survivor Series 1999* and needed to be written off of television.

This is where WWF Creative had to get… creative. Did they stop advertising him for the match they knew he couldn't participate in? No. Did they come clean about the injury and surgery since actual accredited news outlets reported on it? Of course not. No, they didn't do either of those things. You know what they did do though? They hit him with a car.

(Sigh.)

At the pay-per-view event, WWF champion Triple H interrupted Austin while he was giving an interview. This led to Austin chasing Triple H into the parking garage. Unfortunately, Austin did not look both ways in said parking garage and was subsequently plowed down by an unknown assailant.[44] The hit-and-run job did what it needed to do by effectively removing Austin from the advertised championship match and giving him a solid kayfabe excuse for being off television for the foreseeable future. It also gave fans a wild new mystery to solve. Who was driving the car?

---

[44] As I will someday explain to my daughter, we always look both ways for cars before engaging in a parking lot brawl.

Was it The Rock? It did turn out to be his rental car and Austin was his greatest rival. However, the car had been reported stolen prior to the incident. So Rocky seemed clean. Triple H and his D-Generation X buddies had plenty of motive, but they also had solid alibis. Even the McMahons, dastardly as they tended to be, especially toward Austin, had their whereabouts accounted for.

Months went by, and still no one had any idea whodunit, including... wait for it... the WWF Creative team.

"There was no plan," longtime WWF/E producer Bruce Prichard confessed on *Something To Wrestle With* in 2018. "The idea was to pull Steve Austin off of television because of his surgery. When it came time to figure out who drove the car, [Vince] McMahon was asking why it mattered who drove the car? Well, somebody hit him with the car. How can you try and get away from that? It wasn't thought of prior to."

(Longer sigh.)

So they started a story without an ending in mind and were then prepared to willfully ignore a rather significant plot hole afterwards despite being in the business of (checks notes) ... storytelling. We like to call that a "WWE Twofer."[45] Throw in an investigation led by WWF Commissioner Mick Foley and not, I don't know, some form of law enforcement for what was very clearly attempted vehicular homicide, and you've got yourself the time-honored recipe for a wrestling storyline that's not going to make any friggin sense.

And on October 9, 2000, fans were treated to the culmination of

---

[45] It is truly maddening how often this company turns to "hoping fans forget" about storyline details. Wrestling fans *never* forget *anything*. There is somebody reading this book right now fact-checking me about the history between Hannibal and Mannibal in AAW twenty-five years ago. And you know what? I respect that. I often wish the people who book these wrestling shows would respect that a little more, too.

exactly that, as super sleuth Foley – who two short years earlier was wearing a leather mask and falling off steel cages – cracked the case by correctly identifying the culprit of the hit-and-run attack on Austin as: Rikishi.

(Stares into the abyss.)

This reveal certainly succeeded in being unexpected. It was a little like if the Green Bay Packers had said, "Okay, we're going to move on from Brett Favre. But instead of this Aaron Rodgers fellow we've got here who actually plays quarterback and might be pretty good, we're going to give A.J. Hawk a try." And fans would be like, "Hmm. That seems weird. Because in terms of a starting NFL quarterback, A.J. Hawk seems more like an above-average linebacker. So maybe we should let one of the other quarterbacks play quarterback instead." And then the Packers would be like, "No, trust us. This will be fun." And it would actually not be fun at all.

This was kind of like that.

Rikishi – known by many of today's wrestling fans as the father of Jimmy and Jey Uso – had been wrestling in the WWF under other names since 1992. Teaming with his cousin, Samu, Big Keesh went by the name "Fatu" as one-half of The Headshrinkers. He was repackaged as "The Sultan" in 1996, and returned again in his final form, "Rikishi," the night before *Survivor Series 1999*. The 425-pounder became a fan-favorite in 2000 upon aligning with tag team and dance enthusiasts Grand Master Sexay and Scotty 2 Hotty. When it comes to getting over with the fans, the 'big dudes dancing in sumo gear' gimmick always bats a thousand.

Rikishi's babyface run obviously came to a screeching halt when he was revealed as Austin's mystery assailant. His credibility as a heel was then swiftly derailed when he explained that, unsolicited, he "did it for The Rock" – a curious justification, considering The Rock had already been a three-time WWF champion at that point. And any legitimacy he might have had built up as a main eventer was easily squelched when Austin beat the tar out of him at the *No Mercy* pay-per-view a couple weeks later. In summary, this was not good.

It didn't get any better when, after the Rikishi angle bombed, the storyline then pivoted to Triple H being the real criminal mastermind who actually did hire Rikishi to drive the car after all. Why neither one of them ever faced a jury of their peers remains a mystery to this day.

But, there are many things about this storyline that remain mysterious. Like, why continue to advertise a main event once you know one of the participants will be medically unable to perform? Or, why embark on a storyline featuring your company's biggest star without having any idea of an endgame? Or, why spend eleven months developing said storyline only to effectively blow it off in the span of two weeks? Or, most importantly, why Rikishi?

Attempting to apply logic in a largely illogical industry can be a frustrating task. But for the sake of conversation, what if the WWF *had* employed a little bit of logic and a pinch of forethought to this storyline?

* WHAT COULD HAVE HAPPENED *

The Rikishi character debuted on the November 13, 1999 episode of *WWF Metal*, one night before *Survivor Series 1999*. But Rikishi wasn't the only performer to make his in-ring debut around this time. Olympic Gold Medalist Kurt Angle entered a WWF ring for the first time at the November 14 *Survivor Series* event, the same night Stone Cold was run over. Interestingly enough, Angle also won his first WWF championship at *No Mercy 2000*, the same night Austin returned to in-ring competition.

Kurt Angle had one of the quickest ascensions to the top of the card in pro wrestling history, winning the European, Intercontinental, and WWF championships, plus the King of the Ring tournament, all less than a year after debuting in the sport. Would his rise to the main event have been as easy if Steve Austin were still in the picture? Maybe – he did win a gold medal with a broken freakin' neck. But, I might argue that no one benefited more from Austin's hiatus than Kurt Angle. And that's why he would have been the perfect choice to be the man behind the wheel.

Austin's focus upon returning would be on Triple H and D-Generation X, believing they were still somehow responsible for the attack due to how it all went down. This would keep him off Angle's scent as the Olympic Gold Medalist continued his climb to the top of the World Wrestling Federation. The big reveal would happen after Angle had won the WWF championship and Austin was physically capable of fighting him for it.

From here, there are two ways the story could have unfolded. Austin and Angle could have gone at it right away with Austin getting his revenge by the *Royal Rumble* or *No Way Out* so he could head into *WrestleMania X-Seven* against The Rock as the WWF champion. This option would set us back onto the real timeline, with Angle then going into a feud with Chris Benoit while Austin and Rock would fight over the title.

The other way would have been to settle the Austin/Angle storyline at *WrestleMania X-Seven*. This option is the more controversial one, as it would take the second Austin/Rock match away from their *WrestleMania* trilogy. That said, it would also prevent Austin from making a horrible heel turn at the event, which many might consider a net positive.

If Austin and Angle were vying for the championship at *WrestleMania*, a new opponent for The Rock would also be needed. It wouldn't make a ton of sense to make the WWF Championship match a triple threat – Austin and Angle's feud would be personal, while The Brahma Bull would just be in it for the gold. The dichotomy may have been interesting, but it wouldn't provide the one-on-one closure needed to finish the Austin/Angle story.

One option for The Rock at *WrestleMania* might be Eddie Guerrero. We all know the star Eddie Guerrero would become over the next four years, but he wasn't there yet in 2001. We also know Guerrero's 2001 was going to be limited, as he was sent to drug rehabilitation for a painkiller addiction in May and was released from his contract in November following a drunk driving arrest. When Guerrero was able to tame his demons, there were few better in the ring than "Latino Heat." That version of Eddie wasn't the one Rocky would be getting in April 2001, but it's sad to think there was only a single one-on-one contest between the two before Eddie's passing in 2005. So while this option would not necessarily move active storylines forward significantly – both The Rock and Guerrero were off television anyway shortly after *WrestleMania* – it would give fans a dream match of sorts to enjoy in the moment and look back on fondly.

Another potential *Mania* opponent for The Rock would have been Kane, which doesn't sound like a barnburner twenty years later, but in 2001, The Big Red Machine was coming off an outstanding Royal Rumble match performance in which he eliminated a then-record eleven superstars, including The Rock. I've often felt as though the masked version of Kane never quite got the run at the top he deserved. Though he admittedly always hovered around the main event scene simply because of his size and athleticism, he no longer appeared to be a true championship contender by the end of 1998. Perhaps a *WrestleMania* match with The Great One would have elevated Kane back to the level he was at when he debuted back in 1997. And, remember this: The Rock left for four months after *WrestleMania X-Seven* in order to film *The Scorpion King*. A brutal beatdown by The Big Red Machine would have been an easy way to write Rocky off TV, and it would have given Kane the credibility he needed to become the most feared monster in the company once again.

There are obviously several options the WWF could have taken with the *Survivor Series* "Whodunit?" storyline, and any of them would have at least bombed less than what we got. Personally, I like the idea of taking Austin and Angle all the way to *WrestleMania* and elevating Kane back into monster heel territory by having him be the one to sideline The Rock at The Show of Shows.

Regardless, the incorporation of a first-time reigning WWF champion – and one destined to be an all-time great on top of it – makes this path an instant and significant improvement over the Rikishi storyline. No offense meant to Rikishi, but he wasn't a main event star before this angle, his stock didn't rise after it, and his inclusion at all was illogical and convoluted. Angle, on the other hand, had very logical means, motive, and opportunity to be cast as the assailant here. He also would have benefited from the role in both kayfabe and reality, and would have delivered a shocking and satisfying payoff to the storyline.

* WHAT WOULD HAVE HAPPENED NEXT *

The Austin/Angle storyline would have concluded by the spring of 2001, at the latest, wrapping up just in time for the pro wrestling world to get turned on its head when the WWF purchased WCW in March. With WCW then set to "invade" the WWF, Austin and Angle would be pushed into the interesting predicament of having to put their personal differences aside – or not – for the good of the company. Their inability to do that could have been a means for WCW to get the upper hand in the Invasion early on in the storyline. I know every time I've had a co-worker intentionally hit me with a car at work, I've struggled to reconnect. But maybe Austin is a bigger man than me. Then again, it's pro wrestling, so maybe this situation could have lent itself to an Austin/Angle version of the ill-fated "Two Man Power Trip" angle that Austin and Triple H briefly embarked on shortly before Helmsley's quad injury in 2001.

The biggest difference between this timeline and the real one is that

Austin never would have turned heel at *WrestleMania X-Seven*. Austin would have remained a good guy throughout, and Angle would have been, at best, a tweener. And, if we were really doing it right, neither man would have flipped sides and joined the WCW/ECW Alliance, but we'll get to that later on.

Since this storyline is really a direct result of Austin's neck injury two years prior, it does make you wonder what his career might have looked like if Austin had not been injured all. Austin was absolutely over with the crowd before the injury, but his rivalry with the 'Mr. McMahon' character brought him to another level. I would argue that rivalry really began on the September 22, 1997 episode of *Monday Night Raw* when McMahon (in character) wouldn't clear Austin to wrestle due to his injured neck. Austin did not appreciate McMahon's efforts to protect him from himself and hit him with the Stunner.

We still could have gotten to the Austin/McMahon feud without Austin's injury being the catalyst, though. Consider McMahon's post-*WrestleMania* address to Austin in 1998 where the boss tried to make Austin into his version of what a corporate champion should look like. That concept in itself worked fine as the spark to the feud because the foul-mouthed, beer-swilling Austin still wouldn't have fit McMahon's corporate mold. Austin's neck injury didn't change his persona; it changed the way his persona was manifested.

It's hard to tell what impact the lack of Austin's injury would have had on the rest of Owen Hart's career. Of course we all want to find a timeline where Owen didn't die. If we consider how good the Hart/Austin feud was up until Austin's injury, and how negatively the injury affected the pair's trust and friendship moving forward, perhaps it's reasonable to think that the feud could have been revisited again down the road had there been no rift between the two. Maybe that's wishful thinking, but if there were ever a way to avoid Owen taking on the Blue Blazer gimmick, I think we'd all choose that option.

The next question is: how much longer would Austin's career have lasted had he avoided injury in 1997? The answer is likely 'a few years longer,' but he didn't become known as the "Bionic Redneck" only because of the neck injury.

"I came up with that gimmick just because, by the time it came down to it, my right arm wouldn't straighten out, I had some plates in my neck, and I had those two knee braces on, it became part of my gear," Austin recalled on his *The Steve Austin Show Unleashed* podcast in 2017.

Austin had suffered knee damage before he even entered the wrestling business, tearing his left anterior cruciate ligament while covering a kickoff during his college football days at the University of North Texas. He would also tear the posterior cruciate ligaments in both knees over the course of his in-ring career. By 2001, he had taken to wearing double knee braces on both legs, not for the aesthetics, but for the functionality. He needed the additional support in order to work. Because of that, it's likely that Austin's in-ring career would have been winding down by the mid-2000s anyway.

Still, it's fun to consider Austin engaging in an actual program with Brock Lesnar in 2003, or a *WrestleMania XX* dream match with Goldberg in 2004, or a potential "ride off into the sunset" bout against John Cena at *WrestleMania XXI* in 2005. If Austin's knees could handle a few more years, he might have rekindled old rivalries with The Undertaker or Shawn Michaels. Perhaps he could have even popped up for one-off feuds in the 2010s, similar to how Triple H has operated in semi-retirement or how the WWE has used Goldberg since his return in 2016. There's not a wrestling fan alive who wouldn't want to see Austin return to the ring as a "part-timer" for programs with CM Punk or Kevin Owens. It's just crazy to think that Ric Flair won the Royal Rumble in 1992 a month before his 43rd birthday and remained active in the ring for another two decades after that, while Steve Austin wrestled his last match at

WrestleMania XIX in 2003 at the age of 38.

For Rikishi, another run in the Intercontinental title chase would have helped solidify him as a credible singles act. Working with the likes of Eddie Guerrero, Chris Benoit, Chris Jericho, Lance Storm, Jeff Hardy, Rob Van Dam, Edge, and Christian over the next two-to-three years could have been a huge boost for the big man. Perhaps then he would have been able to slide back into the main event picture down the road as each of those men did. The biggest problem with his run – besides the fact that it came out of nowhere – was that nothing about Rikishi changed. Not his ring gear, not his move set. Everything was pretty much the same as it was when he was dancing in the ring with Too Cool, and in order to be taken seriously as the guy who took out The Rattlesnake, he needed something more.

In the end, Rikishi still wound up in the WWE Hall of Fame in 2015, so it couldn't have been all bad. Still, you have to wonder how different things might have been had he not been miscast in the highest profile storyline of his career.

SIX

THE BIG BANG

"People are still anticipating, to this day, the pay-per-view that never happened."

May 6, 2001
Hard Rock Cafe Arena ◉ *Las Vegas, Nevada*
WCW: The Big Bang

* WHAT REALLY HAPPENED *

The Monday Night Wars officially ended on March 26, 2001 when the final episode of *WCW Monday Nitro* aired live from Panama City Beach, Florida. One could reasonably argue the ratings competition had ceased to be competitive for the better part of the previous two years, but this was the moment it all became real. After nearly two decades of a bitter, back-and-forth rivalry with WCW, the WWF now stood atop the wrestling mountaintop, unrivaled.

It would have been inconceivable[46] to picture this scene just a few years earlier when *Nitro* was beating *Raw* in the ratings for 83 consecutive weeks between 1996 and 1998. But a combination of bad creative, backstage politics, and product saturation caused fans to pick up the remote control. Sometimes, WCW even put the idea in their heads.

"Fans, if you're even thinking about changing the channel to our competition, do not," WCW play-by-play man and voice of my

---

[46] You keep using that word. I do not think it means what you think it means.

childhood, Tony Schiavone[47] – at the behest of Eric Bischoff – said on January 4, 1999. "We understand that Mick Foley, who wrestled here at one time as Cactus Jack, is gonna win their World title. Ha! That's gonna put some butts in the seats."

Turns out, it did. An estimated 600,000 fans switched over to WWF television to see Mankind defeat The Rock and win the championship that night. Owing to quality storylines and a deep talent roster approaching its prime, viewing patterns continued to shift in the WWF's favor throughout 1999.

Meanwhile, WCW – which had turned a profit for the first time in company history under Eric Bischoff in 1995 – was now hemorrhaging money. On September 10, 1999, Turner Sports President Harvey Schiller relieved Bischoff of his duties. WCW brought in former WWF head writer Vince Russo – credited with providing direction for much of the WWF's wildly successful Attitude Era during his time with the company – and writing partner Ed Ferrara to take over Creative. This… did not go well… and Russo's initial tenure as head writer for WCW lasted just four months. In April of 2000, WCW reinstated Russo as booker and brought back Bischoff as well, just seven months after sending him home. This too was short-lived and underwhelming. Bischoff would be gone again in July and Russo was out by October.

Listen, I don't want to sit here and bury Vince Russo. The Internet already has that very well under control. And I can't say the opinions of the Internet Wrestling Community are entirely unjustified. Russo's vision of wrestling more closely resembled Howard Stern than Danny Hodge, which upset purist fans, and a significant portion of his angles – even the good ones – often lacked the foresight of an end game, which upset fans of logic and continuity. Still, hear this now: Russo doesn't get nearly the credit he deserves

---

[47] Tony Schiavone is a national treasure.

for giving meaningful screen time and storylines to midcard talent, or attempting to build new, younger stars. Now, he also (somehow) booked a *genuinely unbelievable* total of TEN item-on-a-pole matches[48] in less than twelve months in WCW, and that is objectively indefensible.

Still, it wasn't really any of these things that ultimately doomed WCW. But we'll get there.

On January 11, 2001, the Federal Trade Commission approved a merger between AOL and Time Warner – the media conglomerate that had previously merged with Turner Broadcasting Systems in 1996. That same day, Fusient Media Ventures – a media company led by Eric Bischoff – agreed to purchase WCW from Turner for somewhere between sixty and seventy-five million dollars. Forming Fusient with Bischoff were Classic Sports Network founders Brian Bedol and Steve Greenberg, who four years prior sold their nostalgia-based sports network to ESPN (which rebranded it to ESPN Classic) for upwards of $175 million.[49] Fusient's plan for WCW was to shut everything down for a handful of months and relaunch softly with a clean slate.

With the agreement in place, marketing began for WCW's rebirth, and an intriguing advertisement appeared on the back cover of the April 2001 issue of *WCW The Magazine*.

"*MAY 6TH, TEN BILLION YEARS AGO:*

THE BIG BANG, THE CREATION OF THE

---

[48] In fairness, it was technically nine item-on-a-pole matches and one "Judy Bagwell on a Forklift" match.

[49] After the Fusient deal fell through, Bedol returned to acquiring television – and internet – rights to collegiate sporting events by creating College Sports Television (CSTV). CSTV was acquired by Viacom in 2005 for $325 million and went on to be rebranded as CBS Sports Network.

UNIVERSE

MAY 6TH, 2001

THE BIG BANG, THE CREATION OF THE NEW WCW

This time, it's on Pay Per View"

The event was poised to be the first under the company's new management.

"The plan was that WCW would move to Las Vegas and do weekly tapings out of the Hard Rock Cafe, which was building a 3,000-square-foot arena at that time," former WCW executive in creative John Laurinaitis said.

The plan harkened back to Bischoff's initial turnaround of WCW, when he moved production to the Disney MGM lot to cut costs. WCW was not the only wrestling entity in financial distress at the time, however. Paul Heyman's Extreme Championship Wrestling in Philadelphia was struggling to stay afloat after its weekly national television program on TNN was canceled in October 2000. Just days before Fusient announced its agreement to buy WCW, ECW aired its final pay-per-view, *Guilty as Charged*, on January 7, 2001. Knowing that quality talent – both in and out of the ring – were soon to be available, Bischoff began designing what his revamped roster and announce teams might look like. He even considered out-of-the-box possibilities like – wait for it – working *with* the WWF for crossover pay-per-views, not unlike the working relationship Ring of Honor and New Japan Pro Wrestling launched in 2014 or All Elite Wrestling and Impact Wrestling forged in 2020.

The lynchpin of the plan, though, was distribution. Fusient's offer – which was expected to take between forty-five and sixty days to go from approved to official – was contingent on *Nitro* continuing to air on TNT and *Thunder* staying on TBS. On March 16, 2001, with due diligence on the Fusient deal still incomplete, new Turner Broadcasting CEO Jamie Kellner brought the plans for Bischoff's WCW sale to a screeching halt.

The fact that WCW lost somewhere between sixty and eighty million dollars in 2000 – just three years removed from a $112 million windfall – certainly gave Kellner strong ground to stand on, but – depending on who you talk to – money may not have been the real issue. Despite enduring a creative nosedive over the previous two years, WCW remained a known brand with a loyal – albeit dwindling – fanbase. *Nitro* was still pulling ratings in the high twos and low threes – numbers that wrestling promoters and cable television executives would literally kill for in 2021.[50] The fact of the matter was that AOL Time Warner under Kellner didn't want wrestling. Period. Kellner was transitioning TNT into a drama network and positioned TBS to take on comedy. Pro wrestling didn't fit the profile and because WCW was no longer performing at a respectable level financially, Kellner's case was made for him. And, for as vilified as Kellner has been – possibly justifiably so – for his role in the death of WCW over the years, he wasn't – and isn't – alone in his disdain for pro wrestling.

"If you knew how bad most TV execs did not want professional wrestling on their channels, you'd respect the hell out of WWE, NXT, & AEW for pulling off what they do each week," actor and former WWE writer Freddie Prinze Jr. tweeted in March of 2021.

That's not a shocking revelation to wrestling fans. We know how the world sees us. But back in 2001, with no network willing to air its content, WCW wasn't worth sixty-seven million dollars and the Fusient deal fell through.

With WCW back on the market, an intriguing opportunity suddenly

---

[50] In an admittedly very different media landscape, *AEW Dynamite* hit its stride in 2021 as the top cable program in the 18-49 male demographic on Wednesday nights… with overall ratings regularly between 0.4 and 0.7.

appeared for Vince McMahon.[51] McMahon – in the midst of preparing for what many believe to be the greatest WrestleMania of all-time – had been in negotiations to purchase WCW since at least November of 2000, but wasn't interested in a sixty-seven million dollar acquisition. However, with a thriving television product of his own and a pair of weeknight time slots at his disposal, adding the WCW brand was not such a bad idea, at the right price. Not only could he acquire WCW's trademarks and video library for a fraction of the previous asking price *and* pick up a handful of wrestler contracts, but he – Vincent Kennedy McMahon – could be the man to put the final nail in his competition's coffin. On March 23, 2001, the WWF purchased WCW for a mere four-point-three million dollars.[52] To this day, it remains unfathomable to me that McMahon got all of WCW for next to nothing (relatively speaking). It's even more astounding to consider that he then took the WCW tape library, combined it with his own, leased that collection to cable providers as an on-demand subscription service in 2004, only to

---

[51] Conspiracy theorists may be interested to know that the president of Turner Entertainment Networks and head of WCW at the time, Brad Siegel, was fraternity brothers and former Turner colleagues with a gentleman by the name of Stu Snyder. Snyder just so happened to be appointed president and chief operating officer of the WWF in June of 2000, and helped broker the acquisition of WCW several months later. When the promise of a TV timeslot proved to be the lynchpin of the Fusient deal and simultaneously the lone hurdle for the WWF to make an offer to purchase its competition – with Siegel (by way of Kellner) wielding the influence to either continue or cancel WCW programming – the spidey senses of WCW brass such as Kevin Sullivan, Bob Ryder, and J.J. Dillon started tingling. While no conspiracy or collusion has ever been proven, the circumstances of it all raised has more than a few eyebrows over the years.

[52] The WCW trade name, tape library, and other tangible assets were sold for $2.5 million, with additional acquisition fees coming to $1.8 million. In an interesting twist of fate, the WWF and WCW settled their longstanding disparagement lawsuits regarding Razor Ramon, Diesel, the Billionaire Ted skits, and the like in 2000. WWF attorney Jerry McDevitt later revealed that the money the company was awarded in the settlement with WCW was then actually used to purchase WCW just a few months later.

convert it into his own over-the-top standalone streaming network in 2014… and then sold the digital rights to that network for more than a BILLION dollars in 2021. Incredible.

Three days after the acquisition of WCW ended the Monday Night Wars, McMahon stood in the middle of the ring at Gund Arena in Cleveland, Ohio and, through the television magic of simulcasting, addressed both the *Raw* and *Nitro* audiences at the same time.

"How appropriate is it that WCW's last broadcast is in a beer hall?" Vince rhetorically asked the crowd as he gloated about his purchase.

"WCW is buried," he declared.

And then something special happened. As the crowd began to serenade Vince with a fan-favorite chant that likened the chairman to a rectal cavity, his "No Chance in Hell" theme music hit. Only, it wasn't for him. It was for his son, Shane, who Vince would be facing in a street fight that Sunday at *WrestleMania X-Seven*.[53] Except Shane-O-Mac was not in Cleveland. Shane was in Panama City Beach, Florida. At *Nitro*.

This was a moment. Yes, the WCW storyline would be largely squandered just a few months down the road; however, this night would live forever.

"Surprise, Dad! You're in Cleveland, Ohio and I'm in Panama City Beach, Florida, standing in a WCW ring," Shane said, addressing his father over the TitanTron. "And as usual, dad, your ego has gotten the best of you. You wanted to finalize this deal for WCW at *WrestleMania*. You had the audacity to ask Ted Turner himself to come down and finalize that deal. Well, dad, that's just the opportunity I was looking for. Because, dad, the deal *is* finalized with

---

[53] There was a lot to unpack in this storyline. For the purposes of this chapter, all you really need know is that the McMahon family is a very dysfunctional one.

WCW. And the name on the contract does say, *'McMahon'*..."

The crowd erupted, knowing what was coming next.

"But the contract reads, 'SHANE McMAHON.'"

Vince's eyes nearly popped out of his head[54] as Shane exclaimed, "I now own WCW!"

It was a work of art.

In perfect professional wrestling form, WCW's real-life demise had been spun into an angle on WWF television and used as one final promotion for the following Sunday's *WrestleMania* pay-per-view. If wrestling gods exist, this would have pleased them greatly.

For a host of reasons, the subsequent WCW "Invasion" storyline did not play out the way fans would have liked, but at least *Nitro* was given a worthy sendoff. In the end, maybe it was all inevitable.

"When I look back at it all now, the absolute best thing that could possibly have happened, did happen," Eric Bischoff said in 2016. "...I did such a great job at creating anticipation, that people are still anticipating, to this day, the pay-per-view that never happened."

Still, it makes you wonder. "What if?" What if Bischoff's deal had gone through? What if he had found another television network? What would *The Big Bang* have looked like? Would WCW still be around today? I'm glad you asked.

* WHAT COULD HAVE HAPPENED *

How could this have gone down differently? Well, instead of trying to make a right out of two wrongs by bringing back both Eric Bischoff and Vince Russo in April of 2000, WCW management

---

[54] He's a serial overacter, but damn if that wasn't just what the moment called for here.

could have taken a truly bold approach by trying to acquire Paul Heyman and his Extreme Championship Wrestling enterprise instead. ECW had just begun a three-year television contract with TNN in August of 1999 but the company's financial troubles coupled with the network's acquisition of *WWF Monday Night Raw* led to *ECW on TNN* being canceled in October of 2000. If the brain trust controlling WCW had a genuine interest in improving the product and advancing the company forward, then bringing in Paul Heyman as the head of creative – where he didn't have to deal with the finances, pressures, or minutia of running a real business – and adding a roster full of performers WCW was already picking up à la carte anyway would have been a pretty shrewd move.

If that wasn't in the cards, though, let's start with the premise that Fusient Media's agreement to purchase WCW in early 2001 actually went through. Bischoff would have needed television distribution. If Turner was no longer an option (which it obviously wasn't), Fusient had actually engaged in discussions with FX, which would have been an interesting proposition. With the WWF moving from USA Network to TNN, USA was also about to have a wrestling-sized opening in prime time. Had a deal been struck with either network, it would have been fascinating to see Bischoff's resurrected WCW come to fruition.

Once a television deal was in place, WCW could then center its focus on talent and creative. It is important to note that a majority of WCW's main eventers – Sting, Goldberg, Ric Flair, and the nWo, to name a few – were contracted with parent company AOL Time Warner and not WCW directly. This had a significant impact on WWF/E[55] over the next two years, with McMahon waiting to bring in several marquee names until after their previous contracts had

---

[55] The World Wrestling Federation (WWF) announced it would become World Wrestling Entertainment (WWE) on May 5, 2002. Apparently steel chair-swinging panda bears were causing confusion in the marketplace.

expired, and some performers being content with collecting the guaranteed coin before returning to the ring. This would have been an issue for Bischoff as well; however, a few of those names would have been worth the buyout. Bischoff also had fairly positive relationships with many of the top WCW draws from the glory days of the late 1990s. Names like Hogan, Nash, Sting, Page, and Goldberg all would have been on his radar if circumstances would have allowed for it.

Though it would still be several years before social media would take off, the Internet was becoming an increasingly important element for promotion and information. Given the planned hiatus during the month of April, WCW – which had registered the website www.thebigbangmay6.com – could have used this to its advantage, announcing the match card one by one over a five-week period between the *Nitro: Night of Champions* event on March 26 and *The Big Bang* on May 6, similar to how matches were rolled out via Twitter for the critically acclaimed *ALL IN* event in 2018. Regular website updates over the same time period could have also announced members of the rebooted roster in the same manner that AEW approached the build of its roster in 2019. In the absence of a weekly television program, those tactics would aid in building anticipation and endear the company to the budding Internet Wrestling Community.

To kick off the website announcements, WCW might introduce the announce team for *The Big Bang*. Instead of Tony Schiavone and Scott Hudson, WCW would bring in former ECW voices Joey Styles and Don Callis. Bischoff had already connected with Styles following ECW *Guilty as Charged* in January, hoping to secure him as a play-by-play man. Styles recommended Callis – Impact Wrestling's "Invisible Hand," known then to fans as "Cyrus" in ECW and "The Jackyl" in the WWF – to take on color commentary duties. The third man in the booth would be an exciting surprise reveal at *The Big Bang*, as Jerry "The King" Lawler – who left the WWF in February 2001 – would make his regal debut after the fireworks cleared and Styles and

Callis welcomed fans to the "new" WCW. The familiar voices of Tony Schiavone, Scott Hudson, and Mike Tenay would still remain with the company and be utilized regularly, as Bischoff has spoken at length about wanting to keep the commentary team sounding fresh, even from hour one to hour two of a given program.

For as much as things needed to change, though, there would be a need for some consistency, and a lot of that would come from the talent roster itself. Despite brutal creative throughout 2000, the WCW roster was far from devoid of talent – which, upon reflection, may be what made WCW in 2000 that much more upsetting. Even though it would cost some money, Bischoff would still want WCW to have access to at least a handful of their established stars, specifically Booker T, Goldberg, Sting, Scott Steiner, and Diamond Dallas Page. I'd also be willing to bet that Bischoff could pull off a fairly painless negotiation with close friend, Hulk Hogan. With those six in the fold, the likes of Ric Flair, Kevin Nash, and Scott Hall could all collect their AOL Time Warner money at home for a while and make triumphant returns with refreshed minds and bodies six-to-twelve months into the new era.

Since the final *Nitro* on TNT in the revised timeline would merely be the end of a network contract, as opposed to the end of the company, the *Night of Champions* event would unfold a bit differently to help set up the relaunch on pay-per-view in May. Booker T would not need to unify the United States and World Heavyweight title belts; instead, both Booker and Scott Steiner would hold their respective championships heading into *The Big Bang*, as would Shane Helms (Cruiserweight champion), Elix Skipper and Kid Romeo (Cruiserweight Tag Team champions), and the Natural Born Thrillers (Tag Team champions).

Considering how hard WCW was pushing Booker T in early 2001 – and the fact that he almost immediately feuded with the two top draws in the business, The Rock and Steve Austin, upon joining the WWF later that year – Booker's time on top would come again.

However, Bischoff has indicated in recent years that if the reset had happened as planned, the face of WCW – at least at the start – would have been either Goldberg or Sting, and it's hard to argue with that line of thinking. Say what you might about his technical prowess in the ring, but Goldberg wrestled for the WWE championship at the *Royal Rumble* and again at *SummerSlam*... in 2021. And despite being sixty-one years young when he debuted on AEW *Dynamite* in December of 2020, Sting's t-shirt set the Pro Wrestling Tees record for merchandise sales in a twenty-four-hour period and needed only about twelve hours to do it. As much as WCW needed to elevate its younger talent, it also needed to move the needle, especially coming off of an unprecedented hiatus.

If Bischoff could have negotiated as he planned to, WCW would retain an embarrassment of riches in the main event scene and a solid core in the upper midcard. Lance Storm and Mike Awesome – teammates in WCW's dying days as "Team Canada" – would stand out as strong U.S. title contenders who could elevate to the top of the card with the proper build behind them. Though a bit more seasoned, Bam Bam Bigelow was another established star who could have buoyed between the U.S. and World Heavyweight title scenes. WCW would also have decisions to make with Jeff Jarrett and Shane Douglas – two perennial heels who may have been best suited in the midcard but could certainly slide up to the main event when called upon.

I would also throw Chris Kanyon into the mix here. The "Innovator of Offense" was exactly that in the ring despite his work being criminally underrated in his time. Though the world lost him far too soon in 2010 following a lengthy battle with mental illness, Kanyon's influence on professional wrestling can still be seen today through the work of former mentees and friends like Brian Cage and Matt Jackson.

With perhaps Kanyon being a possible exception, it's fairly easy to see anyone in this group transitioning into a World Heavyweight title feud at some point. Douglas, Awesome, and Bigelow had already held the ECW World title, while Jarrett was a four-time WCW champion. Lance Storm became a belt collector as soon as he set foot in WCW, claiming the United States, Cruiserweight, and Hardcore championships in succession to become the only wrestler in company history to hold three different championships simultaneously. Given that fact, the next logical step for Storm would have been a pursuit of the World title.

The Big Bang would be the perfect spot for WCW to debut two more major heavyweight acquisitions in Steve Corino and Rob Van Dam. Corino had been the ECW World champion until January 7, 2001 and was already signed to a WCW contract courtesy of friend Dusty Rhodes. However, the "King of Old School" had yet to appear with the company before it closed its doors. Corino has since likened himself to wrestling's version of Crash Davis[56], having never quite reached the mainstream success that his ECW run suggested he was bound to have … but with WCW closing its doors, he also never really got the chance. *The Big Bang* would have been the opportunity of a lifetime for Corino.

Rob Van Dam's post-ECW career speaks for itself. The man who held ECW's Television title for an incredible 700 consecutive days headed to the WWF in the summer of 2001 and would go on to become one of the biggest stars of the 2000s before being inducted into the WWE Hall of Fame in 2021. In WCW, Van Dam would have been the kind of performer who could debut at *The Big Bang* in May and headline *Starrcade* by December. RVD was certainly on Bischoff's radar in 2001 and would have been a massive acquisition for the company.

---

[56] "I'm Bull Durham," Corino told Justin Barrasso of Sports Illustrated in 2017. "I had a cup of coffee in the big time, but really, I always stayed in Triple A."

Bischoff would inherit a unique-looking tag team division that in early 2001 was split between Heavyweight and Cruiserweight tandems.

The heavyweight tag division in WCW had seen better days. The Natural Born Thrillers – Chuck Palumbo and Sean O'Haire – would have entered *The Big Bang* as tag champs, and they were capable enough. Palumbo had a decent career, spending the better part of the next eight years in the WWE. O'Haire certainly falls into the 'wrestling what-if' category, though. When Bischoff reflected in 2021 on who might have made his relaunched WCW talent roster, he noted, "[O'Haire] could have been *the guy*." Steve Austin called him one of the "most talented guys that never made it." O'Haire was a big man who could work a cruiserweight style. For modern-day wrestling fans, O'Haire's closest physical comparison might be a taller version of AEW's Wardlow. In 2003, O'Haire even had the makings of an interesting singles run as a devil's advocate character in WWE, ending each of his promos with the line, "I'm not telling you anything you don't already know." But for whatever reason, it never seemed to click. After his wrestling career ended in 2004, O'Haire had a number of run-ins with the law and reportedly struggled with depression and addiction before tragically claiming his own life at the age of 43 in 2014.

In WCW, O'Haire and Palumbo would have limited options to feud with. KroniK – the tandem of Bryan Clark and Brian Adams, which many considered to be a knockoff version of WWF's APA – may have been the best option as challengers heading into *The Big Bang*. Other teams of note during this time would have included Shawn Stasiak and Mark Jindrak, Lex Luger and Buff Bagwell, and Alex Wright and Disco Inferno, who tagged as the Boogie Knights, a team that – for the modern fan – was essentially a less serious version of Breezango. You read that correctly.

Interestingly enough, there was one recently available tag team specialist in attendance at the final episode of *Nitro*. Brian James –

most well-known as "Road Dogg" – was released from his WWF contract in January and showed up looking for work at *Nitro*, only to find out his former employer had just purchased the company. It would have made sense for WCW to bring James into the fold and the tag division was where he was most comfortable. Two years later in TNA, James joined up with Konnan and Ron Killings ("R-Truth" to WWE fans) – to form 3Live Kru. Perhaps Road Dogg and K-Dogg would have hit it off right away in WCW and given the company another feasible tag team to work with.

Short of that, the tag team cupboard was pretty empty due to WCW's recent separation of the weight classes… with one small potential exception. Working in WCW developmental at the time were Chris Harris and James Storm, who would go on to be known as America's Most Wanted the following year as members of the NWA: TNA roster. AMW was named the Pro Wrestling Illustrated Tag Team of the Year in 2004 and crowned tag team champions of the world on six occasions during their five years together. Another legitimate heavyweight team or two would give WCW the depth it would have needed for a quality division, but with AMW not yet ready for prime time, KroniK would seem to be the most realistic contender for O'Haire and Palumbo's titles at *The Big Bang*.

While the Cruiserweight division of 2000-01 was not the same as it was in 1996-97, there was still a wealth of talent available. The cornerstones of the division would have remained Rey Mysterio Jr. and Billy Kidman, who held the WCW Cruiserweight championship a combined eight times between 1996-2000. Late in their WCW run, the pair forged a tag team known as the "Filthy Animals" and won the Cruiserweight Tag Team titles on the final episode of *Nitro*. In the revised timeline, Kidman and Mysterio would be used to help legitimize the Cruiserweight Tag Team championships; however, both were capable of much more as singles competitors. WCW made a critical miscalculation with its cruiserweights the first time around by not pushing stars like Eddie Guerrero and Chris Jericho beyond their kayfabe weight class and into the main event. Perhaps Bischoff would have learned his lesson and allowed Kidman and Mysterio to ascend up the card once their run as a tag team was complete. Oh, and as long as thinking has evolved in this scenario, Mysterio would return to the ring at *The Big Bang* with his mask back on.[57]

Beyond Kidman and Mysterio, the division would also consist of Chavo Guerrero Jr., Jamie Noble, Evan Karagias, Shannon Moore, Kaz Hayashi, Jimmy Yang, Elix Skipper, Kid Romeo, Lash LeRoux, and champion Shane Helms. That list could have grown by May as well with the potential additions of Super Crazy and Tajiri, who finished up with ECW in January. Most interestingly, under WCW contract in 2001 were two other future stars by the names of Christopher Daniels and AJ Styles. Given the careers that Daniels and Styles went on to have over the next two decades, it's intriguing to consider what might have been if WCW were around long enough to have made them the focal point of the cruiserweight division like TNA did in the X-Division four years later.

There are a few other names from WCW's not-too-distant past that would have been worth another look to help bolster the cruiserweight scene as well. Juventud Guerrera and Psychosis immediately come to mind as great options for both the singles and tag team divisions. Even in 2001, La Parka – who now goes by L.A. Park in Major League Wrestling – wouldn't have qualified as a cruiserweight if the weight limit was actually enforced; however, he still would have been a positive and entertaining addition to the division. All three luchadores left WCW in 2000 but remained active

---

[57] Masks have a sacred quality about them in the culture of Lucha Libre, with their roots dating back to the time of the Aztecs. Luchadores traditionally go to great lengths to protect their masks and conceal their identities, like the legendary El Santo, who was buried in his iconic silver mask. In the late 1990s, WCW had a penchant for making match stipulations that involved luchadores being forced to unmask if they lost. Such was the case for Mysterio, who lost alongside Konnan to The Outsiders in a Hair vs. Mask match at *WCW SuperBrawl IX* in 1999. When Mysterio debuted in the WWE in 2002, his mask returned as well.

for years after.

One other longshot cruiserweight to at least kick the tires on is a man who actually retired from the industry in 1999 despite an outstanding rookie year in WCW: Blitzkrieg. He only spent about nine months on television, but his match with Juventud Guerrera at *Spring Stampede 1999* remains one of the greatest pay-per-view opening matches in pro wrestling history. In his review of the match, Dave Meltzer noted, "Blitzkrieg is far from a great wrestler today, but he is more spectacular than Rey Mysterio Jr., [Juventud] Guerrera or any of [WCW's high-profile cruiserweights] were at this same stage of their career."

Jay Ross – who portrayed "The Fabulous" Blitzkrieg – retired in October 1999 to pursue a career in computer technology; however, he did return to the ring five years later to bestow his gimmick upon a young Jack Evans. The future All Elite Wrestling high-flyer worked as "Blitzkrieg II" for some time in tribute to the original Blitzkrieg, whose incredible acrobatics in the squared circle had inspired Evans to become a professional wrestler. While a comeback might not have been in the cards for the original Blitzkrieg in the summer of 2001, the fan in me would want WCW to do its due diligence just in case.

It is clear that WCW had no shortage of talent at its disposal for a relaunch in May of 2001. In hindsight, though, one division is conspicuous by its absence and that is because the early 2000s was not a banner time for women in wrestling. It was still six years before TNA legitimized the division for an American cable-viewing audience and a decade-and-a-half before WWE brought the "Women's Revolution" in sports entertainment to the mainstream. WCW would have theoretically had an opportunity to break some barriers in the name of gender equity around this time, but – in my opinion – the moment passed when they released future WWE Hall of Famer Nora Greenwald (known to WCW fans as "Miss Madness" and "Mona", or WWE fans as "Molly Holly") in August of 2000 and lost her trainer, Madusa,[58] a month later. A true women's division anchored around those two could have worked, especially knowing that the likes of Jazz and Chyna would be leaving ECW and WWF, respectively, by the end of the year, and younger talent like Alexis Laree – later to become WWE's Mickie James – were coming up on the indies. It also would have given the company enough female wrestlers to keep the likes of Torrie Wilson, Stacy Keibler, and Midajah in the managerial roles in which they excelled. Unfortunately, WCW probably wouldn't have much of a women's division assembled by May of 2001 but if the company succeeded in stabilizing itself, it's well within the realm of possibility that a viable core of female talent could have been built within the next year.

So, taking all this roster talk into consideration, what might *The Big Bang* match card have looked like in full? Let's take a look.

WCW *The Big Bang* – May 6, 2001

No.	Matchup
1	Steve Corino def. Chris Kanyon
2	The Filthy Animals def. Elix Skipper and Kid Romeo (c) *Cruiserweight Tag Team Championship*
3	Shane Helms (c) def. Juventud Guerrera *Cruiserweight Championship*
4	Natural Born Thrillers (c) def. KroniK *Heavyweight Tag Team Championship*
5	Rob Van Dam def. Lance Storm, Mark Jindrak, Shawn Stasiak, Mike Awesome, and Ernest Miller *"Face of the Future" Elimination Match*
6	Booker T (c) def. Bam Bam Bigelow *U.S. Heavyweight Championship*

---

[58] Madusa – or "Alundra Blayze" in the WWF – was the first woman ever to be named Pro Wrestling Illustrated's Rookie of the Year when she won the award in 1988. Eleven years later when there was little competition available to her in WCW's women's division, she became the first woman to win the men's Cruiserweight championship.

| 7 | Sting def. Diamond Dallas Page
No. 1 Contender Match |
|---|---|
| 8 | Goldberg def. Scott Steiner (c)
World Heavyweight Championship |

The show might begin with Eric Bischoff in the ring briefly welcoming fans to *The Big Bang*, followed by a hype video for the event, and then enough pyro and ballyhoo to get the Las Vegas crowd worked up into a frenzy. Kanyon would get the party started with his "Who bettah than Kanyon?" schtick, which would set up an unsolicited open challenge to the locker room, similar to how WWE often handles its vagabond brawler, Elias. "The King of Old School" would be a perfect foil for "The Innovator of Offense," as Steve Corino would make his long-awaited WCW debut, defeating Chris Kanyon in a well-wrestled opening bout.

Cruiserweights would take center stage for the next two matches, with Mysterio and Kidman taking the Cruiserweight Tag Team belts off Elix Skipper and Kid Romeo, while Shane "Not Yet Hurricane" Helms would successfully defend the Cruiserweight singles title against a returning Juventud Guerrera. With an already deep roster, WCW could afford to save some surprises for down the road, including additional returns (like Psychosis or La Parka) and debuts (like Super Crazy or Tajiri).

The heavyweight tag team division would likely be the weakest spot on the card and roster. With great respect to all involved, it's unlikely that Palumbo and O'Haire's victory over Bryan Clark and Brian Adams would have garnered a five-star rating on the Meltzer Scale. However, it would have been a believable fight and it would have further solidified Palumbo and O'Haire as the class of the tag team division.

Next on the card would be a "Face of the Future" Six-Man Elimination Match. At this time, WCW would have needed to rely on its established stars on top to secure continued financial viability.

Although many wrestling fans don't like to hear it, name recognition is real and it matters, which is why WCW would need to start its relaunch by marketing names like Sting, Goldberg, and even perhaps Hogan. That said, WCW would also need to do what WCW has been roundly criticized for not doing and that is building *new* top stars. That's what the "Face of the Future" match concept would aim to do – take six guys with main event potential and give them air time to prove it. Lance Storm, Mark Jindrak, Shawn Stasiak, Mike Awesome, and Ernest Miller would all be advertised for the match ahead of time, while the sixth competitor would be revealed at the pay-per-view. When a knockoff version of Pantera's "Walk" blared throughout the arena and Rob Van Dam walked down the ramp as WCW's newest competitor, the crowd pop in Las Vegas would be heard all the way back at Turner headquarters in Atlanta. Of course, to give the concept teeth, the winner would be granted a championship match against an opponent of their choosing at a future WCW pay-per-view. The powers-that-be would need to determine whether that should come at a predetermined event or just at some point over the following twelve months; however, the stakes would show fans and wrestlers alike that the opportunity for upward mobility in the new WCW was real and not just lip service.

The United States championship would be defended next, with Booker T successfully putting his title on the line against Bam Bam Bigelow. The run in WCW for the "Beast From the East" was not forgettable, but not spectacular either. Still, he was a near-four-hundred-pounder who could do backflips off the top rope and had main-evented *WrestleMania* just six years earlier – he could have meant more in WCW than he did. Perhaps a good showing against a champion approaching his prime like Booker T could have helped the big man.

The next match would roll back the clock just a little bit to feature two WCW franchise players in a No. 1 contendership match to determine the next challenger for the WCW World Heavyweight championship. Again, as valuable as "new" is to wrestling fans, "reliable" is more valuable to sponsors and partners. That's why WCW would turn to Sting and Diamond Dallas Page to help deliver some much-needed stability to the brand. Bischoff has said that Sting in particular would have been "near the top, if not the top" of the relaunched roster. In truth, there are probably several names Bischoff and company could slide in to this spot and make it work – Hulk Hogan, Ric Flair, Kevin Nash – but these two names make a lot of sense, especially since they never met one-on-one at a WCW pay-per-view before. Sting would get the win and likely ensure a few more buys as the headlined challenger at WCW's next pay-per-view event.

Goldberg would prevail over Scott Steiner in the main event of *The Big Bang*. These two had surprisingly good chemistry in the ring; they had squared off in one-on-one contests four times previously, with their only prior pay-per-view encounter at *Fall Brawl 2000* ending up as the highest-rated match of either man's career. That bout served to elevate Scott Steiner into World championship contention; this one would position Goldberg as WCW's standard bearer moving forward.

Could there be any more surprises in store at *The Big Bang*? A Hulk Hogan appearance would certainly be within the realm of possibility. Bischoff considered Hogan "a given" to be part of the relaunch, though his return could have been saved to help drive viewership to the company's re-debut on cable television. In terms of other free agents, one unique option might have been the hardcore legend Mick Foley, who briefly left the WWF at the end of 2000 before returning ahead of *WrestleMania X-Seven* the following April. It is theoretically possible that WCW could have swept in during that gap to bring Cactus Jack back home … which, I suppose, would turn this event into *The Big BANG-BANG*. (I'll see myself out…) That said, it might have been difficult for Foley to forgive Bischoff with the sting of 1999's "butts in seats" line still relatively fresh in his memory.

Regardless, the (imagined) match card for *The Big Bang* would have had enough star power and intrigue behind it to get the WCW reboot off on the right foot. The question would then become, "how long could the new WCW survive?"

* WHAT WOULD HAVE HAPPENED NEXT *

It would be safe to say by 2001, the "War" was over; WWF won, clean and decisively. But would WCW still exist today if Bischoff pulled off *The Big Bang*? I'm inclined to ask, 'why not?'

I would predict that the post-*Big Bang* WCW would have traveled a similar path to TNA, but with the benefit of only needing to revitalize a known brand as opposed to building an entirely new one. Jeff Jarrett created NWA: TNA in 2002 and, though the company has certainly lived its nine lives, its latest incarnation, Impact Wrestling, is still kicking two decades later. So, even though TNA at its height was often accused of being "WCW 2.0" or "WCW Lite," its survival would indicate the WCW could have stayed afloat in a similar fashion.

One area where TNA significantly impacted (no pun intended) the wrestling landscape for the positive was its emphasis on the "Knockouts" division. However, the company didn't focus heavily on women's wrestling until around 2007. That's still at least seven years before WWE really began to take its entire women's division seriously as a money-making, viewership-driving entity... though WWE does deserve credit for maintaining a championship-based division and creating capable female wrestlers throughout the 2000s. A refocused WCW could have accelerated the "Women's Revolution" movement in wrestling by building a credible women's division around the likes of Jazz – who joined the WWF in late 2001 and was already the women's champ by *WrestleMania* in 2002 – and Alexis Laree – who was making a name for herself on the independent circuit and debuted on both Ring of Honor and NWA:TNA in 2002. Not to mention, around this time, Chyna was on her way out of the WWF. Though her demands of the WWF were a bit on the grand side at the time (reportedly wanting a million-dollar downside guarantee to be on equal footing with top draw Stone Cold Steve Austin) it is possible that with another viable option available to her in the wrestling industry, perhaps things might have turned out differently for her, both professionally and personally.

Ring of Honor held its first show in February of 2002 – a few months before NWA: TNA debuted – and assembled an impressive first-year roster that featured: AJ Styles, Alexis Laree, Amazing Red, Spanky (Brian Kendrick), Bryan Danielson, CM Punk, Christopher Daniels, Colt Cabana, Eddie Guerrero, Homicide, Jay and Mark Briscoe, Low Ki, Paul London, Samoa Joe, and Steve Corino. It's unlikely that WCW's continued existence would have prohibited the creation of Ring of Honor, as ROH came into being largely as a result of RF Video – ECW's video distributor – looking for a new promotion to sell. The company was co-founded by RF Video's Rob Feinstein and former Paul Heyman protégé and ECW marketer, Gabe Sapolsky. So, while TNA may not have existed had WCW continued, ROH still likely would have. And given the roster they had (and would continue to have), it would be interesting to see how careers might have been altered if WWF/E were not the only cable show in town.

And that's the last piece left to tackle. WWF/E might have won the ratings war, but it would have needed to maintain its focus if WCW were still in the picture. But even Bischoff has said that no one, himself included, would have had the commitment to wrestling that Vince McMahon has had to keep the sport alive and thriving all this time. All other things aside, Vince does deserve credit for not just taking a territorial system national, but building it into the empire of sports entertainment that exists today. There's plenty not to like – feel free to read Twitter on a Monday night, for example – but wrestling fans certainly owe a lot to Vince McMahon. Still, legitimate competition would have not only pushed WWF/E creatively, but it also would have been a massive positive for wrestlers by providing talent with more than one potential employer putting on primetime cable wrestling. In the end, when wrestlers lack leverage, wrestling fans lose.

For the moment, though, let's imagine it all worked out. Bischoff was able to pull off *The Big Bang*. WCW rebuilt around Goldberg, Sting, Scott Steiner, Booker T, and Rob Van Dam. As Billy Kidman and Rey Mysterio Jr. moved on to the heavyweight scene, AJ Styles and Christopher Daniels took up the mantle. And though WWF would remain atop the pro wrestling food chain, it wouldn't be the only show in town.

Would Vince McMahon have handled a disgruntled Steve Austin differently in 2002[59] if there was a chance he might have lost his cash cow to WCW? How would WWE have dealt with CM Punk's walkout in 2014 if a bona fide competitor was able to give him the sort of schedule and shine he felt he deserved?[60] Would NXT or AEW be in the picture if WCW were still on the scene? The entire pro wrestling industry could have changed drastically in one *Big Bang*.

---

[59] Austin no-showed *Raw* after refusing to lose to then-rookie Brock Lesnar in a King of the Ring qualifying match in 2002. McMahon said Austin was "taking his ball and going home" by quitting the WWE. Austin returned to the company for one last run the following year.

[60] Punk quit the WWE – and professional wrestling altogether – in January of 2014. Health, burnout, and creative differences all played roles in his departure. One can't help but wonder if there had been a viable alternative at the time, perhaps wrestling fans might have gotten to enjoy the "Voice of the Voiceless" inside the squared circle a little bit longer than they did.

SEVEN

THE INVASION

"Who in the blue hell are you?"

July 22, 2001
Gund Arena ◉ *Cleveland, Ohio*
WWF InVasion

* WHAT REALLY HAPPENED *

When Shane McMahon stunned the professional wrestling world with his announcement that *he* had purchased his father's rival, World Championship Wrestling, back on March 26, 2001, wrestling fans prepared for an epic invasion of the World Wrestling Federation in the coming days. This… did not happen. At least not in the way fans imagined it might.

Most expected Shane's WCW cohort to make its presence felt at *WrestleMania X-Seven* on April 1, 2001. Given that Shane was slated to face his father, Vince, in a street fight at the event, it would seem a logical place to debut. And, to WWF's credit, this appears to have been the plan. A dozen or so WCW wrestlers were flown into Houston on *WrestleMania* morning, kept on a separate bus, and held there until fans had been seated at the stadium. In the end, none of the secret measures would matter, though.

"Shawn Stasiak did a radio or Internet interview the day before and stooged off the whole thing," Lance Storm recalled on his website in 2011. "The [WWF] office was furious and many of us speculated that it might cost him his job. I was even told that at one point the plan was to have us do a run-in on the Vince-versus-Shane match, but Vince was so mad word had leaked that he killed the angle and almost sent us all home. Thankfully we at least got to stay and watch the show."

And so, the WCW Invasion was doomed from the very start.

Instead of an impactful run-in at *WrestleMania* six days removed from Shane McMahon's bombshell announcement, all fans got was a nod and a wave to a small group of midcard wrestlers watching from the WCW luxury suite. It wasn't until the May 28 episode of *Monday Night Raw* when Lance Storm bolted out of the crowd to superkick Perry Saturn during a mixed tag team match that "The Invasion" seemed to be officially moving forward.

But those hoping for an insurrection of WCW's Millionaire's Club[61] would be sorely disappointed. Jim Ross had been scouting WCW talent in hopes of adding another television program specific to the WCW brand; however, those plans fell through and so too did hopes for any "real" invasion. Not only was there no extra time slot available for WCW, but the majority of WCW's main event-level talent was paid through AOL Time Warner and, as such, were not part of the acquisition. Those wrestlers were presented with the option of staying home and collecting their guaranteed money from AOL Time Warner, or accepting a fifty percent buyout that would allow them to begin negotiating new deals with the WWF. You can imagine how many guys jumped on that opportunity.

The first true "big-name" WCW star made his WWF debut on June 18, 2001, when Diamond Dallas Page revealed himself to have been stalking The Undertaker's then-wife, Sara.[62] DDP's kayfabe

---

[61] When Vince Russo and Eric Bischoff returned to WCW together in the spring of 2000, on-screen they led a group of up-and-coming wrestlers called the "New Blood" against WCW's old guard, branded as the "Millionaire's Club." The latter consisted of the likes of Ric Flair, Hulk Hogan, Kevin Nash, Diamond Dallas Page, and Sting.

[62] The immense respect for WCW within the WWF's creative department was palpable already...

justification for being a disturbed masked trespasser actually had nothing to do with Sara at all, he just wanted to challenge the "biggest dog in the yard." It was a bold strategy, but DDP was a bold man. Page has since noted in interviews that he regrets debuting this way and wishes he would have waited until WWF creative would have had something better in mind, like a feud with The Rock, since both claimed to be their company's respective "People's Champion" during the Monday Night Wars. As a fan of professional wrestling and an adversary of misdemeanor harassment, I wish this too. According to Page, he lost $487,000 by accepting the buyout and coming to the WWF when he did. Whoops.

Business really picked up at *King of the Ring* on June 24. Not only did DDP and The Undertaker brawl through the crowd, but WCW champion Booker T made an appearance, interfering in the main event. The next night on *Raw*, Booker attacked Vince McMahon from behind with a scissor kick, causing the WWF locker room to empty as Booker and Shane escaped through the crowd. Days later on the June 28 episode of *Smackdown!*, WCW Tag Team champions Chuck Palumbo and Sean O'Haire attacked the Hardy Boyz and Dudley Boyz,[63] though the WWF finally got their act together and gave the invaders some comeuppance as they attempted to leave the building.

A pivotal moment for The Invasion came on July 2, 2001 when the WWF first dipped its toe in the waters of a potential brand split. The final twenty minutes of *Monday Night Raw* was given to WCW, with Scott Hudson and Arn Anderson replacing Jim Ross and Paul Heyman at the commentary desk for the main event match between WCW champion Booker T and Buff Bagwell.

---

[63] As I will someday explain to my daughter, in the late 1990s and early 2000s, whenever the letter "Z" replaced the letter "S" at the end of a word, that word's level of coolness increased by a factor of ten. Simple mathematics.

Had things played out differently, the plan - in theory, at least - was for WCW to fully take over the Monday night timeslot, while the WWF would turn Thursday night's *Smackdown!* on UPN into its new flagship show. But again, this… did not happen.

"*Raw is WCW*" lasted all of one night, thanks in no small part to the objectively rough match between Booker and Bagwell. In their defense, the two were really set up to fail. It was a tough enough draw for WCW's in-ring debut to be taking place in Tacoma, Wash. - nothing against Tacoma, it's a fine town full of wonderful people, but it wasn't exactly a stronghold for a company that spent most of its history as a regional entity east of the Mississippi River and south of the Mason-Dixon line. Likely more significant, though, the WWF was positioned as the conquering heroes, while WCW wrestlers were the invading villains, despite an initial effort for the sides to be flipped. I have come to find that one general truth in life is that "good guys" don't scissor kick old men from behind, which Booker T had done the previous week on *Raw*. And anyone who's spent more than three seconds looking at Buff Bagwell would know he's a natural-born heel. So, here these two men were, bad guy versus bad guy, on the good guys' television show. It shouldn't be shocking to anyone that the fans revolted. In fact, one might expect it.

"It was the first time I ever got the 'boring' chant and I was taken aback," Booker T told WWE.com in 2013. "[The fans] didn't like the south, as far as what WCW represented. It was only fitting for them to support the WWE guys over the WCW guys."

And in case any fans were unaware of what an on-screen burial in the wrestling business looks like, two of the WWF's biggest names - Steve Austin and Kurt Angle - ran down to the ring to attack Booker T (with unsolicited assistance from Buff), fought him to the backstage area and literally threw him out the door. When Buff attempted to celebrate with Austin and Angle, he was also tossed to the curb, but unlike Booker, Buff was never seen in the WWF again.

A similar put-down happened a month later on *Smackdown!*. Booker T interrupted a return promo by The Rock, prompting "The People's Champion" to deliver an opening address of, "*Who* in the blue hell are *you*?" While this was an intentional set up for The Rock's "It doesn't matter what your name is" schtick, the insinuation that the WCW champion was a nobody didn't really help build "The Invasion" as a credible threat to the WWF.

In his book, *A Lion's Tale: Around the World in Spandex*, Chris Jericho wrote about the first big lesson he learned about wrestling promos: "Never Totally Bury Your Opponent." A young Y2J had just cut a promo about his first match with "Bulldog" Bob Brown, pointing out how old and slow he was. When Jericho came back to the locker room, Bulldog offered him some advice:

> "What the hell are you doing? Yeah, I'm old and everybody knows it. But I want you to think about this. If I beat you, and I WILL be beating you, then you just got beat by an old man. If you beat me, and you WILL NOT be beating me, then you just beat up an old man."

Sage wisdom from the Bulldog. Now, in fairness to The Rock - who has somehow had a profound influence on both my own youth and that of my daughter's in very different but equally entertaining ways - his gimmick was always pretty much just verbally disrespecting his opponents. However, as a general rule in any competitive endeavor, it behooves you to speak highly of your opponent so if you win, you've defeated someone of significance and if you lose, you've lost to a worthy adversary. Sting has cited the Booker/Rock promo specifically as a key reason he resisted signing with the WWE for so long. He knew what the Sting character meant to WCW and he couldn't be certain that the WWF/E would respect that legacy.

Sting's concerns, by the way, were not unfounded; whether you choose to believe it's coincidence or malevolence, the WWF/E has had a pattern of portraying wrestlers who were big stars in other promotions as second-tier talent. When three-time NWA Worlds Heavyweight champion Dusty Rhodes signed with the WWF in 1989, Vince dressed him in bright yellow polka dots. When WCW's biggest heel of the early 1990s, Big Van Vader, came to the WWF in 1996, he was no longer a monster but instead a stepping stone to put WWF talent over. When the WWF brought in three-time WCW World champion Diamond Dallas Page in 2001, he debuted not as the hardest-working-man in WCW, but as a stalker. And when Sting eventually came over in 2015, though he was admittedly granted a superstar's arrival, by *WrestleMania* he was losing to Triple H in one of the most overbooked, nonsensical matches in wrestling history.[64]

"That was pissing on the grave of WCW," *Busted Open*'s Dave LaGreca astutely summarized.

And therein lies the problem with "The Invasion" as a whole. Despite all these men being *former* WCW talent and *current* WWF assets, it certainly appears that they were still viewed internally as "the other guy's guys." In the eyes of certain decision-makers, it would seem, the WWF and WCW were not equals. And with that mindset, this was just not going to work.

Nevertheless, the angle soldiered on into July, as more and more talent made their WWF debuts. The story took another pivotal turn on the July 9 episode of *Raw*, when a tag team match featuring the WWF's Chris Jericho and Kane and WCW's Lance Storm and Mike Awesome ended in a no contest after Rob Van Dam and Tommy Dreamer - last seen in the now-defunct Extreme Championship

---

[64] Let's table for a moment the bizarre idea that the nWo would come out to *help* Sting (the man they spent fighting for the better part of two years). If somebody hits you with a sledgehammer, you're probably not getting up at all, let alone shaking that guy's hand after you lose… because he hit you with a SLEDGEHAMMER. At least Triple H was able to recover from the match quickly enough to be back in the ring an hour or so later to lay the groundwork for his next feud.

Wrestling (ECW) - began to beat down Jericho and Kane. The cavalry soon arrived, as the WWF's Dudley Boyz, Justin Credible, Tazz, Rhyno, and Raven all rushed the ring to stand between the invaders and Jericho and Kane. But then those men slowly turned around and showed where their allegiances laid, because before joining the WWF, they had each made names for themselves in Paul Heyman's ECW.

"I have been spilling my guts about this Invasion, and it seems to me like everyone has forgotten about the tribe of extreme," Heyman said, leaving his position at the commentary desk and joining his reunited faction in the ring. "It seems to me like these men were too extreme for WWF versus WCW. It seems to me that this man ... and this man ... [referencing Storm and Awesome] left Shane McMahon's WCW. It looks to me like these six men [the Dudleys, Credible, Tazz, Rhyno, and Raven] have left Vince McMahon's WWF. It looks to me like they all have joined E-C-W. So Vince - or Shane - anytime you guys want revenge, we'll take on the WWF, we'll take on WCW. We're not hard to find because this Invasion just got taken to the EXTREME."

The defections caused Vince and Shane to seemingly put their issues aside for the moment and team up. To matchup with the ten ECW wrestlers, Vince selected Bradshaw, Faarooq, Hardcore Holly, Billy Gunn, and The Big Show to represent the WWF, while Shane added Chris Kanyon, Sean O'Haire, Chuck Palumbo, Shawn Stasiak, and Mark Jindrak to carry the WCW banner. In what looked to be a twenty-man tag, the ten ECW wrestlers took the fight to the five from the WWF, while Shane held WCW back. And when the WCW contingent entered the ring, instead of laying down fisticuffs, they went in for the hug. As it turned out, Shane orchestrated the whole thing. But the fireworks weren't quite over yet because Shane had one more surprise in store for his old man. ECW had a new owner, and it wasn't Heyman and it wasn't Shane. It was Vince's daughter, Stephanie McMahon.

It was a shocking end to a great episode. Now, did it shift the focus away from "invasion" and turn it into the McMahon Family Turmoil Show? Absolutely it did. But, it *was* entertaining television at the time. The McMahon power struggle storyline became slightly more exhausting when it was still happening fifteen years later, but in 2001, these were, at worst, interesting dynamics.

"The Alliance" between WCW and ECW against the WWF led to the *InVasion* pay-per-view on July 22, 2001, fittingly hosted at the Gund Arena in Cleveland, Ohio where Vince had first declared victory over WCW back in March. The eleven-match card was booked with perfect balance, as the WWF claimed five wins and The Alliance won the other five heading into the main event, a ten-man tag team match for brand supremacy.

The WCW/ECW Coalition featured Booker T, The Dudley Boyz, Diamond Dallas Page, and Rhyno, while Team WWF lined up Chris Jericho, Kane, Kurt Angle, The Undertaker, and Stone Cold Steve Austin. Austin was the wild card for the WWF. Since turning heel by aligning himself with then-ultimate bad guy and archrival, Vince McMahon, at *WrestleMania X-Seven*, Austin had gone through a change in character. In recent weeks, he had taken on a more entertaining persona, singing and playing guitar backstage. McMahon wanted to bring back the "old Stone Cold" - the one McMahon had done battle with for the last two years - to defeat The Alliance.

"If you want Stone Cold to beat the living hell out of Vince McMahon, give me a 'hell yeah!'" Vince exclaimed to the audience as he tried to appeal to The Texas Rattlesnake's most time-honored personal desires. Austin was not having it. He shook his head and left the ring. But, by the go-home episode of *Raw*, all appeared right again in the WWF world, as Austin made the save in the main event, trash-talking and Stunning anything that moved.

All was not right with the WWF, though. While Austin contemplated

McMahon's request to bring back the "old Stone Cold," McMahon worked through contingency plans. He relied on Kurt Angle in Austin's absence and even made a phone call to The Scorpion King himself in the event that Austin wouldn't defend the WWF. Austin found McMahon's lack of faith disturbing. So, near the end of the main event match at *InVasion*, Austin turned on Angle - and the WWF - kicking the Olympic gold medalist in the head, hitting him with the Stunner, and putting Booker T in position for the cover and victory. The WWF champion had defected to the opposition. The following night on *Raw*, the new leader of The Alliance cited "appreciation" - or a lack thereof - as the reason for his actions.

Post-*InVasion*, all WWF, WCW, and ECW efforts focused on recruiting The Rock, who was set to return to the ring after filming *The Scorpion King*. It did not take long for The Rock to make his decision, though he did offer a brief misdirection by first subjecting Vince McMahon to a Rock Bottom and shaking Shane's hand, before giving the Rock Bottom and People's Elbow to Shane-O-Mac and announcing, "Finally, The Rock has come back... to the W-W-F."

Four days later on the August 2, 2001 episode of *Smackdown!* came the infamous Booker/Rock introduction promo, which set up a match for the WCW World championship at *SummerSlam*. The Rock pinned Booker in 15:19 to claim WCW's top prize for the WWF. A month later at *Unforgiven*, Kurt Angle defeated Austin to take back the WWF championship, though his reign would last just 15 days and he himself would defect to The Alliance on October 29.

As titles - and competitors - began switching back and forth between the two sides, the Invasion neared its conclusion. This led to November's *Survivor Series* pay-per-view serving as a "Winner Take All" blow off to the angle. At the event, Edge's victory over Test[65]

---

[65] The late Andrew Martin was reportedly given the ring name "Test" as a result of his sound check duties while serving as a roadie for the band

unified the WCW United States title and WWF Intercontinental titles, while the Dudley Boyz win over the Hardy Boyz unified the two companies' Tag Team championships. The main event was a five-on-five, winner-take-all elimination match, featuring the WWF's Chris Jericho, The Rock, The Undertaker, Kane, and The Big Show versus The Alliance's Steve Austin, Kurt Angle, Rob Van Dam, Booker T, and Shane McMahon. In the end, The Rock pinned Austin - thanks to an assist from Angle, who turned out to be a double-agent working for the WWF the whole time - to win the match and force The Alliance to disband, officially ending The Invasion.

Though the Invasion angle did offer several memorable moments throughout its eight-month run, most agree that it failed to live up to the high expectations fans had heading into it. The most visible reason for this was that the majority of WCW's main event talent was absent due to their contract statuses. Though fans did get Booker T and Diamond Dallas Page, The Invasion did not include the likes of Hulk Hogan, Kevin Nash, Scott Hall, Goldberg, or Sting, all of whom were major players for WCW in the Monday Night Wars. The lack of credible main-event talent was never illustrated more clearly than in The Alliance's final match, where three of the team's five members - Austin, Angle, and McMahon - were WWF performers, not invading talent from WCW or ECW.

The lack of established WCW stars certainly put the angle behind the eight-ball to begin with; however, the WWF also did very little to elevate midcard talent and create credible new stars. Though there is little argument that the WWF should have overcome the Invasion in the end, WCW and ECW wrestlers were rarely portrayed as being on the same competitive level as their WWF counterparts. In order to compete with the WWF, The Alliance had to rely on interference, disqualifications, and defections. Yes, The Alliance was positioned

---

Mötley Crüe.

to be the heels, but as Matt Borne once astutely noted, "Heels don't cheat because they *have* to; they cheat because they *want* to." These heels cheated because they had to, though, because The Alliance was intentionally booked to be inferior to the WWF.

What might The Invasion storyline have looked like with a little more patience, investment, and consideration for the WWF's competition? Let's imagine.

* WHAT COULD HAVE HAPPENED *

Perhaps no angle has been fantasy booked (or re-booked) as much as the failed WCW Invasion. In truth, what the WWF probably should have done was simply hold off the entire angle until they could play with a full deck of cards in 2002 after most of the AOL/Time Warner contracts had either expired or become more financially attractive to the WWF. However, that would have required immense patience at a time when the company could have used a shot in the arm. Plus, if Shane McMahon had actually purchased WCW for real, he probably would have wanted to either invade or restructure fairly soon after the acquisition. Because of that, this revised timeline of the Invasion would run from *WrestleMania* to *WrestleMania* for a full year of storytelling that would start at *WrestleMania X-Seven* in Houston and wrap up at *WrestleMania X8* in Toronto.

To be clear, Vince McMahon and the WWF should have still gone over in the end; the problem with the angle was never its result, but rather the path to get there. To set us on the right path, let's revisit the original plan: WCW *should* have thrown its first punch at *WrestleMania X-Seven* by interfering on Shane's behalf in his street fight with Vince. This time, though, nobody would tell Shawn Stasiak about it. In fact, let's just go ahead and offer him the Jeff Jarrett treatment[66] because - with all due respect - he wasn't really

---

[66] Vince McMahon infamously fired Jarrett on live television during the

going to figure into our plans anyway.

Given the contract status of the majority of the WCW roster, the core of the WCW group to begin with would have to look fairly similar. That's not all bad, though. In some ways, a staggered invasion is poetic – for a while, *Nitro* was all about the idea of "who's going to show up next?" This wouldn't be a significant departure from that, albeit for different reasons. A new WCW star could debut every month or so. In kayfabe, WCW would be pulling a new rabbit out of its hat every time the odds started to tilt back towards the WWF's direction. In reality, the WWF would be working through contracts one-by-one as each began to make better financial sense.

At the onset, though, the WCW roster would feature wrestlers acquired in the purchase of the company including Lance Storm, Mike Awesome, Mark Jindrak, Sean O'Haire, Billy Kidman, Gregory Helms, Chris Kanyon, Bryan Clark, Brian Adams, and Chuck Palumbo. Perhaps the Natural Born Thrillers - Palumbo and O'Haire - would serve as an insurance policy of sorts for Shane, just in case Vince tried any funny business (which he absolutely would because, at this point, Shane was the babyface and Vince was the heel). So, with the help of the WCW World Tag Team champions, Shane would be able to defeat his father.

But the night would not be over, and as long as we're taking an eraser to history here, we might as well answer one other famous "what if" while we're at it. As the Schrute family adage goes, "If you can snap two chicken necks with a single motion, why use two motions to slaughter those chickens?" Indeed.

WrestleMania X-Seven is regarded by many as the greatest *WrestleMania* in history, with several memorable matches including a clinic

---

March 26, 2001 episode of *Raw*. I guess that's what holding up the Chairman for money at a pay-per-view before leaving to work for the competitor gets you.

between Kurt Angle and Chris Benoit, an incredible Tables, Ladders, and Chairs match that saw Edge and Christian defeat the Dudley Boyz and Hardy Boyz, and the controversial main event in which "Stone Cold" Steve Austin turned heel by aligning himself with Vince McMahon of all people, to defeat The Rock and win the WWF championship.

In the years since, Austin has called his *WrestleMania* heel turn one of the greatest regrets of his career. Not only did it happen in his home state of Texas, where a babyface victory would have led to a massive positive crowd response from the nearly 70,000 fans in the Houston Astrodome, but the alignment with McMahon didn't make a ton of sense and the subsequent heel run was less than stellar.

Austin/Rock II[67] was given a no disqualification stipulation shortly before bell time in order to provide Vince with a legal opportunity to get involved, but if we wanted to keep this a No DQ match, that could still be tacked on at any point before the event so as not to raise any eyebrows.

In this scenario, the stipulation would facilitate the WWF debut of WCW champion Booker T, who would lead the WCW contingent in viciously beating down both Austin and The Rock before being run off through the crowd by the emptying WWF locker room. Vince would be livid as his main event was ruined and his two top stars were pummeled by his son's group of invaders. Nevertheless, this would be a No DQ match and there would have to be a winner. Order would be restored, but with The Rock having taken the worst of the assault (which would be convenient because he needed to take about four months off to film his movie). Austin would soon finish off what was left of the champion to secure the win. There would be no celebration after this win. That wouldn't be how Austin wanted

---

[67] Steve Austin and The Rock headlined *WrestleMania* on three occasions, with Austin winning at *XV* and *XVII*, while The Rock finally got his win in Austin's retirement match at *XIX*.

to take home the title and certainly not the ending Mr. McMahon would have envisioned for his biggest show of the year. Austin and McMahon would lock eyes as The Rock was stretchered out of the arena and a stunned audience looked on to close the show.

The next night, *Raw* would open without pyro and ballyhoo. A somber Vince McMahon, already in the ring, would start by addressing the events of the previous night. He would note that The Rock would be on the shelf indefinitely as a result of his injuries and would vow revenge on his son and WCW for what they did at *WrestleMania*.

Shane McMahon would then interrupt on the TitanTron. 'It felt good,' he might say, to physically decimate his father in their street fight, but it was nothing compared to being able to ruin the one thing Vince took more pride in than anything, *WrestleMania*.

"Credit where it's due - you put together a phenomenal show from top to bottom," Shane would continue. "But in the end, all anyone will remember about the biggest *WrestleMania* in history are the letters W-C-W. See ya later, Vince."

Vince would be determined not to let WCW get the satisfaction of derailing his business operations, so he would schedule a championship coronation to present Austin with his title later that evening. Unlike in 1998, Vince would say that this time around Austin really would be *his* champion and pledge to do everything in his power to ensure the WWF rallied around its new leader as the company faced new and unprecedented challenges. To prove he was serious, he would propose a toast to "new beginnings," inviting Austin's ringside beer man into the ring to provide the two with celebratory Steveweisers, since Austin was unable to celebrate in typical fashion the night before.

But wait! That wouldn't be Mark Yeaton at ringside.[68] It would be Shane McMahon. And with Shane-O-Mac providing the distraction, Booker T would slide into the ring and attack Stone Cold. Pandemonium would reign again. This attack would set the tone for the next month, with WCW wrestlers routinely finding ways to attack WWF talent. Clearly, Vince should have sprung for a real security force instead of local independent wrestlers. Nevertheless, something would have to give, so the McMahons would make a match to settle the matter. If Austin could defeat Booker in an Unsanctioned match (since Booker wouldn't be employed by the WWF in kayfabe) at *Backlash*, WCW would never be seen or heard from again. If Booker won, though, not only would WCW stick around, but the WWF would cede television time every Monday night dedicated to the WCW brand. Unfortunately for Vince, the invaders would need to take this one (otherwise this chapter would be much shorter).

WWF *Backlash* – April 29, 2001

No.	Matchup
1	Jerry Lynn def. Crash Holly (c)
	WWF Light Heavyweight Championship
2	Lita def. Molly Holly
3	Rhyno (c) def. Raven
	WWF Hardcore Championship
4	Jeff Hardy def. Triple H (c)
	WWF Intercontinental Championship
5	Brothers of Destruction def. Edge and Christian (c)
	WWF World Tag Team Championship
6	Matt Hardy (c) def. Eddie Guerrero
	WWF European Championship
7	Chris Benoit def. Kurt Angle

---

[68] Mark Yeaton was a longtime WWF referee and timekeeper, who added another role in the late 1990s as Steve Austin's designated beer can thrower.

30-Minute Submission Match
8   Booker T def. Steve Austin

In the real timeline, Austin and Booker embarked on a pretty fun feud that originally began in December 2001. The revised version would get us into that program a little sooner. Austin would get the better of Booker on TV, but Booker would pick up a key victory for WCW on pay-per-view.

Starting in May of the new timeline, "*Raw is War*" would become "*Raw is WCW*," as WCW matches would be sanctioned on WWF programming. The cruiserweight division would be put on display with matches featuring Billy Kidman, Chavo Guerrero, Gregory Helms, Kaz Hayashi, Jamie Noble, and Jimmy Yang. The Natural Born Thrillers - Chuck Palumbo and Sean O'Haire - would anchor WCW's tag team division, and the company would use the *Judgment Day* event in May to crown a new United States champion in Chris Kanyon. The main event of the pay-per-view – a WWF championship match between Steve Austin and Triple H – would be ruled a no contest after Booker T and a debuting Diamond Dallas Page crashed the party, ending whatever Pax McMahona may have existed between Vince's WWF and Shane's WCW. This would also position Austin and Triple H on the same side for a brief "Two Man Power Trip" run while introducing DDP as a formidable heel without having to resort to stalking anyone's significant other.

WWF *Judgment Day* – May 20, 2001

No.	Matchup
1	Gregory Helms (c) def. Chavo Guerrero
	WCW Cruiserweight Championship
2	Kurt Angle def. Chris Benoit
	2-out-of-3 Falls Match
3	Rhyno (c) def. Big Show and Test
	WWF Hardcore Championship
4	Jeff Hardy def. Chris Jericho (c)

THE INVASION

	WWF Intercontinental Championship
5	Chris Kanyon def. Mark Jindrak
	WCW United States Championship
6	Chyna (c) def. Lita
	WWF Women's Championship
7	Brothers of Destruction (c) def. Dudley Boyz
	WWF World Tag Team Championship
8	Steve Austin (c) vs. Triple H – No Contest
	WWF Championship

As June got underway, so too would the King of the Ring qualifying matches. For the first time ever, the tournament bracket would be split between a WWF side and a WCW side. William Regal, Hardcore Holly, Jeff Hardy, Matt Hardy, Christian, X-Pac, Big Show, and Edge would represent the Federation, while Lance Storm, Buff Bagwell, Chavo Guerrero, Billy Kidman, Chuck Palumbo, Mark Jindrak, and Sean O'Haire would be joined by another familiar face: "Big Poppa Pump," Scott Steiner, debuting as a surprise entrant on *Raw*. Edge, Jeff Hardy, Steiner, and Kidman would reach the semifinals at the pay-per-view, with Edge upsetting Steiner to earn 2001 King of the Ring honors and a big bragging rights win for the WWF.

Down the rest of the card, Lance Storm would claim the WWF European title from Matt Hardy, the Dudley Boyz would defeat the Brothers of Destruction for the WWF World Tag Team championships, Chris Benoit and Chris Jericho would battle for the No. 1 contender position, and Booker T and DDP would prove too much for Austin and Angle's uneasy partnership.

WWF *King of the Ring* – June 24, 2001

No.	Matchup
1	Edge def. Jeff Hardy
	King of the Ring Semifinal Match
2	Scott Steiner def. Billy Kidman
	King of the Ring Semifinal Match

3		Lance Storm def. Matt Hardy (c)
		WWF European Championship
4		Dudley Boyz (c) def. Brothers of Destruction
		WWF World Tag Team Championship
5		Chris Jericho def. Chris Benoit
6		Edge def. Scott Steiner
		King of the Ring Final Match
7		Booker T and Diamond Dallas Page def. Steve Austin and Kurt Angle

Soon after the King of the Ring pay-per-view, the next twist in the Invasion storyline would come – just as it did in reality – with the arrival of Extreme Championship Wrestling. Except this time, ECW would be in no hurry to form an "Alliance" with WCW. Instead, Paul Heyman's tribe would be working in the interest of anarchy.[69] Heyman would play both sides against the middle and seize opportunities wherever they came, no matter who they came against.

Heyman would unleash Rob Van Dam and Tommy Dreamer as new combatants in July, but would also be able to convince the likes of Lance Storm, Mike Awesome, Raven, Rhyno, Tazz, Stevie Richards, Tajiri, and the Dudley Boyz to abandon WCW and WWF and drink the fabled ECW Kool-Aid again.

ECW's mad scientist would talk the McMahons into raising the stakes at July's *InVasion* pay-per-view, challenging the WWF and WCW to compete on ECW turf under "extreme rules." It wouldn't be a hard sell as many a stipulation has been garnered over the years by appealing to toxic McMasculinity. It also wouldn't be a good idea for Vince or Shane. Triple H and Chris Benoit were sidelined by long-term injuries by this point, which was not good for the WWF. Meanwhile, WCW would have begun to hit a wall around this time,

---

[69] Maybe instead of *InVasion*, a more appropriate title for the July pay-per-view would have been *Anarchy Rulez*, an event ECW ran in September 1999 and October 2000.

since a fair amount of its "Invasion" roster was coerced back to ECW.

This would mean good things for ECW, though. At the pay-per-view, Rob Van Dam would defeat Jeff Hardy for the Intercontinental title, Raven would take the United States championship from Kanyon, and the Dudley Boyz and Tajiri would retain their belts in matches against the Brothers of Destruction and X-Pac, respectively. The night would also see Lance Storm and Mike Awesome reunite to defeat Edge and Christian in an All-Canada tag team bout. Not generally lauded for their skills in the ring, Dawn Marie and Francine would be credited with a tag team victory over Trish Stratus and Lita after the former "Miss Congeniality" showed her true colors by turning on Stratus and joining back up with the company that gave Lita her first big break in 1999. The only non-ECW win of the night would come in the main event when Steve Austin, Kurt Angle, and Chris Jericho prevailed over ECW's Tazz, Rhyno, and Tommy Dreamer and WCW's Booker T, Scott Steiner, and Diamond Dallas Page in a nine-man no-disqualification tag team match.

WWF *InVasion* – July 22, 2001

No.	Matchup
1	Rob Van Dam def. Jeff Hardy (c)
	WWF Intercontinental Championship (Falls Count Anywhere Match)
2	Raven def. Chris Kanyon (c)
	WCW United States Championship
3	Dudley Boyz (c) def. Brothers of Destruction
	WWF World Tag Team Championship (Tables Match)
4	Tajiri (c) def. X-Pac
	WWF Light Heavyweight Championship
5	Lance Storm and Mike Awesome def. Edge and Christian
6	Francine and Dawn Marie def. Trish Stratus and Lita
7	Steve Austin, Kurt Angle, and Chris Jericho def. Tazz,

Rhyno, and Tommy Dreamer; and Booker T, Scott Steiner, and Diamond Dallas Page

So July would have been a rough month for both WCW and the WWF. The ECW curveball would have thrown both Vince and Shane off their games and both would be looking for a way to correct that.

For the WWF, help would be on the way. The Rock would make his triumphant return to *Monday Night Raw* on July 30 and he'd have his sights set on one man: the WCW champion, Booker T. Rocky would have been out of action since *WrestleMania* thanks to the beat down Booker and friends levied on him and The Rock would not have forgotten any of that.

WCW would have needed something else. A smart guy like Shane McMahon would have known that he let his ego and emotions get the better of him and that cost WCW at *InVasion*. As a result, Shane would introduce a new general for the WCW army: Eric Bischoff.

The now three-company battle would take a few steps towards consolidation at *SummerSlam* in August, with title unification matches in both the Tag Team and Cruiserweight divisions. The Dudley Boyz would unify the WWF and WCW tag team titles, while Billy Kidman would leave the arena with both the Cruiserweight and Light Heavyweight championships. Edge would reclaim the European title for the WWF from Lance Storm and Diamond Dallas Page would take back the United States title from Raven for WCW. Rob Van Dam, however, would be successful in his Intercontinental title defense against Jeff Hardy, grabbing the belt for ECW in an instant classic ladder match.

The WWF would pick up non-title victories in the middle of the card with The Undertaker and Kane dispatching of Bryan Clark and Brian Adams, while Kurt Angle would outwrestle Scott Steiner in a singles bout. The double main event would shake things up; vengeance would belong to The Rock, who would defeat Booker T for the WCW championship. For a moment, Vince McMahon would be on top of the world, having captured WCW's greatest prize. He would assume that WCW would attempt to retaliate in the main event so in order to protect Chris Jericho, Steve Austin, and the WWF title, McMahon would enlist the services of the APA and Big Show to serve as special enforcers at ringside, just in case anyone from WCW wanted to get involved.

Unfortunately for Vince, Eric Bischoff would still have a trick or two up his sleeve. WCW wrestlers *would* try to get involved… but as a Trojan Horse. The Big Show – always ready to turn at a moment's notice – would flip on the APA before taking aim at Austin and gifting Chris Jericho his first WWF championship. When Vince McMahon entered the ring to question what had just happened, he would be met with a chokeslam before being locked in the Walls of Jericho. Eric Bischoff would then make his entrance, smiling from ear to ear as he entered the ring and hugged WCW's two newest (old) members.[70]

WWF *SummerSlam* – August 19, 2001

No.	Matchup
1	Dudley Boyz (WWF) def. Natural Born Thrillers (WCW) *Tag Team Title Unification Match*
2	Edge def. Lance Storm (c) *WWF European Championship*
3	Diamond Dallas Page def. Raven (c) *WCW United States Championship*
4	Billy Kidman (Cruiserweight) def. Tajiri (Light Heavyweight) *Title Unification Match*
5	Rob Van Dam (c) def. Jeff Hardy *WWF Intercontinental Championship (Ladder Match)*

---

[70] Both Jericho and Big Show departed WCW for the WWF in 1999.

6	Brothers of Destruction def. KroniK
7	Kurt Angle def. Scott Steiner
8	The Rock def. Booker T (c) *WCW Championship*
9	Chris Jericho def. Steve Austin (c) *WWF Championship*

Beginning in September, a soft brand split would develop between WCW and the WWF. This would occur for the same reason the WWE would split up the *Raw* and *Smackdown* rosters in the real timeline the following March: the rosters had grown so large that it became impossible to provide an adequate spotlight to every talent and storyline that deserved it. By employing "brand-specific" pay-per-views a few months earlier, the WWF would have been able to squeeze a little more juice out of the Invasion angle in addition to leveraging a few premier WCW intellectual properties along the way.

The WWF would have the first crack at the brand-specific pay-per-view in September with *Unforgiven*. Of course, there would be some crossover of talent to continue storylines where needed, along with the occasional pop-in from ECW wrestlers who may not have had a home but were always looking for a fight. In addition to The Rock successfully defending the WCW championship against Big Show at *Unforgiven*, Steve Austin would defeat Kurt Angle to become the No. 1 contender for Chris Jericho's WWF title at the new October pay-per-view hosted by WCW: *Halloween Havoc*.

WWF *Unforgiven* – September 23, 2001

No.	Matchup
1	Edge (c) def. Lance Storm *WWF European Championship*
2	X-Pac def. William Regal
3	APA def. Natural Born Thrillers
4	Trish Stratus def. Lita
5	Hardy Boyz def. Dudley Boyz (c)

	World Tag Team Championship
6	Rob Van Dam (c) def. William Regal
	WWF Intercontinental Championship
7	Steve Austin vs. Kurt Angle
	No. 1 Contender for WWF Championship
8	The Rock (c) def. Big Show
	WCW World Heavyweight Championship

At WCW's first standalone event since *Greed* in March, Chris Jericho would defeat Steve Austin with assistance from a debuting Ric Flair. Austin's rivalry with the stylin', profilin', limousine riding, jet flying, kiss-stealing, wheelin' and dealin' son of a gun dated back to the early 1990s when Austin was teaming with Brian Pillman as the Hollywood Blonds. Flair's interference in the match would provide WCW with another main event-level performer to go against a very top-heavy WWF lineup. It would also serve as one of the first admissions by the WWF that life existed beyond the walls of its own carefully curated "universe." For instance, if you only watched WWF programming, you likely didn't realize that the name for Steve Austin's finisher (The Stunner) was a reference to Austin's previous WCW persona, "Stunning" Steve Austin. A subtle jab was usually as close as the WWF ever came to acknowledging a wrestler's past prior to entering a WWF ring. However, Austin's character arc would become much more developed if the audience knew he wrestled in WCW, won multiple championships there, and spent years feuding with Ric Flair and his Four Horsemen, not to mention the fact that Eric Bischoff fired an injured Austin via FedEx in 1995 because he didn't think Austin was marketable. For a company that has always prioritized the "entertainment" side of "sports entertainment," the creative teams should have been salivating at the amount of backstory already written for them.

WCW *Halloween Havoc* – October 21, 2001

No.	Matchup
1	Hardy Boyz (c) def. Jung Dragons

	World Tag Team Championship
2	Billy Kidman (c) def. Gregory Helms
	Cruiserweight Championship
3	Dawn Marie and Lita def. Torrie Wilson and Stacy Keibler
4	KroniK def. Rhyno and Raven
5	Booker T def. Mike Awesome
6	Diamond Dallas Page (c) def. Buff Bagwell
	WCW United States Championship
7	Scott Steiner def. Tazz
8	Chris Jericho (c) def. Steve Austin
	WWF Championship

All three companies would come together for *Survivor Series* in November. Of course, instead of the five-on-five team matchup traditionally held at the event, this year's main event would come with a bit of a twist: three teams, two rings, one cage... WARGAMES!

I'm not sure anyone could introduce WarGames quite like William Regal, but whoever did announce the WarGames match would still get a massive pop. It would also do something that WWF in real life rarely did: admit that WCW had good ideas sometimes, too. It took nearly two decades and the creation of a developmental brand largely directed by someone other than the Chairman for WWE to tap into several of those ideas, but it was a smart move to do so.

Stakes are always important (despite what some promoters might condition you to believe), so whichever company won the War Games match would also secure the thirtieth and final entrant in January's *Royal Rumble* match. The last man standing at the end of the *Royal Rumble* match is (generally) assured the opportunity to headline *WrestleMania*, which makes the No. 30 spot the most coveted entry in the match.

Team WCW – comprised of Jericho, Big Show, Steiner, and Flair – would prevail in the WarGames match and secure the final spot in the 2002 *Royal Rumble* for Eric Bischoff's squad. The *Survivor Series* event would be significant throughout the entire card, though, as new champions would be crowned over the course of the night. Christian would take the European title from his former tag team partner, Edge, in the opening match, while X-Pac would beat Billy Kidman for the Cruiserweight belt, the Dudley Boyz would defeat the Hardy Boyz for the Tag Team straps, Booker T would win the Intercontinental championship from Rob Van Dam, Lance Storm would become United States champion at Diamond Dallas Page's expense, and Jazz would outlast five other women to claim the reactivated Women's championship.

WWF *Survivor Series* – November 18, 2001

No.	Matchup
1	Christian def. Edge (c) *WWF European Championship*
2	X-Pac def. Billy Kidman (c) *Cruiserweight Championship*
3	Dudley Boyz def. Hardy Boyz (c) *World Tag Team Championship*
4	Booker T def. Rob Van Dam (c) *WWF Intercontinental Championship*
5	Lance Storm def. Diamond Dallas Page (c) *WCW United States Championship*
6	Jazz def. Ivory, Trish Stratus, Jacqueline, Lita, and Mighty Molly *WWF Women's Championship*
7	Team WCW (Chris Jericho, Big Show, Scott Steiner, and Ric Flair) def. Team WWF (Steve Austin, The Rock, Kurt Angle, and The Undertaker) and Team ECW (Tazz, The Sandman, Rhyno, and Tommy Dreamer) *WarGames Match*

Starrcade would make its triumphant return to pay-per-view in December and, similar to the real-life WWF Vengeance event in

2001, Chris Jericho would walk out with both the WWF and WCW World championships. Jericho would miss out on defeating both Steve Austin and The Rock in the same night to become the first-ever "Undisputed" Champion in this timeline, but c'est la vie. *Starrcade* would also see Kurt Angle defeat Diamond Dallas Page, Steve Austin top Scott Steiner, and KroniK get a legitimizing victory over the Brothers of Destruction.

WCW *Starrcade* – December 9, 2001

No.	Matchup
1	X-Pac (c) def. Tajiri *Cruiserweight Championship*
2	Sean O'Haire def. Mike Awesome
3	Lance Storm (c) def. Ric Flair *WCW United States Championship*
4	KroniK def. Brothers of Destruction
5	Kurt Angle def. Diamond Dallas Page
6	Steve Austin def. Scott Steiner
7	Chris Jericho (WWF) w/ Big Show def. The Rock (WCW) *Title vs. Title Match*

In the six weeks between *Starrcade* and the *Royal Rumble*, WCW wrestlers would aggressively campaign to Bischoff for why they should be the No. 30 entrant in the match. The arena would come unglued at the *Rumble* when the buzzer rang and after a few seconds of silence, the familiar drumbeat began to introduce GOLDBERG into the WWF. The final four would come down to Goldberg, Kurt Angle, Steve Austin, and the returning Triple H – competing in the ring for the first time since tearing his quadriceps in May.[71] "The Game" would win this match and go on to main event *WrestleMania*; however, the wrestling world would be enthralled by the stare down

---

[71] Triple H tore his left quadriceps muscle in a match on May 21, 2001. His highly-anticipated return at Madison Square Garden on January 7, 2002 remains one of the loudest pops in pro wrestling history.

between Goldberg and Austin. That long-talked about dream match that never happened in real life would be set in motion at the *Rumble* after Goldberg eliminated Austin and Austin returned the favor on Goldberg. Triple H would throw Angle over for the win.

In addition to Triple H's return and Goldberg's debut, fans would also be pleased to see the returns of Mr. Perfect and Bam Bam Bigelow in the Rumble match, as well as the debut of WCW high-flyer Rey Mysterio.

WWF *Royal Rumble* – January 20, 2002

No.	Matchup
1	APA def. Dudley Boyz (c) *World Tag Team Championship*
2	Christian (c) def. William Regal *WWF European Championship*
3	Jazz (c) def. Lita *WWF Women's Championship*
4	Scott Steiner def. Lance Storm (c) *WCW United States Championship*
5	Rob Van Dam def. Booker T (c) *WWF Intercontinental Championship*
6	Chris Jericho (c) w/Big Show def. Kane w/The Undertaker *Undisputed Championship*
7	Triple H won, last eliminating Kurt Angle *Royal Rumble Match*

By February, McMahon and Bischoff would both agree that it was time to end their feud once and for all. No more WCW or WWF – moving forward, there could be only be one. And as André the Giant's beloved *Princess Bride* character, Fezzik, would tell you, there is but one way to settle this: "sportsmanlike." McMahon would finally accept the one-on-one challenge Bischoff laid down at *WCW Slamboree* in May 1998. At *No Way Out*, McMahon and Bischoff would go at it in a Winner Take All Street Fight for total control of the professional wrestling world. If McMahon won, the WWF would absorb WCW like he planned to do a year earlier. If Bischoff won, McMahon and his WWF wrestlers would all work for WCW. And to really do this right, irony would rule the day and pro wrestling's director of chaos, Paul Heyman, would be in stripes to officiate the match.

As we said from the very beginning, though, this was a war the WWF had to win. And so, at some point during the match, Bischoff would go for the pin and Heyman would start to count but invariably stop to give Bischoff a double-finger salute because life imitates art and Heyman was in Vince's pocket the whole damn time. Vince would win the street fight and the WWF would live on Then, Now, and Forever. See what we did there?

But Bischoff has always been a smart guy. He would have figured the odds would be stacked against him and he probably wouldn't come out on top. And because of that, he had one more trick up his sleeve. As is often the case with professional wrestling, the secret is right in front of you but you just don't know it. In this case, the pay-per-view title of *No Way Out* was the tell because the three capital letters in the event's name would be the talk of the wrestling world, thanks to the destructive debut of Bischoff's greatest creation, the nWo. In this timeline, it would be (fittingly) Bischoff – not McMahon – who "injected the poison" of the nWo into the WWF. Chris Jericho would retain his Undisputed championship as a result of a disqualification when Scott Hall, Kevin Nash, and Hollywood Hogan made their way through the crowd and into the ring to destroy The Rock.[72] Jericho – playing the cowardly heel role perfectly – would have been tipped off by the fan response, seen the nWo making their way to the ring, and gotten out of dodge ASAP,

---

[72] Talk about tough luck for Rocky in world title matches. First the *WrestleMania X-Seven* beat down, and now this?

leaving The Rock to deal with Hogan and The Outsiders by himself.

WWF *No Way Out* – February 17, 2002

No.	Matchup
1	Billy Kidman def. Tajiri (c) *Cruiserweight Championship*
2	Diamond Dallas Page def. Tommy Dreamer
3	Kurt Angle def. Lance Storm, Ric Flair, and Mr. Perfect *Fatal 4-Way Match*
4	Brothers of Destruction def. KroniK
5	Edge def. Scott Steiner (c) *WCW United States Championship*
6	Vince McMahon def. Eric Bischoff *Winner Take All Street Fight*
7	Chris Jericho (c) def. The Rock *Undisputed Championship*

After an eventful *No Way Out*, all roads would lead to *WrestleMania X8* where the fans at the Skydome in Toronto, Ontario, Canada would certainly get their money's worth. *WrestleMania X8* would be one for the ages with a host of dream matches on the card, including Austin versus Goldberg, Rock versus Hogan, Angle versus Flair, and The Outsiders versus the Brothers of Destruction.

The night would open with a matchup of two of WCW's greatest cruiserweights, Rey Mysterio and Billy Kidman. Rob Van Dam would also unify the Intercontinental and European championships with a victory over Christian, while Trish Stratus would finally get her coronation day as Women's champion in front of her hometown crowd in Toronto. The WWF would run the table at the top of the card with Austin stunning Goldberg, The Rock taking down Hulkamania, and Triple H getting to be the show-closing, conquering hero, taking home the top prize with a clean victory over Chris Jericho in the main event.

WWF *WrestleMania X8* – March 17, 2002

No.	Matchup
1	Rey Mysterio def. Billy Kidman (c) *Cruiserweight Championship*
2	Scott Steiner and Diamond Dallas Page def. Tazz and Tommy Dreamer
3	Rob Van Dam (Intercontinental) def. Christian (European) *Intercontinental Championship*
4	APA (c) def. Hardy Boyz, Dudley Boyz, and Mark Jindrak & Sean O'Haire *World Tag Team Championship (Elimination Match)*
5	Edge (c) def. Booker T *United States Championship*
6	Kurt Angle def. Ric Flair
7	The Outsiders def. Brothers of Destruction
8	Trish Stratus def. Jazz (c) and Lita *Women's Championship*
9	Steve Austin def. Goldberg
10	The Rock def. Hollywood Hogan
11	Triple H def. Chris Jericho *Undisputed Championship*

For as much well-deserved love as *WrestleMania X-Seven* receives, *WrestleMania X8* could have been even bigger if egos and money weren't in the way. This version of *WrestleMania* at the end of a long and evenly-matched Invasion angle would have provided the one thing every epic story needs: closure. The era of the Monday Night Wars was arguably the greatest time period in professional wrestling history. It deserved a proper sendoff. This path, punctuated by Dream Match Mania, provides just that, even if it only exists on paper and in the minds of wrestling fans.

* WHAT WOULD HAVE HAPPENED NEXT *

The post-WCW World Wrestling Federation would roll on very

similar to how it did in reality. ECW and WCW wrestlers would still assimilate into the WWF roster, the company itself would still split into brands due to roster size and be rechristened the WWE in May, and a trio of blue-chip signees named Brock Lesnar, Randy Orton, and John Cena would still usher in a new era in professional wrestling.

But, as long as we're here... it's worth noting that in the real timeline, Shawn Michaels made his return to the WWE on June 3, 2002 and was back in the ring for the first time in four years that August. It's also worth noting that - though Michaels' back was legitimately injured in 1998 - according to Jim Ross, the WWF paid Michaels a $750,000 annual salary from 1998-2002 to stay home. In other words, the WWF kept Michaels well-compensated as a means to keep him away from WCW. Perhaps the (arguably) greatest in-ring performer of all-time was capable of jumping back in the squared circle a lot sooner than *SummerSlam 2002*. If so, perhaps we could have seen Michaels come back, let's say, conservatively, in March 2002, instead of June. If he was ready even sooner, who knows, maybe he could have been an ace in the hole for the WWF, much like the nWo tried to be for WCW in the alternate timeline.

There's also the issue of "Macho Man" Randy Savage, one of the greatest wrestlers to ever lace up a pair of boots... but who never returned to the World Wrestling Federation after leaving for WCW in 1994. Savage was begrudgingly transitioned from the ring to the commentary booth in early 1993 but, at just forty years old, wasn't quite ready for his days as a wrestler to be over. As the WWF was looking to get younger, WCW was in the market for big name attractions. According to his brother, Lanny Poffo, Savage wanted one more program – a feud with the up-and-coming Shawn Michaels – culminating in a *WrestleMania* match where Michaels would officially send Savage into retirement. When the WWF rejected the idea, Savage said goodbye. His final WWF appearance came on October 31, 1994 and he showed up on *WCW Saturday Night* a month later on December 3. He never returned to the WWF again.

No one knows for certain what happened to cause the relationship between Savage and Vince McMahon to be broken beyond repair, though the Internet has plenty of ideas – some reasonable, some wild. In any case, it would have been nice in a revised version of the Invasion for Savage and McMahon to bury the hatchet and give the Macho Man the proper sendoff he deserved while Savage – who passed away in 2011 – was still alive to receive it.

The one active WCW name conspicuous by its absence in this angle, though, is Sting. The reason for this is two-fold. First, an invading WCW would be a heel WCW, and, for as great as he was, Sting never did 'bad guy' very well. Second, Sting resisted signing with Vince McMahon for the better part of a decade-and-a-half because he wasn't confident in how his character would be handled. In the alternate timeline, perhaps Sting would be more interested in coming on board a whole lot sooner after seeing how the WWF orchestrated the WCW Invasion. If Sting were to make his WWF debut, say, the night after *WrestleMania* in 2002, not only would it have been an incredible moment, but he would have had more than a decade of in-ring time left to spend in the WWE. And, no offense meant to A-Train and Big Show, but I'm guessing most wrestling fans would agree that an Undertaker/Sting matchup at *WrestleMania XIX* in 2003 would have been a slightly more awesome option.

In reality, *WrestleMania XIX* was also the swan song for Stone Cold Steve Austin. The "Texas Rattlesnake" wrestled the final match of his career at that pay-per-view against The Rock in the semi-main event slot. As much as we all love the conclusion of that *WrestleMania* trilogy where The Rock finally got that elusive victory over Austin, this revised timeline could have positioned both men for dream matches against different opponents. For Rocky, he could have had the opportunity at a "People's Champ" versus "People's Champ" feud with Diamond Dallas Page. Page has long stated this would have been his ideal feud upon entering the World Wrestling Federation. For Austin, though, he would have been able to go out on top against the one and only Hulk Hogan, finally settling the debate about who was the biggest star in professional wrestling history. Not a bad way to go out.

My favorite part of this timeline, though, is the light in which it would cast WCW. In this timeline, WCW's biggest event - which predated *WrestleMania*, by the way – wouldn't get turned into a WWE house show. In this timeline, WCW's signature match concept wouldn't be relegated to the WWE's developmental brand. And in this timeline, WCW's greatest stars *would* be given the respect and credibility they deserved instead of lousy gimmicks and weak booking. Yes, history is written by the winners, and yes, late-stage WCW was objectively bad. But in its prime, WCW was *good*. And that's the WCW legacy we should get to remember.

EIGHT

THE REIGN OF TERROR

"Somebody like you doesn't get to be a world champion."

March 30, 2003
Safeco Field ◉ *Seattle, Washington*
WWE WrestleMania XIX

Triple H (c) defeated Booker T by pinfall for the WWE World Heavyweight Championship (12:19).

* WHAT REALLY HAPPENED *

Eric Bischoff had no idea the horrors he was about to unleash on the wrestling world when he presented Triple H with the World Heavyweight Championship belt on September 2, 2002.

Okay, the above statement may be a bit melodramatic. Still, the three-year period that followed that fateful night in Milwaukee, Wis. has not been dubbed the "Reign of Terror" without just cause.

Let's back up. At *Vengeance 2001*, Chris Jericho famously defeated The Rock and Stone Cold Steve Austin in the same night to claim both the WCW and WWF championships, becoming the first-ever "Undisputed Champion" in the process. Jericho carried both the WCW and WWF belts until *WrestleMania X8*, when he was defeated by Triple H.

One week later, the WWF launched its inaugural "brand extension." Since acquiring the assets of its competitors in 2001, the WWF's roster had grown significantly. The brand extension allowed the company to, in essence, "compete" against itself by setting talent rosters exclusive to each of its two weekly cable programs, *Raw* and *Smackdown!*. Vince McMahon assumed control of the *Smackdown!* brand, while Ric Flair - who had returned to the WWF as its (kayfabe) co-owner after *Survivor Series 2001* - was put in charge of *Raw*. On the April 1, 2002 episode of *Raw*, Flair unveiled a new, singular Undisputed Championship belt and presented it to the reigning champion, who - along with his title - was exempt from brand exclusivity, making him free to compete on both *Raw* and *Smackdown!*.

True to WWF form, that arrangement lasted all of about five months. After rookie phenom Brock Lesnar defeated The Rock to win the now-WWE[73] Undisputed title at *SummerSlam 2002*, Lesnar signed an exclusive contract with *Smackdown!*, leaving *Raw* without a champion. So, on the September 2, 2002 episode of *Raw*, Eric Bischoff - who Vince McMahon named *Raw* "General Manager" in July in one of the more surreal moments in pro wrestling history - handed Triple H the "Big Gold Belt" and christened him *Raw*'s World Heavyweight champion.

That happened in front of the camera. Behind the scenes, Paul Leveseque - who likely does not go by "Triple H" or even "Hunter Hearst Helmsley" in his personal life - had been dating Stephanie McMahon - who likely does go by "Stephanie McMahon" in her personal life - for about two years. The pair married in October 2003 and have been (seemingly) happily ever after since. However, the real-life relationship between "The Game" and the boss' daughter did not help decrease speculation that he was leveraging his personal

---

[73] The World Wrestling Federation became World Wrestling Entertainment in May of 2002 following an unfair trade practices lawsuit from the World Wildlife Fund. Chair-swinging panda bears aside, I'm not sure the two entities sharing the same initials caused much confusion in the marketplace, but I also chose to write a historical fiction book about pro wrestling instead of going to law school, so consult your own counsel, I guess.

life for professional gain.

Triple H had already been a WWF champion several times over before he and Stephanie had even begun dating, so any notion that he was only in the main event scene because of their courtship is silly. However, the accusation that he may have used backstage influence to maintain his spot on top was not new in 2002. In fact, it was pretty much the central theme of the whole McMahon-Helmsley storyline throughout the year 2000.

Most fans accepted that run as a pro wrestling angle. But after Triple H was simply gifted a championship and began subsequently rolling over seemingly every top "good guy" contender in the company, fans were not nearly as receptive. Triple H reigned as the World Heavyweight champion five times between 2003 and 2005, holding the belt for a combined 616 days. Not only that, Triple H would headline the WWE or World Heavyweight championship matches at five consecutive *WrestleManias* from 2002-2006 and added two more in 2008 and 2009, with the only thing stopping him from making it eight in a row being a torn quad in 2007.[74] It's little wonder, then, that his heel run on top during much of this time has become known by fans as the "Reign of Terror."

The first victim was Rob Van Dam. "Mr. Monday Night" arrived in the WWF by way of ECW in 2001 and looked poised to become a big-time singles star. He shared the main event spotlight with Steve Austin and Kurt Angle at *No Mercy 2001*, won the Intercontinental title at *WrestleMania X8*, and scored a victory over The Undertaker for the Undisputed championship in May of 2002, though that result was overturned due to officiating error.[75] RVD became the No. 1

---

[74] This was the second torn quadriceps muscle of his career. He popped his left quad in a tag team match with Steve Austin against Chris Jericho and Chris Benoit in May 2001. His right quad was torn in a January 2007 tag match with Shawn Michaels against Randy Orton and Edge.

[75] Undertaker's foot was on the ring rope at the time of the three count. Is

contender to Triple H's World Heavyweight championship in September and challenged for the title at the *Unforgiven* pay-per-view that month. Hunter won after Ric Flair attacked Van Dam with a sledgehammer (as one does).

Van Dam got a modicum of revenge the next month at *No Mercy* when he defeated Flair one-on-one, and returned to the world title scene in November as a participant in the first-ever Elimination Chamber match. A less-than-positive incident occurred when RVD's knee accidentally landed across Triple H's throat when Van Dam attempted his Five-Star Frog Splash finisher from atop one of the Chamber pods. Both men have acknowledged it was a genuine accident, but the fact that RVD only received one televised shot at the World title - a No Disqualifications, Falls Count Anywhere loss to Triple H the following June - between November 2002 and June 2006 would indicate Van Dam fell out of favor with somebody important.

And as it turns out, he probably did. Van Dam himself addressed why his push was halted during a Pro Wrestling Junkies fan Q&A in 2020, noting that Triple H had offered to help him with promos. When RVD rejected the offer, it likely had an adverse effect on their relationship, and his push.

"I should have let him help me," Van Dam said in the interview. "I just didn't want someone else trying to get credit for my success or taking credit for creating me. I was very headstrong and stubborn. Sometimes that was good, but if I could have been a little more flexible on certain things, it surely would have made a difference in a lot of areas."

After RVD came Kane, along with what I am comfortable calling the worst, most deplorable storyline in the long and storied history

---

anyone else troubled by the subjective and inconsistent application of instant replay in pro wrestling? Just me? Never mind then.

of professional wrestling, Katie Vick. The Cliffs Notes version: Triple H alleged that Kane had murdered his – his being Kane's not Triple H's… pronouns, pal – high school sweetheart[76] and then defiled the corpse. And because obviously this story needed visual representation, Hunter dressed up in a Kane mask and mounted a mannequin. It's worth noting that this was done at an *actual* funeral home while an *actual* wake was taking place on the other side of a thin wall. It's also worth noting that neither Triple H nor producer Bruce Prichard wanted this segment to air because of how obviously offensive it was, but they were both emphatically vetoed by Vince McMahon, whose response to the shoot, according to Prichard, was, "Goddamnit, I love it!" He was the only one.

So, that happened. And then Hunter defeated Kane at *No Mercy*, took Kane's Intercontinental title, and unified it with the World Heavyweight championship because why the hell not? Eight months later, he took Kane's mask, too, which was a real bummer because - no offense to the Mayor of Knoxville County, Tenn. - Kane had much more charisma when he was wearing a mask and didn't talk.

In 2003, Triple H formed his own version of the Four Horsemen, assembling Ric Flair, Randy Orton, and Dave Batista as the faction Evolution. Though this group ruled over the WWE as a unit for most of the next year-and-a-half, it also launched the careers of two future Hall of Famers in Orton and Batista, so this development wasn't all bad.

For a good portion of 2003 - maybe because he missed most of the Invasion angle due to injury two years earlier - Triple H took aim at former WCW stars, first dispatching of Scott Steiner after a pair of

---

[76] I had thought Kane was presumed dead but secretly institutionalized as a boy after his brother, The Undertaker, started the fire that killed their parents, so Kane wouldn't have attended high school at all. Maybe I imagined that. Or, maybe the WWE doesn't respect me enough as a fan to maintain foundational levels of historical canon. Who's to say?

pay-per-view matches to start the year, then Kevin Nash over the summer, and later in a four-month feud with Goldberg, who did manage to take the title off Hunter before dropping it back to him at *Armageddon* in December.

However, the most egregious example of a superstar being cut down by the Reign of Terror was Booker T.

A bona fide main eventer and the most decorated champion in World Championship Wrestling history, Booker T had already feuded with Kurt Angle, The Rock, and Steve Austin within six months of coming to the WWF in 2001. After spending much of 2002 in the tag team division, Booker returned to singles competition early in 2003. On the February 24 episode of *Raw*, he eliminated The Rock to win a No. 1 Contender Battle Royal for the opportunity at the World Heavyweight championship at *WrestleMania XIX*.

The following week on *Raw*, Triple H confronted his new challenger in the middle of the ring and cut an incredibly controversial promo:

> Somebody like *you* doesn't get to be a world champion. You see, people like *you* don't deserve it. That's reserved for people like me. See, Book - that's where the confusion is. You're not here to be a competitor. You're here to be an entertainer. That's what you do, you entertain people. Hell, you entertain me all the time. Go ahead, Book. Why don't you entertain? Go ahead. Do a little dance for me, Book. Go ahead, give me one of those spinaroonies. Come on, Book - dance! Entertain me, that's your job. Don't be embarrassed. That's what you do. You're here to make people like me laugh. You know it. That's your role. Your job is to make people like me laugh. And you're very good at it, with your nappy hair, and your 'suckas.' Hell, I was laughing all week long after you won that 20-man over-the-top-rope battle royal. I laughed my ass off thinking about

you challenging me for the World Heavyweight championship."

Those speaking in defense of the promo over the years, including Bruce Prichard, have claimed that Hunter's "somebody like you" referred to "someone from WCW" and the intention was to insinuate that a WCW wrestler had no business headlining *WrestleMania* or holding a WWE world championship. A little odd, considering Hunter's right-hand man at the time was Ric Flair, who was more synonymous with WCW than just about any wrestler alive. So that was weird. Still, there's some credence to the theory that Triple H's promo was meant to focus on WCW, as he also said in the same promo, "Let's face it, that place was a joke," and "you championshipped that place right into the ground."

However, when Triple H used the phrase "nappy hair" - there's no defense for that. Further, there's no ambiguity about it. That's straight up racism. The crowd knew it, too, because the fans immediately groaned in that "oof, too far" kind of way. Even if the rest of the promo *might* have lent itself to other interpretations, as soon as that word was used, there was and is no other context upon which to judge it. There's just not. That word is pretty exclusively applied to people of color, and once Triple H - who, as a reminder, is white - used it, lines like "people like you" and "do a little dance for me" take on a very different connotation when speaking directly to Booker T - who, as a reminder, is black - whether those words were intended to or not.

At the pre-*WrestleMania* press conference, Michael Cole asked Triple H if the promo he cut was deliberately racist. Triple H denied that it was, claiming he was only referring to Booker T's legitimate criminal past. So that would seem to debunk Prichard's claims. According to Triple H, his "People like you" line was not meant to mean "WCW wrestlers" or "people of color" but rather "convicted felons." Alrighty then.

The March 10 episode of *Raw* made any non-racial intention harder to believe, as Ric Flair told Booker T that Triple H had offered to make Booker his chauffeur. When Booker then confronted Triple H in his private bathroom (because of course Triple H had a private bathroom), the champion gave Booker a dollar bill and told the challenger to get him a towel. About the only thing Triple H hadn't done at this point was come out and call Booker "the help."

What is interesting is that this development also bore striking similarities to an angle Bill Watts ran in WCW while Ron Simmons was on his way to becoming the company's first-ever African-American World Heavyweight champion. While managing Big Van Vader, Harley Race told Simmons in a promo, "Seven different times I was world champion, and I had a boy like you carrying my bags." Simmons immediately - and rightfully - beat the snot out of Race for that comment. However, Watts booked that promo intentionally as a means to rally support for Simmons who would indeed soon make history by becoming champion. I find it extremely difficult to believe that Hunter Hearst Helmsley - a wrestling historian, well-known admirer of Harley Race, and WCW performer himself two years after that angle - was unaware of the commonalities between the Simmons build and the angle he found himself in with Booker T.

To be clear, this is not to say that the man Paul Levesque is or was racist at all. We are talking strictly about a pro wrestling angle (which was very obviously racially-charged). The incredible thing about pro wrestling, though, is that the racism storyline could have been permissible: as long as Booker T won in the end.

Unfortunately, that was never going to happen.

"The plan was always for Hunter to go over at WrestleMania," Prichard said in 2018. "Vince was adamant from the very start. There was one major title that was going to change hands in his eyes that night and that was Brock [Lesnar]. We were crowning one guy, one new babyface, that was it. It was going to be Brock's night."

And so, Hunter went over at WrestleMania. Not only did the bad guy win, but he won by hitting his finisher once and delaying a full twenty-two seconds before covering for the three-count. Booker T hit every move in his arsenal. Triple H hit one Pedigree.

As Conrad Thompson said to Prichard following his attempted explanation for the result, "You can't defend this. The babyface should have won."

Instead, the bad guy did. Definitively. And the story was, for all intents and purposes, over.

Triple H held onto the World Heavyweight championship until dropping it to Goldberg at *Unforgiven* in September. He won it back at *Armageddon* in December and held it until *WrestleMania* the following March. Then, after a six-month reprieve, the title was back around his waist from September to December 2004 after he effectively killed off Randy Orton's babyface run, and again from January to April 2005 when Batista mercifully brought an end to the "Reign of Terror."

Booker T eventually did have his moment in the sun with the World Heavyweight title, winning it from (former WCW wrestler) Rey Mysterio at (former WCW pay-per-view) *The Great American Bash* in 2006. It would be the only post-WCW world title run of his Hall of Fame career.[77] The good news is, when Booker T and Triple H met again at *SummerSlam 2007*, Booker T was able to get his win back, defeating The Game as he returned from injury. Just kidding; Triple H won that match, too. At least that outcome made sense, though.

Not surprisingly, the result of the *WrestleMania XIX* World Heavyweight championship match continues to irk fans, though

---

[77] Booker's fifth WCW championship victory came during the Invasion storyline under the WWF banner when he defeated Kurt Angle for the belt on the July 30, 2001 episode of *Raw*.

Booker T himself remains at peace with the match.

"I don't lose any sleep over it," Booker said on his Reality of Wrestling podcast in 2021. "I've always looked at wrestling like movies, like Hollywood. When you're watching a movie, sometimes the bad guy wins. The movie goes off and the bad guy gets away with the crime. That's just the way I look at that night."

If it doesn't bother Booker, maybe it shouldn't bother us either. Then again, maybe it should. Not to get too soap boxy, but I'm about to because I personally view professional wrestling in the same way that the great philosopher and theologian G.K. Chesterton viewed fairy tales:

"Fairy tales do not tell children that dragons exist," Chesterton said. "Children already know that dragons exist. Fairy tales tell children the dragons can be killed."

Too often in real life, the hero doesn't win; the dragon does. Ignorance does. Racism does. Disease does. It turns out, dragons are hard to kill in real life. And that's why we choose to escape to this world of fiction, where there exists a payoff that is anything but. We *need* a world where Fiends and Giants and Beasts Incarnate can be beaten; where saying your prayers and eating your vitamins can actually make a difference; where hustle, loyalty, and respect can help you rise above hate; and where if you fight for your dreams, then your dreams will fight for you.

Professional wrestling is intrinsically emotionally manipulative, but that's a power than can be used for noble means instead of nefarious ones. As Stephen Amell's[78] character "Jack Spade" summarized in

---

[78] Best known for his work as Oliver Queen on the hit CW series *Arrow*, Amell is 2-1 in pro wrestling matches. He and Neville defeated Wade Barrett and Cody Rhodes' Stardust character in an excellent tag team match at *SummerSlam 2015*. Two years later, Amell joined Rhodes and The Elite (Kenny Omega and The Young Bucks) to defeat Flip Gordon, Scorpio Sky, Christopher Daniels, and Frankie Kazarian at Ring of Honor's *Survival of the*

the 2021 Starz series *Heels*: "They're coming tonight because they trust me to tell them a better story than what they have to live with every day."

Sometimes pro wrestling is so much more than pro wrestling. Sometimes we really need the good guy to win. So let's fix that now.

* WHAT COULD HAVE HAPPENED *

Fortunately, this is one of the easier corrections to make: Booker T just had to win. There was nothing "wrong" with the build to *WrestleMania*. I mean, yes, certainly, the dog-whistle racism was morally reprehensible, but through the lens of performance art, we could work with it and actually make it work for us. Again, Booker just had to win.

The *WrestleMania* match itself was also just fine until the referee's palm hit the mat for the third time. That solution is simple, too: Booker T would kick out just before the count of three. And, again, Booker had to win.

If, as Bruce Prichard has claimed, the WWE was fully against the World Heavyweight title changing hands on the same night as Brock Lesnar's coronation - which, by the way, is ridiculous, but let's play along for the moment - then there are two other routes they could have gone down. The first would be to avoid all racial overtones in the build. That means no "people like you," no "do a little dance for me," and obviously no use of the word "nappy."

I personally don't think the WCW burial would be a great direction, either, if for no other reason than the fact that Ric Flair was a cornerstone of WCW. Delegitimizing Booker's achievements because they occurred in WCW also delegitimizes Flair's, which I don't believe is the intended result. One could argue there was a

---

Fittest before coming up short against Daniels in his first and only one-on-one match at *ALL IN*.

difference between Flair's WCW era and Booker's, which Triple H may have been alluding to when he referenced the company's "illustrious champions" David Arquette and Vince Russo. That path may have had a bit more validity to it, but it also would have required Hunter to acknowledge WCW's period of superiority over the WWF, which I'm not sure Vince McMahon could ever bring himself to do. But, let's just say hell froze over and it happened. Triple H would have to talk about the "glory days" of Ric Flair's WCW and how the company imploded when Ric left and the likes of Scott Steiner (who Triple H had just defeated and is, not inconsequentially, Caucasian) and Booker T started running the show. Late-stage WCW is fairly easy to insult; Triple H just would have needed to make it clear that that was the version of WCW he was putting down.

Now, this route doesn't do anything about stopping the "Reign of Terror," but it would make it so no one would really care about the outcome twenty years later. It would be just another *WrestleMania* match, which would have been an improvement on this result.

The other way to give Triple H the win at *WrestleMania* would be to continue the feud beyond *WrestleMania*... but before the feud was over, Booker would have to win the belt. An easy way to achieve this would be to have Triple H clearly cheat to win at *WrestleMania*, setting up a rematch at *Backlash* where the stipulations would prevent any shenanigans from happening again. If Ric Flair had interfered at *Mania*, perhaps Evolution would be barred from ringside. If Triple H got himself disqualified at *Mania*, perhaps he would lose his championship if he got DQ'd at *Backlash*. If we just wanted a cool visual, perhaps a Lumberjack match would be the stip of choice. It sure felt like there were enough killed-off babyfaces during the "Reign of Terror" to fully surround the ring and give Triple H his comeuppance. In the end, though, Booker T would have to win.

Of all the options, my preference is to follow Occam's Razor - the simplest answer is the right one. Booker T should have won at *WrestleMania*. He should have kicked out after the 22-second post-

Pedigree pause, recovered, hit another one of his own signature maneuvers, and ended Hunter's reign.

* WHAT WOULD HAVE HAPPENED NEXT *

After defeating Triple H at *WrestleMania*, Booker T would have held the championship through the spring, all the way until *SummerSlam* when Goldberg was ready to take over. Booker T would have replaced Randy Orton in the Elimination Chamber match, which still could have come down to Triple H and Goldberg as the final two participants in order to set up their program. The difference in this timeline, though, is that Goldberg would go over a month earlier and win the title at *SummerSlam* when the fans were ready for it, instead of at *Unforgiven*, with Triple H still being able to win the belt back at *Armageddon*.

Booker T's championship challengers up until *SummerSlam* could include the likes of Chris Jericho, Ric Flair, or even Scott Steiner, while Triple H could maintain his same slate of opponents - namely Shawn Michaels and Kevin Nash - from May through August. Hunter did not need a title belt in order to feud with the Two Dudes with Attitudes; that storyline would have been plenty interesting without it. Booker's career, on the other hand, could have used a signature win and championship run to establish him as a *WWE* main event player, not just a WCW one. Instead, we got Triple H telling Booker T that somebody "like" him was inferior... and then proving it at the pay-per-view.

There is one silver lining to how badly the WWE botched the Booker T/Triple H outcome in 2003: it made Kofi Kingston's WWE championship victory at *WrestleMania 35* in 2019 that much more special.

"KofiMania" wasn't supposed to happen. He was never even supposed to be in the championship picture. But an injury to Mustafa Ali ahead of the 2019 Elimination Chamber match opened up a spot that the eleven-year WWE veteran was able to fill. Kofi brought his in-ring game to a new level, the fans reacted, and WWE, to its credit, listened. Mr. McMahon himself entered the storyline, putting Kingston through his own Twelve Labors of Hercules after McMahon-splaining why the perennial fan-favorite was not WWE championship material on the March 12, 2019 episode of *SmackDown Live*.

Kofi then addressed the elephant in the room by using language eerily reminiscent of Triple H's promo to Booker T sixteen years earlier: "I have never complained about the fact that you have never allowed *someone like me* to compete or contend for the WWE title."

This time, that line left little room for interpretation. Since Buddy Rogers' inaugural World Wide Wrestling Federation (WWWF)[79] championship victory in 1963, The Rock had been the only man of African-American heritage to claim the title with the company name on it for more than fifty years, and, though his Blackness should not be disregarded, many believe The Rock is more generally celebrated for his Samoan lineage.

Representation matters. That was no more evident in the world of pro wrestling than when Xavier Woods and Big E slid into the ring with their eyes filled with tears to celebrate Kofi Kingston as the new WWE champion. It wasn't just because their friend had realized his dream. It was because that dream was the same dream shared by thousands of people who looked "like him" and who until that moment believed that dream to be unattainable. WWE commentator Byron Saxton summarized it well when Woods and E

---

[79] Vince McMahon Sr.'s wrestling promotion in the Northeast United States was known as the "World Wide Wrestling Federation" from 1963-79. When Vince Jr. founded Titan Sports in 1980, he also shortened the acronym of his father's company to WWF by eliminating "Wide" from the name. Junior officially purchased the WWF from his father two years later and the rest is history.

presented Kingston with his new championship belt.

"I call this sight right here a symbol of accomplishing your goals, achieving your dreams, no matter who you are, no matter where you come from, no matter what you look like," Saxton proclaimed in what will no doubt be the greatest call of his commentary career. "If you believe, you can make it happen."

That is the magic of pro wrestling in action, and when the story is told well, not only does good conquer evil, but the audience feels like they can, too. Daniel Bryan showed fans how to shake off labels and stand up to unjust authority. Becky Lynch proved there's no gender barrier to being "The Man" and taught little girls that they too can grow up to be lass kickers. Shoot, fifty years before either of them, Bruno Sammartino served as an icon for immigrants in America because he *was* the American Dream.[80]

The lesson here is that before you can be it, you have to see it. So when Kofi Kingston hoisted the WWE championship above his head, it didn't just mean that *he* was championship material; it was a

---

[80] In an industry built on hyperbole and fiction, Bruno Sammartino was a real-life "Living Legend." Sammartino grew up chronically ill and in poverty in Pizzoferrato, Italy. The youngest of seven children, four of his siblings died in childhood. When the Nazis invaded Italy during World War II, Sammartino's family was captured and lined up to be executed before being saved by fellow villagers. After the War, the Sammartinos fled to America, arriving at Ellis Island and settling in Pittsburgh, Penn. where Bruno faced constant prejudice and bullying as an immigrant. When a local landscaper introduced him to weightlifting, everything changed. Nine years later, the once sickly, undersized Sammartino set an unofficial world record in the bench press at 565 pounds and caught the attention of both professional football and professional wrestling in the process. Sammartino pursued a career in the latter and went on to become one of the most well-known and beloved celebrities of his time. Dave Meltzer best summarized Sammartino's impact in his 2018 eulogy for The Italian Superman: "There's a saying about being careful to meet your heroes because you end up disappointed. Millions grew up with Bruno Sammartino, and the ones who got to know him, they were not disappointed."

signal to every other person of color that they could be as well.

Hopefully, we - both in the pro wrestling world and society as a whole - are continuing on a trajectory of awareness and inclusivity. Not only is it the morally right path, but it's an entertainingly gratifying one. There was no better pro wrestling storyline in 2019 than Kofi Kingston overcoming all odds, obstacles, and prejudices to win the championship at *WrestleMania*. It's just disappointing to think we should have been given that satisfaction sixteen years sooner.

NINE

THE ALPHA MALE

"He was letting everybody know, 'I'm the king here, not Monty Brown.'"

January 16, 2005
Impact Zone ◉ Orlando, Florida
TNA Final Resolution

Jeff Jarrett (c) defeated Monty Brown by pinfall for the NWA Worlds Heavyweight Championship (16:17).

* WHAT REALLY HAPPENED *

When World Championship Wrestling met its demise in 2001, Jeff Jarrett was at a career crossroads.

He was, in no uncertain terms, "unwelcome" to return to the World Wrestling Federation. If Jarrett wanted to wrestle, he was going to have to hustle on the independent circuit - which he did, for a bit, claiming the World Wrestling All-Stars (WWA) Heavyweight championship during a tour of Australia in October 2001. But for a guy who had spent the last ten years wrestling under the brightest lights and largest crowds the industry had to offer, Jarrett had limited interest in working community centers and convention halls if he didn't have to. And then he thought that, indeed, *he might not have to.*

The WWF had swallowed up its competition and, as a result, limited employment avenues for wrestlers in 2001. Jarrett saw this as an opportunity. Alongside his father - longtime wrestling promoter Jerry Jarrett - and Internet wrestling pioneer Bob Ryder, Jeff Jarrett founded a professional wrestling company in June of 2002 that would not rival the WWF, but instead serve as a potential mainstream alternative to Vince McMahon's sports entertainment monopoly.

Ryder pitched the concept of a wrestling product exclusive to pay-per-view, and in lieu of launching a new line of company-branded championships, the trio forged a partnership with the National Wrestling Alliance (NWA) to seize creative control over the NWA Worlds Heavyweight and Tag Team championships. Longtime Jarrett supporter Vince Russo also came on board as the company's creative writer. Together, they are credited with naming the promotion "TNA" (strikingly similar to "T&A") because the company would theoretically have more latitude to push the envelope on pay-per-view than the WWF could on basic cable. "TNA" was originally meant to be an acronym for "Tuesday Night Attitude" in reference to the day of the week events were to be held; however, because event replays brought in good revenue on Tuesdays, pay-per-view companies pushed for a Wednesday night show. Instead of changing the initials, Jarrett and Russo changed the acronym and TNA became known as "Total Nonstop Action."

TNA quickly began calling the Nashville Fairgrounds in Nashville, Tenn. home. Actually, what they called it was the "TNA Asylum" and they held weekly pay-per-view events there for two years until relocating to Universal Studios in Orlando, Fla. in June of 2004. Location was far from the only change that year, though. When TNA went from "The Asylum" to the "Impact Zone," it also transitioned from a four-sided ring to a six-sided ring, and finances necessitated the abandonment of weekly pay-per-views in favor of a weekly cable television program on Fox Sports Net called *TNA Impact*, along with more traditional three-hour pay-per-views each month.

Though the changes represented a massive departure from TNA's original vision, they also helped usher in the most successful period of the company's history. A television deal with Fox Sports Net led to a timeslot on Spike TV, which made TNA an attractive destination for well-known stars like Team 3D (formerly known as the Dudley Boyz), Sting, Christian Cage, and Kurt Angle to sign with the company.

Coveting thy competition's roster occasionally had its benefits. By the mid-2000s, TNA was signing a new established star seemingly every other month. At the same time, the company was developing a strong core of "homegrown talent"[81] and future world champions, but struggled to find balance between pushing the known commodities and elevating its own creations. With an ever-expanding talent roster, only so many main event spots available, and not everyone at the top of the card interested in sharing the spotlight, TNA was perfectly primed to miss the boat on a blossoming superstar.

And in 2005, it did. His name was Monty Brown.

Brown had been an All-American linebacker on Ferris State University's football team in the early 1990s before heading to the NFL for a four-year professional career that included an appearance in Super Bowl XXVIII as a member of the Buffalo Bills in 1994. Despite his obvious prowess on the field, however, football was not Brown's first love.

"As a kid growing up, I never had posters of football players in my room," Brown told Alex Marvez of the South Florida Sun-Sentinel in 2004. "I always had posters of wrestlers. This isn't something where I thought one day, 'You know what? I want to wrestle.' This is something I've planned all along."

As an NFL free agent in 1996, Brown signed with the New England Patriots, citing the ability to play closer to World Wrestling

---

[81] I know Eric Bischoff hates this phrase, but I'm going to use it anyway because it's the best terminology available to distinguish TNA performers who did not gain their fame in WWE, WCW, or ECW.

Federation headquarters in Stamford, Conn. as a primary reason for his relocation. Pro wrestling has never had a shortage of men who dreamed of gridiron glory seeking a second life in the squared circle; it's much rarer for a professional football player to leverage *that* career so as to make a pro wrestling dream come true.

But that's exactly what Brown did. Trained by Dan "The Beast" Severn and Sabu, Brown's wrestling dreams were realized in 2000 when the Saginaw, Mich. native made his in-ring debut at the local All World Wrestling League. It was around this time that the six-foot-one, two hundred-forty pounder attended a party following an episode of *WCW Monday Nitro* and introduced himself to Jeff Jarrett. When Jarrett launched TNA in 2002, he offered "The Alpha Male" - Brown's pro wrestling alter ego - his first big break.

"Still one of those headscratchers how [Brown] didn't become a really, really big superstar," Jarrett said of Brown during a 2021 episode of his *My World* podcast with Conrad Thompson.

Brown appeared on five of TNA's first eleven pay-per-views, even challenging Ron Killings for the NWA Worlds Heavyweight championship in August of 2002. Though Brown certainly looked the part, something wasn't quite clicking with the audience. He spent the next eighteen months honing his craft on the independent circuit and returned to TNA on March 10, 2004 with the volume on his "Alpha Male" persona turned up to eleven.

Now being billed from "The Serengeti," Brown dressed in leopard print and put the locker room on notice that it was "open season" with The Alpha Male at the top of the food chain. His promos were intense and over-the-top but the charisma he exuded was also undeniable. Pro Wrestling Illustrated named Brown the publication's Rookie of the Year in 2004 in recognition of his work.

Thanks to a violent-looking shoulder tackle maneuver known as "The Pounce," Brown rolled through the likes of Sabu, BG James

(Road Dogg), D'Lo Brown, Antonio Burks (MVP), and Ron Killings over his first six months back in TNA. As the wins piled up, a showdown between The Alpha Male and the NWA champion Jeff Jarrett appeared increasingly inevitable. By November of 2004, Brown and The Pounce had respectively become the most over wrestler and move in the company. This was owed partly to how hated Jarrett's character was, partly to how impressively Brown's opponents sold The Pounce as a high-impact finisher, and partly to Brown himself being so endearingly ridiculous that fans couldn't help but appreciate him.

With momentum squarely behind him, Brown joined Jarrett, AJ Styles, and Jeff Hardy on the promotional poster for TNA's inaugural three-hour branded pay-per-view, *Victory Road*, in November 2004, a marketing decision that seemed to indicate the company had big plans for The Alpha Male. After defeating Raven and Abyss in the first-ever Monster's Ball[82] match at the event, Brown found himself in line to challenge Jarrett for the NWA Worlds Heavyweight championship on the December 3, 2004 episode of *Impact*. The first Brown/Jarrett championship match came complete with: a ref bump, a guitar shot[83] to Brown's head, a kick-out of Jarrett's finisher, a roll-out of the ring after Brown's finisher, interference by Scott Hall on Jarrett's behalf, and two chair shots to Brown's back before Jarrett scored a pinfall victory. It was a massive night for all those playing Overbooking Bingo. However, it can also be (mostly) forgiven because the match happened on cable television and succeeded in getting Brown over further as a

---

[82] The "Monster's Ball" concept was a specialty of Abyss in TNA and involved (kayfabe) sequestering combatants in locked rooms without lights, food, or water for the twenty-four hours preceding the match in order to induce maximum aggression. The match would then take place under "hardcore rules" wherein weapons were not only legal, but encouraged. It was fun for the whole family.

[83] The guitar is to Jeff Jarrett as the gun is to Anton Chekhov. If you see it in Act I, best believe it's being used by Act III.

sympathetic babyface. It also set the scene for a return bout in which people would pay money to see Monty Brown overcome and defeat Jeff Jarrett to become the NWA Worlds Heavyweight champion.

Everything seemed to be lining up exactly that way. Brown alone adorned the December *Turning Point* pay-per-view poster, which featured the tagline "Destiny Awaits." At the event, Brown took down Abyss in a "Serengeti Survival" hardcore match. By the time *Final Resolution* rolled around in January, the stage was set for Brown's coronation.

In order for that to happen, though, Brown would first have to go through a pair of industry legends at the pay-per-view in Kevin Nash and Diamond Dallas Page, with the winner of their three-man elimination match moving on to face Jeff Jarrett for the NWA Worlds Heavyweight championship in the main event. Fans in the Impact Zone jumped to their feet with elation when Brown countered the Diamond Cutter and drilled Page with The Pounce for the 1-2-3, securing his place as the No. 1 contender.

As Jeremy Borash made his ring introductions ahead of the main event later that night, chants of "Next world champ!" rang throughout the arena. You have likely already guessed that this… did not happen.

For a while it looked like it might, though. Brown and Jarrett worked a solid match for eleven minutes or so. Then came the first ref bump. That was followed by a guitar shot to Brown's head - kick-out. When referee Rudy Charles turned away to wince in pain as a result of the bump, Jarrett hit Brown in the head with a steel chair - another kick-out. When Charles turned away again, this time to remove the chair from the ring - never stopping to contemplate how it got there, mind you - Jarrett hit Brown with the championship belt… and another kick-out.

Frustration was boiling over for everyone witnessing this unfold.

You see, pro wrestling operates with a fundamental requirement for the suspension of disbelief. (Most) fans know what they are watching is fiction, but within the moment itself, we need it to feel like it's real. We're all familiar with the age-old phrase, "*Mundus vult decipi, ergo decipiatur.*" No? Well, in English, it means: "The world wants to be deceived, so let it be deceived." That, in a Latin nutshell, is pro wrestling. We know the magic isn't *magic*, but we want to believe it is while we're at the show. And that works... so long as the magician doesn't rub the audience's nose in the act.

So sure, referees can miss calls; that happens in "real" sports all the time. Referees cannot be outwardly incompetent, however; that causes fans to revolt as the suspension of disbelief collapses. Can you imagine a football line judge missing a call because he was literally facing opposite the action? Or a basketball referee leaving his post to clear an item off the court while play was occurring? No one would accept that kind of behavior from an official in competitive sports; why then, do we accept it in our fictional ones?

Not only that, but when Rudy Charles turned away from the match, he only happened to turn back around at the exact moment his services were needed to count a pinfall attempt. Few pro wrestling tropes challenge the suspension of disbelief quite like the inattentive official who suddenly remembers they have a job to do at the most convenient, coincidental, or opportune times.

Still, Monty Brown's defiance in the face of a deck clearly stacked against him only riled the crowd up more. As Brown continued to battle, the fans could feel that this was surely his night. He was going to overcome all the obstacles, all the chicanery, all the underhanded tactics... and that's when the second ref bump came.

To Rudy Charles' credit, he sold The Pounce like a champ. That poor man *flew* across the ring when Jarrett ducked and Brown hit him with a shoulder tackle. For anyone who wants to claim The Pounce wasn't a devastating finishing maneuver, go watch this hit on Rudy Charles.

It was majestic.

Less majestic was what happened next. With the metaphorical tables now turned, Brown blasted Jarrett in the head with a guitar. After some time, a new referee, Andrew Thomas, then ran down the ramp and into the ring to count the pinfall attempt, which Jarrett managed to kick out of.

Okay. With a referee incapacitated, we can all understand the desire for a replacement. Fair enough. But how come it took Andrew Thomas more than a minute to get to the ring? The Impact Zone ain't that big. Further, if Thomas had been watching the match, which (in kayfabe) clearly *somebody* was in order to know the original referee was down, then Thomas should have been aware of the shenanigans Jarrett had been pulling throughout the match. Or even the guitar shot Brown had delivered, which happened a solid 15 seconds before Thomas slid into the ring for the pinfall attempt.

More importantly - though I have not personally attended referee training school - I have to imagine "keep your eye on the action at all times" has to be included in the curriculum. And yet, as soon as Jarrett kicked out, Andrew Thomas turned his back to the combatants to tend to Charles. 1) TNA was not recruiting the best and brightest from the officiating world; 2) Where the hell was the medical staff? 3) Never trust a man with more than one first name. That's a classic blunder, right up there with getting involved in a land war in Asia or going in against a Sicilian when death is on the line.

As Andrew Thomas (two first names) stepped away to literally check Rudy Charles (!) for a pulse, Jeff Jarrett (!!) grabbed his guitar again and smacked Brown in the face with it. Right on cue, Thomas turned around to see Jarrett subsequently hit his finisher once... and twice... And after the second time, Thomas noticed a guitar shard in the ring, so he turned around to dispose of it. I can't say whether or not Thomas ever wondered how or why the back of an acoustic guitar made its way into the middle of a wrestling ring. But in the eight full seconds it took for Thomas to remove an item that he could have just swept to the side with his foot, Jarrett was able to kick Brown in the groin and hit The Stroke for a third time, putting Brown down for the count, 1-2-3.

There would be no tickertape parade for Monty Brown on this night. He did not overcome the obstacles, chicanery, or underhanded tactics. Instead, TNA doused its hottest act with a bucket of cold water, a decision many have come to view as intentional to keep the spotlight - and the title - on the company's founder.

"He would have been a star," TNA veteran Konnan said of Brown in 2010. "[Jarrett] was letting everybody know, 'I'm the king here, not Monty Brown.'"

In many respects, what Triple H's "Reign of Terror" was to the WWE, the "Planet Jarrett" era was to TNA; however, as Rich Fann (accurately) pointed out on the PWTorch Dailycast on October 26, 2019, "Jeff Jarrett was never over when he did these things." To make matters worse, at the *Destination X* pay-per-view in March, Brown turned heel, joining up with, of all people, Jeff Jarrett. This arrangement lasted about five months, after which time the TNA creative team, with all the self-awareness of Gob Bluth, realized they'd made a huge mistake. Brown broke away from Jarrett by September and refocused on his own singles career, once again setting off in pursuit of the NWA Worlds Heavyweight championship.

He was on his way, too. At the *Genesis* pay-per-view in November, Brown defeated Jeff Hardy to become the No. 1 contender for the heavyweight title. That same night, though, Christian Cage made his TNA debut. A resident of the upper mid-card for years in WWE and one of the first wrestlers to leave for a different company by choice since the end of the Monday Night Wars more than four years prior, Christian immediately moved into the world title picture. This meant that Monty Brown was about to be the victim of some really bad timing.

The Alpha Male put his No. 1 contender spot on the line against Christian at December's *Turning Point* event. Christian won and would go on to defeat Jeff Jarrett for the title at *Against All Odds* the following February. In his first major title defense, Christian defeated Brown in a singles bout at *Destination X* in March of 2006. It was Brown's last title match in TNA; six months later, he was gone from the company.

Brown signed with the WWE in November 2006 and in January of 2007, he made his in-ring debut as "Marcus Cor Von" on the company's relaunched ECW brand.[84] Brown-er… Cor Von… still had looked like a potential superstar and even cracked the *WrestleMania 23* card in April as a member of the New Breed faction, teaming with Elijah Burke, Kevin Thorn, and Matt Striker against Rob Van Dam, Tommy Dreamer, The Sandman, and the man who trained him, Sabu.

This made it all the more shocking that his in-ring career would be over forever by the end of June. To this day, the June 19, 2007 loss to CM Punk in the ECW World Heavyweight Title Tournament remains the last match The Alpha Male Monty Brown ever wrestled. He took time off following the match to tend to unspecified family issues and officially retired from professional wrestling several months later.

The reason for Brown's sudden and, as it turned out, permanent departure was reportedly that his sister passed away. In lieu of returning to the ring, Brown retired, electing instead to stay off the road and care for his sister's children. His story remains one of wrestling's more interesting cases of unrealized potential and "what might have been." More than a decade after his last televised

---

[84] His name was originally spelled "Marquis," but that lasted all of one week.

wrestling appearance, Brown's name is still top of mind for fans and wrestlers alike.

"Monty Brown is someone that I've called out several times, but I think Monty Brown is scared of Moose," Impact Wrestling's Moose[85] said in 2020.

Brown himself made headlines later the same year by recording a promo on Twitter in support of his former TNA rival Lance Archer as the big man prepared to challenge Jon Moxley for the AEW championship. Between that video and Moose's not-so-subtle callout, the Internet was abuzz with speculation - and hope - that perhaps fans hadn't seen the last of The Alpha Male after all.

Nostalgia is powerful everywhere, but especially in the world of professional wrestling where nothing pops a crowd like the surprise return of a hero from yesteryear. The case of Monty Brown feels much different than other potential comeback stories, though. While fans would surely love to see another Pounce or wild promo, for many it will still be bittersweet. Because they'll always wonder, "what if?"

* WHAT COULD HAVE HAPPENED *

In this instance, we won't focus on "what if" Monty Brown hadn't abruptly retired in 2007, but instead on what if TNA had struck while the iron was hot and ran with Brown back in 2005 when they had the chance. Personally, I have often felt, as Monty Brown did in one of his first interviews as a full-time TNA wrestler: "As far as The Alpha Male goes, the future is limitless."

TNA made a critical error in not putting the belt on Brown at *Final Resolution 2005*. Jeff Jarrett was already seven months into his third

---

[85] Like The Alpha Male before him, Moose came to pro wrestling by way of the NFL. Quinn Ojinnaka – as he was once known – started twenty games at left tackle for the Atlanta Falcons from 2006-10.

NWA title reign at this time, so his run on top had already been plenty long. Then again, this was a man who named his finisher "The Stroke" in WCW due to the backstage influence he was known to possess with lead creative writer Vince Russo, so Jarrett's stranglehold on the world title belt may be upsetting, but far from surprising. To his credit, though, Jarrett made Brown look strong in the loss. It took every dirty trick in the book, plus three finishers to put Brown down for good. However, a win in the match would have meant significantly more because he would have *actually* overcome the obstacles, as opposed to just being a tough guy to knock out.

It also would have been a significant step in the right direction for TNA as a company. By this point in TNA history, AJ Styles had won the NWA title on two occasions, with his third reign set to begin in May 2005. But Styles and Abyss were the *only* homegrown talents to hold the NWA Worlds Heavyweight championship during TNA's entire run with the title from 2002-07. Every other world champ had previously made their names in WWE, WCW, or ECW. After the relationship with the NWA dissolved in May of 2007, a "TNA Original" wouldn't win the TNA World Heavyweight championship until April of 2008 when Samoa Joe won the belt from Kurt Angle. A Monty Brown championship victory in 2005 would have gone a long way in, if not breaking the habit, at least changing the narrative that TNA could not create its own main event stars, or that the company's homegrown talent was inferior to the free agents coming in from the competition.

So what would have needed to change at *Final Resolution 2005* to put us on a better timeline? Not a lot, really. Most of Jarrett's heel tactics throughout the match were good storytelling elements… assuming the babyface were to win in the end, of course. And, just because Rudy Charles did such a fantastic job of selling The Pounce, we should keep that as well. Revisions wouldn't be needed until the second ref bump.

So let's pick up there. First of all, Alpha Males don't need weapons.

Instead of using Jarrett's guitar against him, Brown should have smashed it on the mat and tossed it aside because apex predators are dangerous enough as they are. Jarrett would know that, too, so we would get the added visual of a villain who deserved no mercy, on his knees begging for it.

Second, it shouldn't take more than a minute for a substitute referee to appear. Within thirty seconds of Rudy Charles going down, Andrew Thomas should have been sprinting down to ringside to assume officiating duties, and someone with a degree in medicine should have been tending to Charles. Listen, folks. These referees took an oath to serve and protect the integrity of the match, not to look after their fallen colleagues.[86] Much like every cook will tell you that you can't make an omelet without breaking a few eggs, every pro wrestling referee will tell you that you can't book a heel champion's title run without assaulting a few unsuspecting company officials. I don't make the rules.

Third, Brown needed to Pounce Jarrett out of his boots. PERIODT.[87] One option would be for the match to play out as it did, with Jarrett hitting two Strokes on Brown, but before he could hit the third, Brown would counter, push Jarrett off into the ropes, bounce off his own set of ropes, and explode into the Pounce for the 1-2-3. The problem with this route is that it prostitutes Jarrett's finisher, which I personally am not a fan of doing. A finisher needs to be sold as the certain conclusion to a match, except on the rarest of occasions, otherwise the move ceases to remain a "finisher." In baseball terms, a finisher is a lot like a closer. When the closer comes in, the ballgame is almost assuredly over; when a closer starts

---

[86] I can't verify that professional wrestling referees take oaths of any kind, but I like to believe they do.

[87] Almost every Monty Brown promo ended with the words, "POOOUUUUNNNNCCCCEEEE! PERIODT." Spelled just like that.

blowing saves, it's probably time to move on from the closer.

Another way to get Brown the 'W' would be for him to counter out of the first Stroke (protecting Jarrett's finishing maneuver), have Jarrett duck The Pounce a second time (showing he was still a crafty ring veteran who appears to remain one step ahead of the less experienced challenger), but have Brown land in a four-point stance instead of outright missing (showing he had learned and was actually a step ahead of the champion). From his coiled, ready position, Brown would connect with Jarrett, who would be completely blindsided by The Pounce. Andrew Thomas would count to three, Monty Brown would fulfill his destiny as the "next world champ," and the Impact Zone would celebrate the dawning of a new era in TNA.

* WHAT WOULD HAVE HAPPENED NEXT *

How different might the rest of Monty Brown's career turned out had he been given the NWA title run in 2005?

It's difficult to project in full, given how fate intervened in 2007. However, as far as TNA would be concerned, at least, he would have been a homegrown, bona fide main event player. After winning the championship at *Final Resolution*, I would envision a Monty Brown title run lasting at least until *Hard Justice* in May, or possibly *Slammiversary* in June.

In the real timeline, The Alpha Male tagged with Diamond Dallas Page against Eric Young and Bobby Roode at February's *Against All Odds* event. In the revised timeline, we might want to insert Brown right into the main event against Jeff Jarrett and Kevin Nash in a triple threat match. Along with Scott Hall, Jarrett and Nash formed the "Kings of Wrestling" stable the previous year. Though the group split in early 2005 due to Nash's desire to compete for the NWA title (which Jarrett possessed at the time), their closeness would make for an interesting storyline throughout the match - and, possibly, yet

THE ALPHA MALE

another obstacle for the babyface Brown to overcome.

Instead of teaming with Brown at the pay-per-view, Page would have to find a different partner. Locating a partner on DDP's level would have been a challenge, so the announcement would likely be a game time decision, so to speak. Fortunately, TNA happened to have a well-known star coming into the company that very night: Sean Waltman. The artist formerly known as X-Pac (and Syxx, and The 1-2-3 Kid) actually debuted at *Against All Odds* by attacking Jarrett. Since TNA main events were often overbooked enough, perhaps The Kid's presence might have been more positively utilized as DDP's mystery tag team partner.

Back in reality at *Destination X* in March of 2005, Brown battled a gentleman by the name of "Trytan" to a no contest. If you're having trouble picturing Trytan, you're not alone. He only wrestled fifteen matches on-record in TNA, and aside from a handful of house show or dark matches in WWE under the name "Jacob Duncan," Trytan spent most of his wrestling career on the independent circuit. For a short time in early 2005, though, Trytan used a "Terminator" gimmick that culminated in a match against Monty Brown at *Destination X*. No offense intended to Trytan, but in our new timeline, he would likely not be getting a shot at the champ on this night.

However, I do like the path TNA was (probably unintentionally) going down here. Monty Brown wrestled in twenty-one pay-per-view matches of the one-on-one variety during his time in TNA. Seventeen of those matches came against former WCW, ECW, or WWE talents. We never got to see The Alpha Male in true singles programs against other homegrown talents like AJ Styles, Christopher Daniels, or Samoa Joe. When it came to one-on-one bouts, Brown was almost always pitted against an incoming talent. So, at *Destination X*, it might have been nice to see The Alpha Male take on a new face.

Bobby Roode is one name that immediately comes to mind when considering potential challengers for Brown. A future TNA and NXT champion, Roode was booked in an eight-man tag match as a member of Team Canada against 3Live Kru and America's Most Wanted; however, I would have been okay with swapping Johnny Devine in for Roode here, provided Devine didn't blow out his knee while working a tag match in Memphis Wrestling that March.

If Devine's injury would have prevented us from getting Brown versus Roode, another opponent to look at might be Lance Hoyt. AEW's Murderhawk Monster was tagging with Kid Kash at the time and would actually go on to have a pay-per-view bout with Monty Brown at *Bound For Glory* later that year. However, simply due to Hoyt's size and athleticism, he should have been inserted as a plug-and-play challenger much sooner in his career than he actually was, as evidenced by his outstanding work in both NJPW and AEW.

Jarrett and Page could still fight in their singles match at *Destination X*; however, since Jarrett would not hold the NWA Worlds Heavyweight championship, the match would just be a rivalry bout. The most significant outcome of this version of *Destination X*, though, is that Brown wouldn't be killing off his momentum by turning heel for no good reason.

At *Lockdown* in April, Brown might be held off the card and instead used to do guest commentary for the main event, a No. 1 contender's match between AJ Styles and Abyss. This would give Brown a chance to be entertaining on the microphone, in addition to providing a kayfabe opportunity for The Alpha Male to scout his next prey. It also wouldn't hurt to have a stare down between Styles (who would win the match) and Brown - two TNA Originals - to close the show.

In the real timeline, Brown was teaming with Jeff Jarrett and The Outlaw (formerly known as Billy Gunn) against B.G. James (formerly known as Road Dogg), Diamond Dallas Page, and Sean

Waltman in a Lethal Lockdown match.[88] Who might have been a suitable replacement for Brown in this match? Well, if Chyna were available, there could have been an even bigger D-Generation X reunion. Or if Scott Hall were available, the Kings of Wrestling storyline might have been revisited. An even farther fetched option might have been TNA's first world champion, Ken Shamrock, who had aligned with Jarrett in a ten-man tag match the year before, but left the company shortly thereafter.

The idea of a one-night rental here has appeal, since these were all established stars from other companies; not to mention, Jarrett's team lost. When the new teammate didn't result in a squad victory, there would be no pressure for the ringer to maintain a relationship with Team Jarrett afterwards. Had Kevin Nash not been removed from the match due to a staph infection, it might have been fun to reunite the New Age Outlaws on Team Jarrett. Given B.G. James' previous WWF relationships with both men (having served as the "Roadie" for Double J and the longtime tag partner of Billy Gunn) there would already be a built-in storyline to pursue following the team's failure at *Lockdown*.

At *Hard Justice* in May, Brown would defend the NWA championship against No. 1 contender AJ Styles. In the real timeline, Styles defeated Jarrett for the title here. In our timeline, Brown would go over in the main event, while Jarrett would simply slide into Brown's spot teaming with The Outlaw against DDP and Ron Killings. It would be a bigger deal for Brown to beat Styles than for Styles to beat Brown. Styles was a two-time NWA Worlds Heavyweight champion at this point and in the real timeline, his third reign only lasted a month. We also know that nothing would stand in the way of AJ Styles becoming one of the five-to-ten greatest in-ring

---

[88] The Lethal Lockdown was somewhat similar in concept to WCW's WarGames match, as teams of combatants fought inside a steel cage. In TNA's version, the cage had weapons hanging from it.

performers of all-time. Styles' career survived a paternity test blackmail angle during a particularly #TNAwful period in 2012;[89] a clean main event loss to Monty Brown in 2005 wouldn't hurt him. Conversely, this match would have been big for Brown, who could have classified this as a signature victory. Plus, Styles flipping inside-out for The Pounce likely would have been one for the highlight reel.

The Alpha Male's NWA title run would conclude at *Slammiversary* in June. The only difference between the real timeline and the revised one is that this time, Brown would enter the King of the Mountain ladder match as champion instead of Styles. In the end, Raven would still go over to win the NWA championship for the first and only time in his career.

Post-*Slammiversary*, Monty Brown spent the next three months of the real timeline teaming with the Artist Formerly Known As Billy Gunn. In the alternate timeline, the reunion of the New Age Outlaws – known in TNA as the "James Gang" – would have already been accelerated. Because of this, Brown would be removed from that feud and B.G. James would take his place. With the new champion, Raven, preoccupied with Abyss, the most recent former champion would be slotted into a No. 1 contendership match at July's *No Surrender* event. His opponent? Sorry to say, but it's TNA in 2005, which means it would be about time to welcome back J-E-Double-

---

[89] The Claire Lynch angle began with the (kayfabe) rumor that Styles was having an affair with TNA President Dixie Carter. It was later revealed that the two were not having an affair, but instead working together to assist a drug-addicted pregnant woman named Claire Lynch in straightening out her life. Then, Christopher Daniels and Frankie Kazarian - feuding with Styles at the time - claimed that Styles was the father of Lynch's unborn baby. Styles went on to defeat Daniels in a Last Man Standing match for the right to a paternity test, because that's how that works. Then, it was revealed that Lynch wasn't even pregnant at all and Kazarian was just trying his hand at blackmail. Ladies and gentlemen, TNA.

F J-A-Double-R-E-Double-T, Jeff Jarrett![90]

The match would work here because they would both have a direction to go in after it. Jarrett would get the win at *No Surrender*, likely in typical Jarrett fashion. After Raven defeated Abyss, Jarrett would also get to unveil his newest recruit, Rhino, who would debut just as he did in the real timeline by attacking Raven and setting up the main event at August's *Sacrifice* event. Some will scoff at the notion of bringing Jarrett back into the title scene, but I'm okay with main event Double J in moderation. Being a lifelong wrestling heel probably didn't help his reputation with wrestling fans, perception being reality and all. Buuuut, reality is reality, too, and Jarrett had the power to step aside in order to make new stars and out of fear, jealousy, or general self-interest, he usually did not. So I do understand the skeptics here.

It's also important for the skeptics to recognize that TNA was entering a period of mainstream appeal where television contracts were being negotiated and there was a natural desire to have a known commodity as world champion. Though Jarrett was never the draw he purported himself to be, he *was* a recognizable name, and as TNA headed to Spike TV in the fall of 2005, name recognition mattered. Not only that, but when Jarrett was accused of "burying" talent, it was generally because he was halting momentum unnecessarily. If both involved parties had clear storyline trajectories that benefited everyone in the end, there would be less to complain about. Don't get me wrong, wrestling fans would still complain. There would just be less of it.

A loss to Jarrett would send Brown over the edge and play off the real-life criticisms fans had for TNA booking. Brown already wouldn't have been pleased to have lost his championship at *Slammiversary* without having been personally defeated by pinfall or

---

[90] Ain't he great?

submission. Now, he would have lost to Jarrett, and probably through nefarious means. Brown would wonder aloud how Jarrett continued to find himself in championship matches, bringing out into the open the issues fans have complained about for ages. He would also question why TNA had rules at all if they were just going to be broken without enforcement? For the previous ten months, Brown tried to be a model citizen. Now, he would be done with that. Now he would live by the law of the jungle. No rules... no mercy... and "no limits."

You heard that right, folks. Playing off the company's tagline, it wouldn't be about weight limits, it would be about no limits because Monty Brown would head over to the X-Division! For the uninitiated, TNA's X-Division was intended to spotlight the fast-paced, high-risk, lucha libre style of wrestling typically utilized by cruiserweight wrestlers. However, the inclusion of heavyweight wrestlers (who were also athletic enough to move in the ring) alongside the majority of sub-200-pounders made for unique clashes, and as the old adage goes, "styles make fights." Never had that been truer than in the summer of 2005 when Samoa Joe arrived in TNA. A 280-pound freight train, Joe competed with reckless abandon when he set his sights on the X-Division title. It would be fun to see Monty Brown go down a parallel path, culminating in a pay-per-view matchup between The Alpha Male and the Samoan Submission Machine somewhere down the line.

That matchup would take months to develop, though. In the immediate future, Brown would focus on the smaller, more traditional X-Division stars. Names like Austin Aries and Alex Shelley come to mind as potential opponents at August's *Sacrifice* and September's *Unbreakable* events. At *Bound For Glory* in October, it would have been interesting to see Brown compete in - and even win - the Ultimate X match. Rarely did heavyweight competitors participate in the high-risk, gravity-defying match, so Brown's entry would have been unique and - given his athleticism and general disposition - likely entertaining.

Brown's win at *Bound For Glory* would turn into a title shot against X-Division champion AJ Styles the following month at *Genesis*. However, this time around, Styles would retain. It would also end Brown's X-Division run, at least for the time being. At *Turning Point* in December, Brown would have fought Christian Cage for the No. 1 contendership to the NWA championship. Unlike in the real timeline, Brown wouldn't have already been the No. 1 contender and voluntarily gambled away his title shot; instead, Brown would serve as the fill-in for Jeff Hardy, who cited travel challenges as the reason he no-showed the event. I know many fans will object to booking the former WWE star over the up-and-coming talent, but here's the harsh reality: as *Impact* transitioned from Fox Sports Net to Spike TV during the fall of 2005, the company needed to rely on established stars. In the short-term, for sure, that strategy paid off. *Impact*'s Spike TV debut on October 1, 2005 garnered an audience of 850,000 viewers. By the time the contract was renewed less than two years later, that audience had grown to more than 1.5 million weekly. So yes, to some degree at least, the additions of known commodities like Christian Cage, Sting, and Kurt Angle did hold homegrown talents like Monty Brown closer to the midcard; however, those moves also made good business sense.

With the loss to Christian at *Turning Point*, Brown's TNA career would then come to the same crossroad it did in reality. That's not all bad, either. Even if Brown ended up bolting for the WWE, he still had time in the TNA spotlight. He was in the main event of *Final Resolution* in January, tagging with Jeff Jarrett against Christian Cage and Sting in Stinger's first big return to the ring in nearly five years. Two months later, he was battling for the NWA Heavyweight title against Christian Cage at *Destination X* in March. His last match in TNA came against Rhino at *Victory Road* in July and he signed with WWE that November. Those are all solid matches against world championship caliber opponents.

Had Brown stayed in TNA, matches against Bobby Roode, James Storm, Christopher Daniels, and Samoa Joe would have been obvious to book, plus Scott Steiner came into TNA just as Brown was on his way out, and Kurt Angle debuted just after Brown left. Brown's WWE career likely turned out about as well as it could have, given the circumstances, but as far as TNA was concerned, there likely would have been a decent amount of meat left on the bone for the rest of 2006 and 2007, at least.

It is interesting to consider if anything would have or could have changed long-term had Brown stayed in TNA instead of leaving for Stamford, Conn., though. Brown retired from the ring to be with his family, which is certainly a noble decision. Maybe it's possible that due to TNA's significantly lighter travel and taping schedule, that arrangement might have lent itself more easily to having both a limited wrestling schedule and a full family life. Then again, Monty Brown doesn't strike me as a guy who's not one-hundred percent in on whatever he's doing. Plus, if he truly signed with the New England Patriots in 1996 to be closer to WWF headquarters - at a time when the WWF wasn't the only or best wrestling show on the market - then that was his dream landing spot all along, and kudos to him for realizing it.

Even if it was inevitable that Monty Brown's pro wrestling career was going to be complete by the middle of 2007, a revised 2005 would have changed a whole lot for The Alpha Male and his legacy. He would have received the world championship title run fans felt he deserved, engaged in singles feuds with other TNA Originals that fans never really got to see, and still would have remained high enough on the card to share the ring with some of the biggest stars of the time period. His own star still might have burned out faster than fans would have liked, but there would be a measure of solace in knowing that at least some of his massive potential was realized. We still would have wanted more, but perhaps we would wonder less about "what might have been."

TEN

THE NEW MONDAY NIGHT WARS

"TNA has held me back from TNA. They're not ready for me."

January 4, 2010
Impact Zone ⏺ *Orlando, Florida*
TNA Impact

* WHAT REALLY HAPPENED *

With fans and media gathered in the heart of Manhattan at the "World's Most Famous Arena," TNA Wrestling president Dixie Carter stood at a podium on October 27, 2009 to make an announcement that would change the trajectory of her company forever.

"A little over seven years ago, TNA Wrestling started," Carter said. "We were a television show that broadcast weekly pay-per-views to tens of thousands of people. And here we are today, at Madison Square Garden, announcing the biggest acquisition you can have in the history of wrestling."

Hulk Hogan was coming to TNA.

"We're not going to settle," Carter continued. "Until we become the number one wrestling company in the world."

The news was seismic. Age and injuries aside, Hogan remained the biggest and most recognizable wrestling star on the planet. He wouldn't be coming to TNA alone either. Former WCW president and longtime Hogan confidant Eric Bischoff actually brokered the deal and would be joining The Hulkster in Total Nonstop Action.

For a company already nearing two million weekly viewers for *Impact* on Spike TV, this - Carter believed - could put TNA over the top. Armed with an exceptional roster, a weekly cable television show, and respectable ratings already, it seemed that adding the biggest wrestling superstar of all time to the mix might be the final piece of the puzzle for TNA to go from programming alternative to justifiable competition for Vince McMahon's WWE.

Less than two months later, in a live interview with Ultimate Fighting Championship (UFC) announcer Joe Rogan on Spike TV's *The Ultimate Fighter*, Hogan upped the ante with a declaration that made wrestling fans across the globe giddy with anticipation.

"On January 4, TNA *Impact* - we're going wide open, we're going head-on-head, we're going to battle with the WWE," Hogan proclaimed.

For the first time since March 2001, WWE's flagship program, *Monday Night Raw*, was going to have direct pro wrestling opposition. At least for one night. TNA's live three-hour episode of *Impact* was merely a trial run to see how the company really stood up against the WWE machine in a head-to-head fashion.

And you know what? TNA delivered. *Impact* did not beat *Raw* in the ratings that night - *Raw* drew an average audience of 5.6 million viewers and a 3.37 rating among the key 18-49 male demographic. However, *Impact* registered an average of 2.2 million viewers and a 1.5 rating over the three-hour special, making the January 4 episode of *Impact* TNA's most-watched program ever.

TNA likely benefited from a one-hour head start on WWE, as *Raw* was only a two-hour show at the time.[91] As such, TNA had a prime opportunity to reel a larger audience before *Raw* got underway an hour later, which is why *Impact* began with the shocking return of

---

[91] It was a simpler, happier time.

perennial fan-favorite, Jeff Hardy. The "Charismatic Enigma" had left TNA for the WWE in 2006. In December 2008, he won the WWE championship and claimed the WWE World Heavyweight championship twice in 2009. Hardy's contract expired in August of 2009 and WWE officials had hoped to have him back in the fold for the Road to *WrestleMania* in early 2010. TNA scooping up one of WWE's most popular main event players was a huge win for the start of the Bischoff/Hogan era.

A second surprising debut came soon after, as the legendary Ric Flair emerged from a limousine and made his way to AJ Styles' locker room. Flair got a (well-deserved) hero's sendoff from WWE following his retirement match against Shawn Michaels at *WrestleMania XXIV* in 2008. He remained on good terms with the company through June of 2009, but when six months passed without contact from the WWE, the Nature Boy entertained - and accepted - an offer from TNA.

As the nine o'clock hour approached, so too did Hogan's limousine, as the Hulkster's TNA debut was matched up to go head-to-head with the start of *Monday Night Raw*. Meanwhile, WWE wisely counter-programmed with the well-advertised return of Bret Hart after a more than twelve-year absence from the company. This would be The Hitman's first time back in a WWE ring since the fabled Montreal Screwjob at *Survivor Series 1997*, and an event most wrestling fans never imagined they would see. On *Raw*, Hart opened his address appropriately with the words, "Well, I guess hell froze over." Soon after, he called out Shawn Michaels and the two "buried the hatchet," ending the unforgettable segment with a handshake and a hug.

That piece of wrestling history was going to be nearly impossible to top. Still, Hogan's segment managed to peak with a TNA-record 2.9 million viewers for the 9:00 to 9:15 p.m. EST quarter-hour. This was thanks to not just Hogan's debut, but also the short-lived New World Order reunion that followed, as Hogan was quickly joined in the ring by Scott Hall, Sean Waltman, Kevin Nash, and Eric Bischoff. While Hall, Waltman, and Nash looked to get the band back together, Hogan insisted that things were different now and that he and Bischoff had come to TNA for business, not a party.

As Hall, Waltman, and Nash made their exit, Bischoff and Hogan began to talk about "change." It's a word the pair used seven times in the final three minutes of their promo. At one point, the camera panned to a fan wearing a red and yellow Hogan "CHANGE" t-shirt, designed in the style of Shepard Fairey's iconic Barack Obama poster from the 2008 U.S. Presidential campaign. On the surface, the rhetoric was far from uncommon. Whenever a babyface authority figure seizes power in the world of pro wrestling, the talking points almost always focus on some combination of change, justice, and opportunity. However, as fans soon realized, "change" was not what TNA needed.

In hindsight, that "change" promo should have been seen as the first red flag because TNA had already reached the point of being able to stand on its own in a mainstream pro wrestling landscape dominated by WWE. The company was flawed, of course, but it didn't need a complete overhaul just as it was approaching real competitiveness; what it needed was more of what was clearly already working. Alas, Bischoff's closing remarks were his most prophetic: "What we're going to do is turn this company upside down."

Indeed, they would.

In defense of "Easy E," Bischoff came to TNA as an on-screen character. "I had nothing to do with management of TNA," Bischoff recalled on *83 Weeks* in 2020. "I was there to oversee creative as it related to Hulk Hogan."

Bischoff soon discovered, though, that *everything* in TNA was going to relate to Hulk Hogan. Bischoff went on to add Executive Producer duties behind the scenes and formally became the head of

Creative in 2013.

Less than two weeks after their TNA debut, Bischoff and Hogan opened the *Genesis* pay-per-view by greeting fans to a "brand new" Impact Zone, which featured a traditional four-sided ring instead of TNA's signature six-sided ring, which had been a staple of the company since *Impact* debuted in 2004. That alteration was met with a chorus of boos from the crowd, followed by a loud chant of, "We want six sides!" The fan response undoubtedly caught the new TNA proprietors off guard. Hogan attempted to calm the crowd by asserting, "You had it and it only got you so far," which, while accurate to some degree, did not go over well.

Now, did the number of sides on the ring *really* matter? Probably not. Bischoff wasn't necessarily wrong when he assessed the six-sided ring years later as an "odd idea with no rational purpose." However, TNA management did misjudge how much the six-sided ring meant to fans in terms of brand identity. It was a huge differentiator for the company and fans took pride in that uniqueness. The move back to four sides may have been the right decision, but Hogan and Bischoff were ill-prepared for what should have been predictable fan backlash. The lack of foresight led to Hogan proclaiming the less-than-ideal off-the-cuff line that would come to define his TNA legacy: "We're changing it whether you like it or not."

After eight weeks back on Thursday nights, *Impact* made a "permanent" move to Mondays, sliding into the 9:00 p.m. Eastern time slot opposite *Raw* on March 8, 2010. This change lasted just two months, as the writing appeared all over the wall by the second week of the ill-fated experiment. After pulling a 0.98 rating with 1.4 million viewers on March 8, the March 15 episode of *Impact* scored TNA's lowest rating since November of 2006 at 0.84 and saw an overall decrease in viewership by 21.4 percent from Week One to Week Two. In the same time period, *Raw* saw its overall viewership *increase* by ten percent. *Impact*'s ratings briefly bounced back in April when the program shifted to an 8:00 p.m. ET start, but plummeted to a brutal 0.5 rating on April 26. It was no surprise then when *Impact* returned to its usual Thursday time slot in May.

"Our fans made it clear that they preferred the Thursday night time period," Dixie Carter said in the explanatory press release, which also announced the program would be rebranded as *"Thursday Night Impac*t*."*

There is some truth in Carter's statement, since the replay of *Impact* on Thursday, March 13 pulled a 1.0 rating, actually outperforming the live episode by 0.02 points. It's also true that head-to-head competition divides an audience, so both WWE and TNA stood to gain viewers by airing their content on different days. However, when it came right down to it, fans saw the kind of "change" the Bischoff/Hogan era was bringing to TNA and they just did not like it. Why, you ask? Well, perhaps it was because during this brief and underwhelming Second Coming of the Monday Night Wars - when TNA had no choice but to bring its A-game every week - Creative's premium segment offerings included a Sting heel turn (the next one that works will be the first), up-and-comers Ric Flair (age sixty-one at the time) and Hulk Hogan (age fifty-six at the time) going head-to-head in main event matches, and opening a show with Eric Bischoff playing acoustic guitar. I'm not saying that TNA went into this experiment without a long-term plan, but I would call what fans got to be something along the lines of "bottle rocket booking": a momentary spectacle geared towards instant reaction.[92] Everything appeared to be built toward popping a Monday night rating instead of laying the groundwork for compelling storytelling over an extended period of time. Less than three months into the new regime, TNA's gamble backfired spectacularly and all the momentum the company had coming into the year was destroyed.

---

[92] Also like bottle rockets, simple enough to be done at home but dangerous enough that someone was bound to lose a few fingers.

In fairness to this era, there were a few interesting things that happened during Hogan and Bischoff's tenure in TNA. The Aces & Eights storyline that featured a *Sons of Anarchy*-esque vigilante biker gang with its eyes on a company takeover may have been polarizing and flawed, but it was occasionally compelling and - with a seventeen-month arc - certainly long-term.[93] The Bound For Glory Series was a unique concept that added an element of "real" sports feel through its point system format. Most significantly, though, with Hogan and Bischoff in charge, James Storm, Bobby Roode, Austin Aries, Bully Ray, and Chris Sabin were all elevated to main event status with each claiming the TNA World Heavyweight championship between October 2011 and July 2013. That was definitely some positive change. The problem was that it took nearly two years for the "change" Hogan and Bischoff boasted about in January 2010 to happen. And by that point, it was too late.

To Dixie Carter's credit, she knew by the spring of 2010 that TNA was in trouble. The company's creative direction was clearly not working so she began to explore other options to shake up TNA's leadership team. First to mind was Jim Ross, whose WWE contract was set to expire at the end of April and who Eric Bischoff actually recommended for the job. The legendary play-by-play announcer and longtime talent relations executive was said to be open to jumping ship to the competition if he could play the role of a real-life general manager. However, Ross allegedly requested that Vince Russo be removed from the company's creative team before J.R. would take any offer from TNA seriously. Russo remained and Ross was back behind a WWE announce desk by November.

When conversations stalled with Ross, TNA brass set its sights on a new target - someone who had been out of the wrestling business for more than three years but possessed the credentials and creativity

---

[93] The Aces & Eights angle was simultaneously voted the Feud of the Year by Pro Wrestling Illustrated in 2012 and the Worst Gimmick of the Year by the Wrestling Observer Newsletter in 2012 and 2013. (Jordan shrug.)

to succeed where the Hogan/Bischoff experiment had failed.

His name was Paul Heyman.

TNA began courting the former Extreme Championship Wrestling owner in May of 2010, less than six months into the Hogan/Bischoff era. Heyman had been on the market since December of 2006 when he parted ways with the WWE following a less-than-stellar *December to Dismember* pay-per-view event.[94] Heyman was content with pro wrestling in his rearview, but was intrigued by the options TNA may have been able to offer, which - at least in Heyman's mind - included a personal contract with Spike TV[95] and stock ownership in TNA.

Now, Heyman may have believed TNA was too far gone already so he asked for something he knew he couldn't get (ownership) just so he could say he turned their offer down. Much like Abraham Lincoln's belief that "It is better to remain silent and be thought a fool than to speak and remove all doubt," for Heyman, it may have been better to remain a free agent and be thought a savior than to accept a Herculean task and fail. Nevertheless, he pitched Carter his five-year plan for the company, but just like with Jim Ross a month earlier, a directional request was made that proved to be a deal breaker for both sides.

---

[94] Vince McMahon sent Heyman home less than twenty-four hours after the event, citing "slumping television ratings and a disgruntled talent roster as causes for Mr. Heyman's dismissal." Heyman and McMahon allegedly engaged in a spirited disagreement over the booking of the ECW championship match in the main event, with Heyman strongly advocating for CM Punk to win and McMahon staunchly supportive of Bobby Lashley. For Heyman, this latest WWE-ification of his ECW creation was the straw that broke the camel's back.

[95] Not unlike WCW's relationship with AOL Time Warner, Spike TV covered salary expenses for some of TNA's top stars, including Sting and Hulk Hogan.

"I don't want a bunch of guys in their 40s," Heyman said.

Heyman told Carter if he was hired, she could keep just one "legend" on the active roster. He didn't care which one, but it could only be one. Flummoxed by the proposal, Carter could not agree to Heyman's terms and the deal was dead.

"TNA has held me back from TNA," Heyman explained to Ariel Helwani on The MMA Hour later that year. "They're not ready for me."

Two years later, Heyman returned to the WWE in an on-screen capacity as the "advocate" for Brock Lesnar. Carter, meanwhile, stayed the course with Hogan and Bischoff in TNA until late 2013, but the ratings never recovered. The company that had more than two million viewers to begin 2010 saw that audience dwindle to less than a million by the end of 2014. The plummet from grace was swift and staggering, especially considering the amount of talent - both established and developmental - that performed for the company during this span. This is not to say that Hogan and Bischoff were solely to blame for TNA's downfall; there are plenty of blood-soaked hands in that conversation, and those two weren't even "creatively" in charge of everything for a decent portion of their time in the company. However, it's clear that Hogan and Bischoff were not the men to take TNA to the next level and because a deal couldn't be reached in the spring of 2010, wrestling fans will always wonder if Heyman was.

* WHAT COULD HAVE HAPPENED *

What might Paul Heyman's TNA have looked like? One thing we know for certain is it would have looked younger. In his August 2010 interview with Ariel Helwani for AOL Fanhouse, Heyman compared handling TNA's roster to how he would have wanted to manage the New York Yankees at the time.

"My first move, I let A-Rod go, I let Derek Jeter go, I get a whole team of twenty-one-, twenty-two-year-olds," Heyman said. "Cause A-Rod's already hit six hundred home runs. He's not going to hit six hundred more. I want to find a kid who's going to hit six hundred for me in the next fifteen years."

For the sports fans in the house, this would be a mildly concerning statement. The Yankees had literally just won their 27th World Series title less than a year earlier with Alex Rodriguez and Derek Jeter playing pivotal roles throughout the championship run. Not only that, teams that sell off their star players tend to have given up on the present in favor of preparing for the future. That can work in pro sports because even though coaches and general managers may lose their jobs, the entire team isn't going to go under if there are a few rebuilding seasons. In pro wrestling, if you don't have star power, you're not going to have a television show for very long either. Knowing Heyman's affinity for hyperbole and shock value, my guess is his position was intentionally bold to overtly illustrate TNA's need to focus its energy on developing new, younger stars.

Now, this ended up being where TNA found itself out of necessity by the time Hogan and Bischoff were officially on the outs. Scott Hall, Kevin Nash, and Sean Waltman left the company in 2010; Mick Foley wrapped up his TNA run in 2011; Scott Steiner was released and Ric Flair returned to the WWE in 2012; Rob Van Dam followed suit in 2013; Jeff Jarrett resigned from TNA Entertainment in December of 2013; and Hogan and Sting both joined the WWE in 2014. TNA lost double-digit main eventers over a four-year period, effectively forcing the company to create its own stars. Had Heyman come aboard in 2010, that process would have been more deliberate instead of survivalist, which would have had its benefits.

Heyman planned to spend the first eighteen months of his time in TNA building up a roster of talented upstarts. One would assume such TNA "originals" as AJ Styles, Samoa Joe, Bobby Roode, James Storm, Christopher Daniels, and Frankie Kazarian all would have fit in well with Heyman at the helm. There was one man not on the

TNA roster who Heyman believed would have been central for the plan to succeed, though: the "American Dragon" Bryan Danielson.

The darling of independent wrestling from 2002-09, Danielson signed with the WWE in the summer of 2009 and made his television debut as the creatively named "Daniel Bryan" on the inaugural episode of the company's new faux competition program entitled *NXT* on February 23, 2010.[96] When the NXT rookies made their shocking *Raw* invasion as The Nexus on June 7, 2010, Bryan - in the eyes of WWE management - took his instructions to "go out and raise hell" a bit too far when he choked out ring announcer Justin Roberts with Roberts' own neck tie. Bryan was fired for the incident four days later and immediately became the most sought after free agent in the industry. Instead of signing an exclusive contract with another major promotion right away, Danielson elected to return to the independent scene. By the end of August, though, he was back in the WWE, participating in the main event of *SummerSlam* and would of course go on to become one of the company's biggest stars over the next five years.

"I don't know if Bryan would have signed with TNA, but I do think there was a window in June/early July of last year where he probably would have if Heyman and I went there," Gabe Sapolsky said in 2011. "Now the window on everyone is slammed shut. Just another 'what could have been.'"

Sapolsky would know. Heyman's former marketing man in ECW went on to become the co-founder and head booker for Ring of Honor during the majority of Danielson's run in the company. Post-ROH, Sapolsky launched Dragon Gate USA in 2009, which became one of the handful of independent promotion's Danielson chose to work with during his hiatus from the WWE. Adding to the intrigue

---

[96] Though far from a "rookie" in terms of pro wrestling experience, Bryan was appropriately paired with former MTV *Real World* reality television star The Miz as his pro, which the Internet *hated* (as was the intent).

is the fact that Sapolsky said, "...if Heyman **and I** went there." Apparently, if TNA could have landed Heyman, they would have gotten Sapolsky as well. For a company looking to solidify its creative direction, picking up the Wrestling Observer Newsletter's "Best Booker" award winner for four straight years (2004-07) would have been a pretty big get. Not only that, it's worth noting that the fresh-faced roster Sapolsky assembled for Dragon Gate USA in 2010 included Tommaso Ciampa, Sami Callihan, Johnny Gargano, Chuck Taylor, Ricochet, Adam Cole, Rich Swann, Akira Tozawa, and Jon Moxley. Though this would have been very early in each of those men's careers, it's not far-fetched to think many would have been interested in following Sapolsky to TNA if circumstances would have allowed it.

Danielson, though was clearly ready for prime time. If things had gone according to Sapolsky's theory, Heyman would have rebuilt TNA around the American Dragon as an unbeatable submission specialist. Danielson would have gone on a Goldberg-esque run for the next year, culminating in a one-on-one instant classic with 1996 Olympic Gold Medalist Kurt Angle at *Bound For Glory 2011*.

Before getting there, though, Danielson would still need a proper build. Perhaps he would debut in TNA as an ally and tag team partner of Brian Kendrick. There would be a real-life storyline built in there, as Danielson and Kendrick were classmates and trainees of Shawn Michaels at the Texas Wrestling Academy a decade earlier. In TNA, the two might tag together for the first few months of Danielson's time in the company, possibly taking on Ink Inc. at July's *Victory Road* and Generation Me – who bore a striking resemblance to The Young Bucks – at August's *Hardcore Justice* before earning a shot at the Motor City Machine Guns' tag team titles at *No Surrender*. Kendrick would take the pinfall in the match with the Guns, resulting in Danielson turning on him for failing the team. This would set up a one-on-one match between the two at *Bound For Glory* and begin Danielson's singles run heading into 2011.

Over the next six to eight months, Danielson would focus his attention on the X-Division, taking on - and tapping out - the likes of Amazing Red, Eric Young, Robbie E, Jay Lethal, and Doug Williams. At *Lockdown* in April of 2011, Danielson would win the Xscape cage match to become the No. 1 contender for the X-Division title and would claim the belt from Frankie Kazarian at *Sacrifice* the following month. This would lead to a two-month program with Samoa Joe, who began his TNA career on a similar tear. Up until this point, Danielson would have generally been staying in his own weight class. The program with Samoa Joe would have been his first foray into the heavyweight scene and put him on track to follow in the footsteps of AJ Styles towards the company's primary singles title.

After conquering Samoa Joe, Danielson's next challenger might be Rob Van Dam - one of the few elder statesmen left on the TNA roster by this point. RVD would be a prime candidate here, as he wrestled like an X-Division competitor but had the resume and credibility of a heavyweight champion, making Danielson's victory over him at *Hardcore Justice* all the more meaningful.

Leading up to *No Surrender*, Heyman would alert fans that he planned to make a major announcement regarding Danielson and the X-Division championship at the September pay-per-view. Heyman would praise Danielson for his work over the last year, noting how the X-Division had always been the backbone of TNA and that Danielson had added great prestige to the title through his impressive run. He would wonder, though, if there might be a way to make the X-Division title even more valuable to its holder. That would be when Heyman would institute a new rule for the X-Division championship. Moving forward, the X-Division champion would have the ability to exchange the title belt for a shot at the TNA World Heavyweight championship. TNA actually branded this concept as "Option C" in 2012 when elevating Austin Aries to the main event scene. Lucha Underground employed a similar idea with the "Gift of the Gods" title belt in 2015 as well. To me, it's a good play if there are stakes involved in order to keep the X-Division title from appearing "less-than." Perhaps there would be a caveat that once a wrestler "cashed in" the X-Division title, they could not contend for that championship again for the next calendar year, which would mean not only would they lose out on the prestige of holding a title, but if they didn't succeed in winning the world championship, then they would have gambled away their chance at a champion-level salary for twelve months. Wrestling is always better when the wins and losses actually matter if for no other reason than winners get paid more than losers.

Danielson would then take a few days to make his decision before declaring he would be challenging TNA World Heavyweight champion Kurt Angle at *Bound For Glory* in October. This would vacate the X-Division title, allowing TNA to crown a new champion at the company's marquee event, in addition to setting the stage for what would promise to be an incredible match between Angle and Danielson in the main event. Danielson's victory over Angle would cement Heyman's "new era" in TNA and position Danielson as the now unstoppable heel *world* champion.

It's worth noting that though he would have run through many X-Division stars in his first year, Danielson would have never touched AJ Styles, Christopher Daniels, Bobby Roode, James Storm, Magnus, Austin Aries, or Jeff Hardy during this time, leaving plenty of show-stealing feuds on the table for his world title reign and beyond. It is disappointing - for a host of reasons - that Desmond Wolfe (better known in non-TNA circles as Nigel McGuinness) had his career cut short for medical reasons in 2010, otherwise it would have been a no-brainer for he and Danielson to rekindle their legendary Ring of Honor rivalry in TNA. Still, Danielson would have no shortage of fresh opponents to tell new stories with.

Simultaneous to Danielson's journey to the top in 2011 would be the cementing of the "TNA Originals" as no longer the future, but the present of the company. AJ Styles, Christopher Daniels, James

Storm, and Bobby Roode would all be thrust into the main event picture over the course of the year, working with - and going over against - established, mainstream stars along the way.

Many of the high-priced veterans previously in those spots would indeed be on the chopping block, as Heyman requested (demanded?) in his 2010 proposal to Dixie Carter. There would be a handful of names worth keeping around, though.

As it relates to the overused term "legend," Sting (age fifty-one) would have been one to actually qualify for the category and be worth retaining. Sting played a huge role in legitimizing TNA and meant enough to Spike TV that they helped pay his salary. Admittedly, sentimentality would also play a role in this decision, so I'll admit my bias there. I think TNA could have also negotiated a pair of additional concessions to retain Kurt Angle (age 41) and Rob Van Dam (age 40). Established stars were still necessary to create new ones, and both Angle and Van Dam were athletically capable enough at this point to keep up with the younger talent. I get the sense that Heyman's feelings about the youth movement had more to do with *Impact* main events featuring sixty-one-year-old Ric Flair and fifty-six-year-old Hulk Hogan rather than a hard stop when a wrestler turned forty. If guys can still put on quality matches, then age is just a number.

Though not quite approaching the forty-year mark, thirty-three-year-old Jeff Hardy and thirty-four-year-old Ken Anderson would have been two established names to keep on the roster as well. Both men ended up being multi-time TNA World Heavyweight champions and both would have served a purpose in lending credibility to the up-and-coming talent Heyman would be looking to push.

If I were Heyman, I also would have kept Bully Ray (age thirty-nine) and Devon (age thirty-eight) around for a couple more years. Bully ended up doing good work during his singles run in 2012-13, and Team 3D still had some gas left in the tank as a team. TNA usually had a fairly solid tag team division, which would only improve in the coming years with the additions of The Wolves and The Hardys. It would therefore make sense to retain one of the greatest tag teams in wrestling history at a time - again - when they could still work at a high level.

By the time 2012 rolled around, Heyman would have had his roster right where he wanted it, with Bryan Danielson on top and a slew of hungry new faces ready to chase him for the title - all legitimized by the work of a few capable veterans used to prepare the next generation of wrestlers for the main event.

* WHAT WOULD HAVE HAPPENED NEXT *

The great unanswerable question remaining is, of course… "but would it have worked?" To TNA's credit, the company continues to appear virtually unkillable. Exceptionally few professional wrestling promotions could have or would have withstood the misfortune and occasional mismanagement TNA - or Impact Wrestling, as it is now (thankfully) known - has encountered over the last two decades. With that said, the answer to our question is probably dependent on how we choose to define success. If success means maintaining a cable television program with one to two million viewers each week, I would say the odds are pretty good that Heyman's vision would have at least kept the company's momentum, if not improving it a bit. If success means dethroning WWE as the No. 1 professional wrestling company in the world, then I would say Heyman was probably not the answer TNA was looking for - but I'm also not sure anything or anyone would have achieved that goal.

WWE had what amounted to a market share monopoly for almost a full decade and Vince McMahon wasn't going to willingly hand over any part of it. As Heyman once described McMahon's competitive drive: "He competes with his own sneezes."[97] It wasn't a coincidence

---

[97] Stephanie McMahon has confirmed this: "The fact he can't control the

that Bret Hart returned to WWE on the same night that *Impact* aired on a Monday. Nor was it a coincidence that years later that WWE just happened to adjust NXT to become a live, two-hour broadcast every Wednesday night on USA Network two weeks before All Elite Wrestling was set to debut Dynamite on TNT. Even during the "Wednesday Night War" era, AEW had an engaged and supportive billionaire owner, a weekly prime time slot on a premiere cable television network, and a roster composed of some of the best wrestling talent in the world, and its head-to-head competition remained with WWE's *third* brand. Anyone who thinks WWE is only the top dog because there's not another wrestling show airing on Monday nights is sorely mistaken. Vince McMahon has built a behemoth with the roots and resources to defend its turf whenever it needs to. McMahon heard TNA loud and clear when his biggest star (Hulk Hogan) stood in what he believed to be his home arena (Madison Square Garden) and challenged the WWE to a fight. Unfortunately, TNA wasn't ready to take a punch.

In my opinion, the reason the Hogan/Bischoff era in TNA flopped was because their goal was to compete with WWE immediately. Instead of laying out and committing to a deliberate multi-year plan for how to prepare the roster and audience to compete at the WWE's level, TNA threw whatever money and creative it had at week-to-week programming in a ratings war they were ill-equipped to win. Had the creative been better, it *might* have played out more positively for TNA in the short term, but by investing primarily in stars on the back-nine of their careers, TNA had no long term plan for the future.

"I don't think [Hogan] knew the roster that was in front of him," AJ Styles said of the time period on the Two Man Power Trip of Wrestling podcast in 2015. "[Hogan and Bischoff] wanted me to dye my hair blonde and be 'Little Ric' just because they didn't know me.

---

sneeze makes him upset." This is what we're dealing with, people.

Instead of being Ric Flair, I needed to be AJ Styles *with* Ric Flair."

And therein lies the issue. Instead of *leveraging* veterans to *elevate* the next generation, the legacy of the Hogan/Bischoff era to many fans is *relying* on veterans at the *expense* of the next generation. While Heyman's plan may or may not have worked, it was at least from a different playbook from the one that helped doomed WCW a decade prior.

Of course, the downside to the Heyman plan is that if Bryan Danielson went to TNA, Daniel Bryan wouldn't have come back to WWE, and fans wouldn't have gotten his epic run to *WrestleMania XXX*, inarguably one of the greatest moments in wrestling history. That might be the trade-off for getting Paul Heyman in charge of TNA in 2010 - Bryan Danielson would have received his superstar status much sooner, but it would have happened in front of 3,500 fans at the Liacouras Center in Philadelphia instead of 75,000[98] fans at the Superdome in New Orleans. Heyman and Danielson in TNA would certainly be a huge win for TNA; however, more than a few wrestling fans might debate whether it would be a net win for the industry. That is the double-edge sword of the "what if" game, though. The ripple effects are plentiful and the solutions to one problem might create even bigger issues elsewhere.

In the end, TNA suffered through several rough years as a result of decisions made during the Hogan/Bischoff regime, but the company survived. Bryan got his *WrestleMania* moment and became one of the biggest stars of his era. And the wrestling world got Heyman back

---

[98] The actual attendance number has been disputed. The announced attendance was 75,167, but the Wrestling Observer Newsletter reported paid attendance at 59,500 and actual attendance somewhere between 60,000-65,000. Having worked in the sports industry for the majority of my professional life, unless you're counting turnstiles, attendance figures tend to be either tickets off the system or eyeball estimates. Regardless, *WrestleMania*'s physical audience was close to twenty times bigger than that of *Bound For Glory*.

on television in a managerial capacity for three all-time greats in Brock Lesnar, CM Punk, and Roman Reigns. Perhaps, in this case at least, everything worked out as well as it could have. For fans of TNA Wrestling, though, the missed opportunity to land Heyman - and possibly Danielson - in 2010 will always leave them wondering, "what if?"

ELEVEN

NEXUS

"I'm afraid I've got some bad news."

November 21, 2010
American Airlines Arena ⦿ *Miami, Florida*
WWE Survivor Series

Randy Orton (c) defeated Wade Barrett by pinfall for the WWE Championship (15:10).

* WHAT REALLY HAPPENED *

Four years before NXT TakeOvers became the hottest event in professional wrestling, the original "NXT takeover" transpired at the conclusion of the June 7, 2010 edition of *Monday Night Raw*.

It featured a shocking debut that had been set in motion back in February when Vince McMahon introduced WWE's new developmental division as "the **next** evolution of WWE." On February 2, the Chairman alerted fans that a program called "NXT" would be replacing WWE's weekly ECW show in the Syfy channel's Tuesday night timeslot. Two weeks later, the press release made it official:

> "World Wrestling Entertainment and Syfy today announced the next generation of reality television with the debut of WWE NXT, Tuesday, February 23, 2010 at 10:00 PM ET on Syfy.
>
> WWE NXT is a hybrid live event/reality show featuring eight well-known, popular WWE Superstars ("Pros") mentoring eight WWE "Rookies." These Rookies, who are

learning the ropes, are athletes who epitomize pop culture and personify strong attributes — they are opinionated and aggressive — which means inherent conflict between Rookies and other Rookies, conflict between Rookies and Pros, as well as, conflict between Pros and Pros. The trials and tribulations of the WWE NXT cast ensure action-packed, innovative entertainment — WWE Style."

Over the next fifteen weeks, eight Rookies competed in a variety of matches and skill competitions under the kayfabe tutelage of their Pros. On the June 1 season finale, a former British bare-knuckle boxer by the name of Wade Barrett emerged from the competition victorious. His reward was a WWE contract and a championship opportunity at a future pay-per-view event.

Six days later, as WWE champion John Cena battled CM Punk in the *Raw* main event, Barrett appeared at the top of the entrance ramp and made his way down to ringside. He was soon joined by fellow rookies Michael Tarver, David Otunga, Heath Slater, Justin Gabriel, Skip Sheffield, Darren Young, and Daniel Bryan. Led by Barrett, the NXT Eight proceeded to lay waste to everyone and everything in their path, attacking both Cena and Punk, as well as Luke Gallows (Punk's heavy at the time), commentators Matt Striker and Jerry Lawler, timekeeper Mark Yeaton, and ring announcer Justin Roberts before literally tearing apart the ring in front of a stunned audience at the American Airlines Arena in Miami, Fla.

The group had been instructed to "go out and raise hell," a directive Daniel Bryan took to heart, as he choked out Justin Roberts with the announcer's own necktie. Bryan was fired for the non-PG incident four days later. His sudden departure was explained in kayfabe the following week on *Raw* by Barrett claiming Bryan was expelled from the group for having expressed remorse for his actions. Contrition may be a moral virtue, but it will get you nowhere with gang warfare or WWE corporate.

When Barrett demanded full-time contracts for his six remaining underlings, *Raw* General Manager Bret Hart[99] refused, fired Barrett, and removed the NXT contingent from the building. Naturally, the group returned later in the evening to try the more traditional contract negotiation strategy of abducting the boss and throwing him into the back of a limousine for the driver to play a high-speed game of bumper cars in the parking lot. Barrett and company ended their assault by pulling the unconscious Hall of Famer out of the limousine and demanding approval on their contracts by the *Fatal 4-Way* event the following Sunday. Considering they already played their felony kidnapping, false imprisonment, and attempted vehicular homicide on live television cards, one can only imagine what was left up their sleeves in the event of an unfavorable decision at the pay-per-view.

The rookies ended up costing John Cena his WWE championship at *Fatal 4-Way* and were officially welcomed to the main roster the following evening when Vince McMahon relieved Bret Hart of his duties and installed an Anonymous *Raw* General Manager[100] as the program's new authority figure. For those unaware, the Anonymous *Raw* General Manager reigned from June 21, 2010 through July 18, 2011 and communicated generally unpopular decisions via emails to a laptop maintained by play-by-play man Michael Cole. Who was this Anonymous *Raw* General Manager?

"To my knowledge, there never was a firm plan regarding the identity of the GM," former WWE writer Kevin Eck confessed in

---

[99] Hart served as *Raw*'s General Manager for about a month in the summer of 2010. Some consider it legacy-defining. Most have blocked the entire "General Manager" era from their memories.

[100] Throughout the process of writing this book, I have occasionally questioned if my booking ideas are any good. Then I remember the Anonymous *Raw* General Manager and I think to myself, "That ran on primetime cable television for more than a year." This always gives me the confidence boost needed to keep writing.

2016. "Every now and then during my first several months on the job, someone on the creative team would pitch an idea to tie up the loose end and reveal who the anonymous Raw GM was... Whenever we presented one of those ideas to Vince McMahon, he would always shoot them down and say that the audience had moved on and didn't really care anymore who the anonymous Raw GM was."

(Deep exhale.)

Side note: In 2012, WWE revealed its resident under-the-ring leprechaun, Hornswoggle, to be the Anonymous *Raw* General Manager.[101] This was pitched as a joke because of how poorly fans received Hornswoggle's previous mystery-reveal storyline of being Mr. McMahon's illegitimate leprechaun son,[102] but McMahon ended up approving the *Raw* GM payoff (because of course he did) and ending the storyline promptly upon reveal (because of course he did).[103]

This is all to say that later in the June 21, 2010 episode of *Raw*, McMahon served as the special guest referee in Cena's return match for the WWE title against new champion Sheamus. McMahon was viciously attacked by the NXT faction during the match. This was

---

[101] We don't have time to explain why a leprechaun lived under the ring.

[102] We don't have time to explain why Mr. McMahon had an illegitimate leprechaun son.

[103] Eck revealed in a 2016 blog post, "The idea was that after Hornswoggle was outed as the GM, he'd reveal who he truly was. Saying that his name was Lou Manfredini (the last name of one of the writers), he would speak with a W.C. Fields-like accent, chomp on cigars and refer to women as 'dames.' He would say that he hated being the lovable Hornswoggle character, but playing the role was what he had to do to get a job with WWE. Being the anonymous *Raw* GM gave him the opportunity to mess with all the Superstars that (in his mind) laughed at him because of his size and treated him more like a mascot than a person. We had planned on making Hornswoggle a heel manager going forward." My God, what might have been.

very much a heel move at the time, but after living through the Anonymous *Raw* General Manager era, I'm not so sure it really was.

On the July 5 episode of *Raw*, Barrett's group was christened "The Nexus" and competed in their first official contest in WWE the following week, defeating John Cena in a six-on-one handicap match. The Nexus would not be so fortunate a month later at *SummerSlam*, when "plans changed" and Team WWE - including the surprise return of the now re-hired Daniel Bryan- defeated The Nexus in a seven-on-seven elimination tag team match.

"It died way too soon," Heath Slater recalled on Busted Open Radio in 2020. "SummerSlam, we should have taken over. Period. We should have won. As soon as [we lost], we shifted from fourth to second gear in a matter of one night."

Slater claimed the plan heading into the pay-per-view was for The Nexus to go over, which would have been the logical decision. But then, "a couple matches before, we weren't." Why the sudden change? According to fellow match participants Edge and Chris Jericho on the latter's 2013 *Talk is Jericho* podcast, John Cena wanted a different outcome and he got it.

> Jericho: John wanted to do things a certain way and we told him 'you're wrong.' Remember that? And he did it anyways, and it sucked. And then afterwards he came over to us and said, 'I should have listened to you, but I wasn't seeing it that way.' And sometimes you just don't see it that way, you know?
>
> Edge: It's one of those things where he was adamant about what he wanted to do. And I remember, I was like, 'fine, I'm out of the match by that point.'
>
> Jericho: Exactly. He wanted to get DDT'd on the floor by Barrett, then kick out and beat them both. And you and I were like, 'that's the dumbest thing. That's just throwing it

away for no reason.'

Edge: [The Nexus] should have gone over because they were so hot.

Jericho: We were fighting for Barrett to go over. And, in all fairness, where's Wade Barrett now? They should have listened to us.

Instead, Cena got a win he didn't need and The Nexus' credibility and momentum were both shot. The next night on *Raw*, Darren Young was exiled from the group when he lost to Cena in the main event. Two days later, Skip Sheffield suffered a catastrophic ankle injury that kept him out of action for the next two years, which dropped The Nexus down to five active members by the end of the summer. To WWE's credit, however, they did continue to run with Wade Barrett in the main event. At least for a little while.

At September's *Night of Champions* pay-per-view, Barrett cashed in the championship match he earned by winning the NXT competition. Unfortunately for Barrett, the Anonymous *Raw* General Manager immediately made his title shot part of a Six-Pack Challenge match with Chris Jericho, Randy Orton, John Cena, and Edge all also vying for the championship. So, technically Barrett still got his match; however, this should serve as a reminder for all aspiring title challengers to always get the "one-on-one" stipulation in writing. In truth, the cash-in would have been pretty solid if Barrett had won the match, as his credibility as a competitor would have skyrocketed with a championship victory against five future Hall of Famers just four months into his main roster tenure. Of course, if you've made it this far into the book, you've probably already guessed that this did not happen. Barrett did eliminate Cena from the match but was taken out himself by Randy Orton, who went on to defeat Sheamus for the title. In the end, the whole thing felt as if Barrett's guaranteed title shot was something of an albatross for creative, rather than an opportunity to create a new top star. It's almost as if they knew Barrett belonged in the title picture, but decided halfway through the story to change how to get him there.

At *Hell in a Cell* in October - thanks to help from NXT Season 2 competitors Husky Harris and Michael McGillicutty - Barrett defeated John Cena to force the thirteen-time WWE champion to join The Nexus. Why WWE felt a pair of third generation wrestlers like Windham Rotunda and Joe Hennig - better known these days as Bray Wyatt and Curtis Axel - should debut with names like "Husky Harris" and "Michael McGillicutty" will forever be a mystery. On the *Raw* after the pay-per-view, Barrett successfully leveraged his new stablemate to win a twenty-man battle royal and become No. 1 contender for the WWE championship, instructing Cena to eliminate himself from the match so Barrett could claim victory.

Barrett got his one-on-one title shot three weeks later at *Bragging Rights*, where the stipulation was that if Barrett lost, Cena would be fired. The outcome, of course, was fairly predictable to longtime fans. Barrett only had to win the match, not the title, and since titles don't change hands on disqualifications, all Cena had to do to keep his job was attack Barrett, whom he did not like to begin with. Because Cena's actions benefited Orton, the champion was disqualified, granting Barrett a hollow victory. It's the sort of stipulation you add in order to advance a storyline from a minor pay-per-view to a major one, enabling Barrett to challenge Orton for the championship again in the main event of November's *Survivor Series*.

A strong argument can be made that the outcome of *SummerSlam 2010* was the costliest misstep in The Nexus story arc. For the group as a whole, there is likely no doubt about that. But for Wade Barrett in particular, it was *Survivor Series* a few months later that ended up being the most pivotal moment of his career. With John Cena as the special guest referee - and the stipulation set that if Barrett won the title, Cena would be granted his freedom from The Nexus, but if Orton retained the title, Cena would be fired - Barrett lost. Cena pushed Barrett into Orton's RKO finishing maneuver, counted the

1-2-3, and rolled the dice on kayfabe unemployment.

The next night on *Raw*, Barrett was granted a rematch, which Cena also interfered in, leading to The Miz cashing in his Money in the Bank briefcase on Randy Orton to become the new WWE champion. After several more weeks of Cena interfering in Nexus business (and WWE security failing to protect its wrestlers from attacks by former employees), Barrett rehired Cena - because apparently he had that kind of stroke - and challenged him to a "Chairs" match at the *TLC: Tables, Ladders, and Chairs* pay-per-view in December. Cena won that match with an Attitude Adjustment on top of two rows of chairs. Barrett proceeded to crawl on all fours back up the ramp, but was caught by Cena, who then beat him down with a chair some more, dragged a pallet on top of him, and dropped some twenty-three steel chairs on top of said pallet, both literally and figuratively burying Barrett. "A symbolic gesture by John Cena tonight," exclaimed Michael Cole on commentary. Indeed…

The match was Barrett's last as the leader of The Nexus. When he returned to WWE television on January 3, 2011, CM Punk had usurped his position. Barrett went on to form a short-lived spinoff of the group called "The Corre" on *Smackdown* with Ezekiel Jackson and former Nexus members Heath Slater and Justin Gabriel. The group dissolved in a matter of months and Barrett became a solo act for the majority of his remaining tenure with the WWE.

Barrett appeared to be onto something potentially special when he debuted a new gimmick in December of 2013 known as "Bad News" Barrett, where he would stand at a podium and declare, "I'm afraid I've got some BAD NEWS" before insulting the fans, their city, or his upcoming opponent. Barrett's schtick soon became among the most entertaining segments on WWE television each week. And – some would argue - that is why it went away.[104]

---

[104] Instead of listening to the crowd, as it successfully did with the likes of

"I was kind of told by the powers that be that I had to knock it on the head for a while as too many people were joining in and cheering me for it," Barrett told Sky Sports in 2015.

Barrett claimed victory in the 2015 King of the Ring Tournament and spent his final years as an active wrestler in WWE using the moniker "King Barrett." Despite being a television regular during his six-year run with the company and winning the Intercontinental championship on five different occasions, Barrett never again reached the heights he seemed destined for when he debuted in 2010, leaving fans to wonder what might have been if WWE had struck while the iron was hot.

* WHAT COULD HAVE HAPPENED *

Looking back on the Nexus storyline, there are two significant results that should have shaken out differently: Nexus should have won at *SummerSlam 2010* and, at some point, Barrett should have won the WWE championship.

First things first - while the *SummerSlam* victory alone likely would not have significantly altered the long-term careers of the men involved, it would have definitely helped in the short-term. Instead, the loss killed their momentum on the spot. So what if it didn't go down that way?

SummerSlam delivered big with the surprise return of Daniel Bryanon Team WWE, but what if the match ended with Bryan revealing himself to be a double-agent, still a member of The Nexus the whole time? With Team WWE down to two men, Bryan might betray Cena and rejoin Barrett's squad, giving Nexus the win and setting the table for what could then have been a pivotal *Night of Champions* pay-per-

---

Daniel Bryan and Kofi Kingston, WWE chose to shut down the organic momentum of the Bad News gimmick.

view in September.

The Nexus would turn the momentum from *SummerSlam* into gold at *Night of Champions*, with Bryan claiming the United States championship from The Miz, Heath Slater and Justin Gabriel winning the WWE World Tag Team championships from the Hart Dynasty, and Wade Barrett emerging victorious in the Six-Pack Challenge. However, I would not book Barrett to cash in his free title shot coupon until after a five-man match had already been made. Changing the stipulations after Barrett declared his intentions made him look foolish; Barrett inserting himself into a match he wasn't booked for (and then winning) would make him look like an opportunistic heel.

October's first pay-per-view event, *Hell in a Cell*, was largely booked as a rematch show[105] in 2010 and could serve the same purpose in our alternate timeline, especially with another pay-per-view, *Bragging Rights*, coming at the end of the month. At *Hell in a Cell*, Bryan would successfully defend against The Miz, Slater and Gabriel would defeat the Hart Dynasty, and Barrett would top Sheamus inside the Cell in a hard-hitting main event.

Bragging Rights would close out the month of October. This was an event originally conceived with the vision of "brand supremacy" in mind, wherein *Raw* wrestlers would match up against *Smackdown* wrestlers. Since (in theory) performers were exclusive to one brand or the other during this era, a win against a competitor from the opposite brand would bring with it "bragging rights." It's a fair enough concept assuming A) rosters were actually exclusive and B) *Survivor Series* didn't do the exact same thing.

Side bar: when it comes to "bragging rights," I feel like WWE has missed an opportunity in recent years to capitalize on what is likely the most worldwide and diverse roster in the company's history.

---

[105] "Is there any other kind?" -WWE fans, presumably.

How could one celebrate this fact? How about a World Cup event?[106] Despite wrestling promoters seemingly despising tournament formats, I personally loved what WWE did in 2016 against the backdrop of the Summer Olympics with the Cruiserweight Classic (having competitors "representing" their home countries) and their *Battleground* pay-per-view (where the marketing for the event focused on flags that featured the logos of the involved superstars). Consider that the Olympic Games and FIFA World Cups each play to global audiences well beyond three billion people; the niche of professional wrestling obviously wouldn't garner anywhere close to those numbers, but that data point should give some indication that people do take pride in their nationalities, especially when put in a competitive setting. Not only that, such an idea would grant the opportunity to bring a major event - or series of events - to historic stadiums and arenas (and, obviously, fanbases) around the world. Even if it were just a twelve-man company-wide tournament featuring the likes of AJ Styles (United States), Finn Bálor (Ireland), Drew McIntyre (Scotland), Shinsuke Nakamura (Japan), Andrade (Mexico), Aleister Black (Netherlands), Cesaro (Switzerland), Kevin Owens (Canada), Buddy Murphy (Australia), Pete Dunne (England), WALTER (Austria), and Ilja Dragunov (Germany) - can you tell me you wouldn't watch that? Or a women's field that included Asuka (Japan), Becky Lynch (Ireland), Bianca Belair (United States), Nikki Cross (Scotland), Rhea Ripley (Australia), Natalya (Canada), Toni Storm (New Zealand), and Xia Li (China)? Things I think about. Anywho.

Back at the non-nationalism-focused *Bragging Rights 2010* event, it would seem fitting to book champions versus champions in order to maintain the original theme of the pay-per-view. Therefore United States champion Daniel Bryan would face Intercontinental champion

---

[106] What Culture Pro Wrestling pulled this off in 2017, assembling an impressive collection of independent talent from fifteen countries around the world for a sixty-four man tournament.

Dolph Ziggler and WWE champion Wade Barrett would match up with World Heavyweight champion Kane. The actual card had Kane write The Undertaker off television in a Buried Alive match; however, I would push The Deadman's send off to *Survivor Series*. Not only is that a tentpole event, but this path would also enable Barrett to get an undeserved win against Kane, maybe even thanks to some supernatural tomfoolery from Taker.

Since the WWE World Tag Team titles were no longer tied to a single brand by this point, it would make sense to employ a Tag Team Turmoil match at *Bragging Rights* (instead of at *Night of Champions*, as it was in the real timeline). The *Night of Champions* Turmoil match included the Hart Dynasty, The Usos, Santino Marella and Vladimir Kozlov, Evan Bourne and Mark Henry, and Cody Rhodes and Drew McIntyre. I would swap out Marella and Kozlov for Slater and Gabriel, and the bizarre tandem of Bourne and Henry for another Nexus pairing: David Otunga and Darren Young (who would not have been exiled from the group in this timeline).[107] The inclusion of a second Nexus team would be the start of the group's splintering, as Otunga and Young would end up winning the match and taking the titles off Slater and Gabriel.

For the five-on-five *Survivor Series* elimination match in November, Barrett would entrust Daniel Bryan to captain the team of Slater, Gabriel, Otunga, and Young; however, bad blood between the Slater/Gabriel and Otunga/Young teams would prove costly and Nexus would lose the match to, let's say, CM Punk, The Miz, John Morrison, Sheamus, and Ezekiel Jackson. Or whoever. Doesn't *really* matter. The point is that Barrett would blame the loss on Bryan for his "poor leadership." Angered and disappointed, Barrett would demand the five losing Nexus members get out of his sight as he prepared for his title defense against No. 1 contender John Cena.

---

[107] Additional Nexus members Skip Sheffield and Michael Tarver were on the shelf with injuries.

This would be a critical mistake on Barrett's part. Without the rest of the Nexus in his corner, no one would be around to save Barrett (and his title) from The Miz cashing in his Money in the Bank contract and leaving *Survivor Series* with the WWE championship.

Over the next month, tensions would begin to boil over between Barrett and Bryan, as well as between the Slater/Gabriel and Otunga/Young teams. During Bryan's United States championship match against Sheamus at December's *TLC: Tables, Ladders, and Chairs* pay-per-view, Barrett would bark orders to the champion, distracting Bryan and "inadvertently" costing him the title.[108] Bryan would return the favor in the main event, not by distracting Barrett, but by outright assaulting him. Bryan would disobey a direct order from Barrett to interfere on his behalf in the WWE championship triple threat match against The Miz and John Cena, turning babyface instead by betraying Barrett. This would officially set us on the course for a Bryan versus Barrett match at *WrestleMania XXVII*, as the two would eliminate each other in the Royal Rumble match in January and be unable to settle their differences inside the Elimination Chamber in February.

Bryan would win the 'Mania match and Barrett would resurface as a main-event level singles competitor on *Smackdown* shortly thereafter. Meanwhile, the teams of Slater and Gabriel and Otunga and Young would continue battling within the tag team division before being separated out in the 2011 WWE Draft that April. Though Otunga and Young were likely best suited to be career tag team performers, Slater and Gabriel both could have seen some success as midcard acts in contention for the Intercontinental and United States titles from time to time. The big win in this timeline, though, is that both Bryan *and* Barrett would be on the path to world championship contention for years to come.

---

[108] "Bad Move" Barrett, amirite?

* WHAT WOULD HAVE HAPPENED NEXT *

While the Nexus storyline was hot in the short-term, it failed in building new stars over the long haul. Would that have changed if something as simple as the Nexus winning at *SummerSlam 2010* had happened? It wouldn't have hurt, that's for sure. It is very easy to envision Wade Barrett - after a successful *SummerSlam* and, at some point between *Night of Champions* and *Survivor Series*, a WWE title reign - advancing on a similar course as Sheamus: a multi-time world champion, best suited for the semi-main event level but able to step in as a primary villain when called upon. For the rest of the group, though, it's worth considering exactly how much a Nexus win at *SummerSlam* could have realistically altered the trajectories of those involved.

Darren Young was sent back to NXT in early 2011 and repackaged as one-half of the Primetime Players tag team with former Arena Football Leaguer Titus O'Neil for the majority of his remaining six years with the company. A win at *SummerSlam* could have kept Young in the group and tag team scene a little longer, but Nexus wasn't proving to be his vehicle to success.

Michael Tarver wrestled his final match on the WWE main roster in October of 2010. After rehabbing an injury, Tarver was sent back to developmental with Florida Championship Wrestling and was released from his WWE contract in 2011. He went on to perform in the National Wrestling Alliance and New Japan Pro Wrestling over the next several years, but has yet to return to mainstream cable wrestling in the United States. Due to injury, a different *SummerSlam* experience likely would not have changed much for Tarver.

Skip Sheffield was injured three days after *SummerSlam* and the outcome of that match likely would not have affected his health either. Furthermore, the Skip Sheffield gimmick wasn't going anywhere in WWE. When he was repackaged in 2012 as "Ryback," that character actually did have legs. Author David Shoemaker once astutely described the gimmick as, "Goldberg meets the Ultimate Warrior meets Rob Van Dam's tights." Ryback racked up a thirty-eight-match winning streak before headlining multiple pay-per-views as a babyface challenger for CM Punk's WWE championship. Though he never won the title, the company clearly saw serious star potential in him… just not as Skip Sheffield.

Out of all the original Nexus members, David Otunga was the only one to remain continually employed by the company more than a decade after the group's debut. However, Otunga has now spent more time as a commentator and panelist than he did as an in-ring performer, having last wrestled in 2015. Given that fact, it's unlikely that the two-time tag team champion would have enjoyed a significantly different in-ring career with a *SummerSlam* win under his belt.

I might contend that out of anyone (aside from Wade Barrett), Justin Gabriel and Heath Slater stood to gain the most from a different outcome at *SummerSlam 2010*. Slater went on to be a four-time WWE Tag Team champion, winning the belts three times with Gabriel. The "One Man Band" was mostly used as an enhancement talent and comic relief after the Nexus and Corre storylines concluded, though. Slater stayed with the company for fourteen years until his release during the COVID-19 pandemic in 2020.[109] "Heath" then dropped the "Slater" portion of his name and debuted with Impact Wrestling ninety days later.

Gabriel may have had the best shot to be a singles standout, thanks in no small part to his high-flying, daredevil move set. He was a

---

[109] WWE released more than thirty performers from its active roster and reportedly let go of triple-digit employees from its corporate staff in April 2020, despite having more than $500 million in cash on-hand and being declared an "essential business" by the state of Florida at the time. WWE then went on to report its most profitable year in company history by the end of the third quarter of 2020. Late-stage capitalism went over big in 2020.

participant in the 2011 Money in the Bank ladder match and went on to challenge for both the United States and Intercontinental championships in 2012 and 2013. Unfortunately, he soon became a victim of the dreaded "creative has nothing for you" routine. His remaining years with the company were spent as an enhancement performer before being let go in 2015. Now known as "The Darewolf" PJ Black, the Cape Town, South Africa native has carved out a solid "off-Broadway" career on the periphery of mainstream with TNA, Lucha Underground, NWA, and Ring of Honor. Gabriel's biggest problem in WWE might have been that he just got there five years too soon. Blessed with the same measurables and relative move set as Seth Rollins, perhaps the "Darewolf" might have fit in better with Finn Bálor's NXT than Wade Barrett's.

But the man who stood the most to gain from a better-booked Nexus was always Wade Barrett. Barrett's WWE career was good; as of 2021, only nine men have held the WWE Intercontinental championship at least five times and Barrett is one of them. That's nothing to scoff at. Still, of those nine men, Barrett is the only one to have never held a world title. He was in position to do it in 2010, but the company didn't pull the trigger and the moment never came again. Barrett was pigeonholed as a midcard heel for the rest of his career when he was capable of being much more. And though fans saw it that way, the company never would, leaving us to only imagine what might have been.

TWELVE

BEST IN THE WORLD

"After I'm gone, you're still going to pour money into this company. I'm just a spoke on a wheel."

September 18, 2011
First Niagara Center ◉ *Buffalo, New York*
WWE Night of Champions

Triple H defeated CM Punk by pinfall (24:10).

* WHAT REALLY HAPPENED *

On June 27, 2011, CM Punk sat cross-legged at the top of the WWE *Raw* entrance ramp and cut the single greatest professional wrestling promo of his generation.

With his contract set to expire the following month, Punk - the first true "indy darling" to reach star status on the sport's biggest stage - had tweeted earlier in the night: "I'm in full 'what-are-they-gonna-do-fire-me?' mode." And, boy, was he.

Punk's career up to that night had been good, perhaps even great. His 2004 trilogy of matches with Samoa Joe in Ring of Honor and subsequent "Summer of Punk" storyline in 2005 propelled him onto the Mount Rushmore of independent wrestling. The following July, he debuted to much internet fanfare on WWE's version of ECW and embarked on a six-month-long undefeated streak before eventually winning the ECW Championship in September of 2007. The following March, he won the Money in the Bank ladder match at *WrestleMania XXIV*, and then successfully cashed in his Money in the Bank contract to win the WWE World Heavyweight championship in June. That reign was admittedly short at just sixty-nine days; however, Punk was not without championship gold for long, as he and Kofi Kingston would win the WWE World Tag Team titles in October. Punk then added the WWE Intercontinental championship to his waist in January 2009 to become a WWE Triple Crown winner faster than any man in company history. He went on to win the Money in the Bank ladder match for a second time at *WrestleMania XXV*.

By the end of the summer of 2009, Punk had won the WWE World Heavyweight championship twice more. In November, he formed his own heel stable known as "The Straight Edge Society." Long before Seth Rollins became the "Monday Night Messiah," CM Punk had drawn up the blueprint as *Smackdown*'s "Straight Edge Savior," pontificating on his real-life straight edge lifestyle and offering all those misguided by drugs and alcohol an opportunity for a spiritual rebirth by pledging their devotion to Punk.

But, like I always say, there's no epidural in a spiritual rebirth. Despite the first three years of Punk's WWE tenure being quite impressive, he had never really been put in a position to be *the guy*. By the time 2010 rolled around, it was starting to appear that he never would.

Punk was unsuccessful in his quest to convert Rey Mysterio to the Straight Edge Society that year, first losing to the masked superstar at *WrestleMania XXVI*, then losing his hair in a Pledge vs. Hair match at *Over The Limit*. Embarrassed to be seen without his long locks, Punk began wearing a black mask himself until the hood was swiped by Big Show in July. The Straight Edge Society went on to lose a three-on-one handicap match to the giant at *SummerSlam* when Punk abandoned the team, and he himself lost a one-on-one match to Big Show the following month at *Night of Champions*. Soon after, Punk's congregation disbanded. He briefly joined the *Raw* commentary team while working through a hip injury late in the year, then usurped control of the splintering Nexus faction in an effort to exact revenge on Randy Orton for costing Punk his first World

Heavyweight title several years earlier.

While a *WrestleMania* feud with the "Apex Predator" was nothing to scoff at, it wasn't where Punk felt he belonged either. Where he wanted to be was the main event... and it seemed increasingly more unlikely that he would ever get there. At *WrestleMania XXVII*, Punk and Orton were lower on the card than the Michael Cole versus Jerry Lawler match - a bout between commentators that was universally panned as the worst match in *WrestleMania* history. Not only that, but the actual main event of the show featured The Miz - a former reality television star turned pro wrestler[110] who first gained notoriety as a cast member on MTV's *The Real World* - defending the WWE Championship against John Cena in a match that really only existed in order to set up the following year's *WrestleMania* main event between Cena and the guest host for the evening, The Rock. One can imagine why Punk - a wrestler's wrestler who paid his dues for years on the independent circuit working matches in exchange for a hotdog and a handshake - might have felt a bit miffed at the landscape he saw unfolding before him in 2011.

And so, on June 27, with an expiring contract and a lot on his mind, CM Punk donned a Stone Cold Steve Austin t-shirt, cost John Cena his main event tables match against R-Truth, grabbed a microphone, and dropped a promo that has since come to be known as the "pipe bomb."

> John Cena, while you lay there - hopefully as uncomfortable as you possibly can be - I want you to listen to me. I want you to digest this because before I leave in three weeks with your WWE Championship, I have a lot of things I want to

---

[110] The Miz went on to win over the hardcore pro wrestling fanbase through his dedication to the craft over the years, but his run as champion in 2011 was *not* well received. Miz got the last laugh, though, putting together a Hall of Fame caliber career and, more importantly, marrying two-time WWE Divas champion, Maryse. You win, Miz. You win.

get off my chest.

I don't hate you, John. I don't even dislike you. I *do* like you. I like you a hell of a lot more than I like most people in the back. I hate this idea that you're the best. Because you're not. *I'm* the best. I'm the best in the world. There's one thing you're better at than I am and that's kissing Vince McMahon's ass. You're as good at kissing Vince's ass as Hulk Hogan was. I don't know if you're as good as Dwayne [The Rock], though. He's a pretty good ass kisser. Always was and still is.

Whoops! I'm breaking the fourth wall! [Punk waves to the camera]

I am the best wrestler in the world. I've been the best since day one when I walked into this company. And I've been vilified and hated since that day because Paul Heyman saw something in me that nobody else wanted to admit. That's right, I'm a Paul Heyman guy. You know who else was a Paul Heyman guy? Brock Lesnar. And he split just like I'm splitting. But the biggest difference between me and Brock is I'm going to leave with the WWE Championship.

I've grabbed so many of Vincent K. McMahon's imaginary brass rings that it's finally dawned on me that they're just that, they're completely imaginary. The only thing that's real is me and the fact that day in and day out, for almost six years, I have proved to everybody in the world that I am the best on this microphone, in that ring, even in commentary! Nobody can touch me!

And yet no matter how many times I prove it, I'm not on your lovely little collector cups. I'm not on the cover of the program. I'm barely promoted. I don't get to be in movies. I'm certainly not on any crappy show on the USA Network.

I'm not on the poster of *WrestleMania*. I'm not on the signature that's produced at the start of the show. I'm not on Conan O'Brien. I'm not on Jimmy Fallon. But the fact of the matter is, *I should be*. This isn't sour grapes. But the fact that Dwayne is in the main event at *WrestleMania* next year and I'm not makes me sick!

Oh hey, let me get something straight. Those of you who are cheering me right now, you are just as big a part of me leaving as anything else. Because you're the ones who are sipping out of those collector cups right now. You're the ones that buy those programs that my face *isn't* on the cover of. And then at five in the morning at the airport, you try to shove it in my face so you can get an autograph and try to sell it on eBay because you're too lazy to go get a real job.

I'm leaving with the WWE Championship on July 17th. And hell, who knows, maybe I'll go defend it in New Japan Pro Wrestling. Maybe, I'll go back to Ring of Honor.

Hey, Colt Cabana, how you doing? [Punk waves at the camera again]

The reason I'm leaving is you people. Because after I'm gone, you're still going to pour money into this company. I'm just a spoke on the wheel. The wheel is going to keep turning and I understand that. Vince McMahon is going to make money despite himself. He's a millionaire who should be a billionaire. You know why he's not a billionaire? Because he surrounds himself with glad-handing, nonsensical, douchebag yes-men like John Laurinaitis, who's going to tell him everything he wants to hear. And I'd like to think that maybe this company will be better after Vince McMahon is dead. But the fact is, it's going to be taken over by his idiotic daughter and his doofus son-in-law and the rest of his stupid family.

> Let me tell you a personal story about Vince McMahon, alright? We do this whole bully campaign-- [microphone cuts off]

And in that one worked-shoot segment, CM Punk instantly became the biggest wrestling star on the planet.

Two weeks later - after serving a kayfabe suspension for his comments - Punk joined Mr. McMahon in the ring for a contract negotiation on the go-home episode of *Raw*. The first handful of Punk's demands were intentionally outlandish, as he asked for things like his own private jet, "CM Punk: The Movie," and turnbuckle pads featuring his face. He also wished for WWE to bring back the old "Ice Creamania" ice cream bars which had been popular in the 1980s and '90s. WWE actually followed through on that one, albeit six years after Punk retired. But then came two final demands that to this day remain unfulfilled and seemed to be less from CM Punk the television character and more from Phil Brooks, the man who portrayed him. First, he wanted to be in the main event of *WrestleMania*; and second, he wanted a personal apology from Vince McMahon.

More than a decade later, if there were any way left to heal the relationship between CM Punk and the WWE, those last two demands might be a good place to start.

Punk acknowledged the drawing power that a fantasy matchup between The Rock and John Cena would have, but he also truly believed himself to be the "best in the world" when it came to his craft and at *WrestleMania*, he wanted to go on *last*.

That July 11, 2011 episode of *Raw* was also the night CM Punk first proclaimed himself to be the "Voice of the Voiceless" when he demanded an apology from Vince McMahon. The initial request came in response to Punk's storyline suspension but it quickly transitioned into a far more authentic grievance when he invoked the names of friends and former colleagues Colt Cabana and Luke Gallows, who had been fired by the WWE - in Punk's words - "because you don't know what makes a superstar in 2011." Since they could no longer stand up to McMahon themselves, Punk positioned himself as the mouthpiece for those wronged by WWE's corporate vision of the wrestling world.

After several minutes of public needling, McMahon begrudgingly offered a sincere apology. And by sincere, I mean that his exact words were, "I apologize, you son of a bitch," phrasing I myself regularly use to express contrition to those closest to me. Punk appreciated the anger it caused McMahon to say at least the first two words of that sentence, but before his renegotiated contract could be signed, out came John Cena to complicate the matter. Looking beyond the goofy, juvenile attempts at humor that made Cena's character occasionally insufferable and polarizing to much of the fanbase throughout WWE's "PG Era," the future Peacemaker made a pretty salient point: "Listen to them, man - they love you. And they'll love you in your hometown of Chicago. And that's the night you walk out on each and every one of them. ... I get it, you feel mistreated at work and you hate this guy. I hate him, too! ... But I show up for work every day. ... If I don't show up, sure, it shortsides him, but these people paid a lot of good money to be here tonight and they're the ones who really take it on the shin."

Cena called Punk a hypocrite for claiming to speak for the fans while planning to take the belt and go home. Punk told the ten-time champ that Cena had lost his perspective because he was no longer an underdog, but a dynasty. The exchange soon became physical, causing Punk to slide out of the ring, swipe the contract out of McMahon's hands, and return to his seated position atop the stage.

"I'm glad you just punched me in the face, John," Punk said. "I'm glad it went down this way because it hit me like a bolt of lightning, exactly why I no longer want to be here, why I want to leave. It's because I'm tired of this. I'm tired of you. I'm just tired. So ladies and gentlemen of the WWE Universe, Vince, John - Sunday night, say goodbye to the WWE title, say goodbye to John Cena, and say goodbye to CM Punk."

Punk tore up his proposed contract and said to the camera, "I'll go be the best in the world somewhere else," as *Raw* went off the air.

That's some pretty compelling storytelling to close a go-home show. Even better, the pay-per-view lived up to the hype. Jerry Lawler accurately compared the atmosphere to if the Chicago Bears were playing in the Super Bowl and the Super Bowl was in Chicago. Though "C-M-Punk" chants would go on to become time-honored favorites of WWE audiences over the next decade, rarely have they ever been louder or more impassioned than they were on this night.

Punk and Cena put on a five-star, instant classic - one of the best performances of either man's career. Towards the end of the match, with Punk locked in Cena's STF submission hold, Mr. McMahon signaled for the official to call the match - reminiscent of the Montreal Screwjob at *Survivor Series 1997*. Seeing what was about to transpire, Cena - always living the hustle, loyalty, and respect gimmick - broke the hold to prevent a tainted win. Cena took down John Laurinaitis, McMahon's right-hand man who was sent by the Chairman to ring the bell and end the match, but when the champ rolled back into the ring, Punk was waiting with his Go-To-Sleep finishing maneuver. Punk pinned Cena to become the new WWE champion.

McMahon then had to turn to Plan B. Two matches earlier, Alberto Del Rio had won *Raw*'s Money in the Bank ladder match, entitling him to a WWE championship match at a time of his choosing. In this case, it came at a time of McMahon's choosing, as the Chairman ordered Del Rio down to the ring to immediately cash in his title shot and win the belt back from the soon-to-be departing Punk. That match never officially took place, though, as Punk kicked Del Rio in the head and fled through the crowd, blowing a kiss to McMahon on his way out of the WWE.

But not really. Though Punk did indeed have an expiring contract, he actually signed a new deal that night at the venue once known as the Rosemount Horizon. Rest assured, John Cena absolutely would have had his hand raised at the end of the night if Punk didn't reach an agreement to remain with the company. Fortunately, Punk *did* secretly sign a new contract and the story ended exactly as it should have.

Or at least that chapter of the story, anyway.

What unfolded in the weeks following Punk's escape through his legions of fans at *Money in the Bank 2011* was less ideal in the eyes of many.

The night after the pay-per-view, a resolute Mr. McMahon announced an eight-man tournament for the WWE Championship, as Punk was (in storyline) no longer employed by the company. The Miz and Rey Mysterio ended up in the finals later that night, but before the match could take place, McMahon returned to the ring and ordered John Cena to join him. As McMahon prepared to fire Cena for insubordination, the former champion let the Chairman know, "I love this. This is what I do. And if you make me walk tonight, then I will walk on someone else's television show and keep doing this, BROTHER," a not-so-subtle reference to Hulk Hogan, who had seized power in TNA the previous winter.

Before McMahon could say his two favorite words, his son-in-law, Triple H interrupted. The Game informed McMahon that there had been an emergency Board of Directors meeting that morning, and the Board had issued a vote of no confidence for McMahon's leadership following the Punk debacle. The Board appointed Triple H to take over day-to-day operations of the company and instructed Hunter to inform McMahon that he had been relieved of his duties. The show ended with McMahon standing alone in the ring, in tears.

The July 25, 2011 *Raw* began with Rey Mysterio being crowned the new WWE champion by defeating The Miz in the main event that never happened the week before. Later in the night, the WWE's newly appointed Chief Operating Officer, Triple H, announced that Mysterio would be in action again to close the show, this time defending his title against John Cena. Poor Rey Mysterio's reign as champion lasted less than two hours, as Cena reclaimed the belt in the main event. Cena, too, had little time to celebrate, as his theme music was cut off in favor of Living Colour's "Cult of Personality" - the song CM Punk used during his 2005 "Summer of Punk" farewell tour in Ring of Honor. After several bars played, Punk emerged on the ramp with the WWE title around his waist. The episode ended with Punk and Cena, face to face in the ring, each raising their respective titles in the air.

So Punk was back on television eight days after hightailing it out of the Allstate Arena with the WWE's top prize. That seemed a bit rushed, but he did leave *Money in the Bank* as the hottest property in pro wrestling, so it made sense for WWE to want to bring him back as soon as possible. Case in point, Punk was already making the media rounds the week he returned to TV - and doing so with major outlets.

"Real" sports entities like ESPN - whose acronym (for the haters) stands for ***E****ntertainment and* ***S****ports* ***P****rogramming* ***N****etwork* - rarely went anywhere near professional wrestling… but on July 27, 2011, CM Punk was the featured guest for forty-one minutes on Bill Simmons' *B.S. Report* podcast. Simmons - who called Punk's angle at the time "the most brilliantly executed storyline in recent wrestling history" - praised Punk for re-energizing the casual fan.

"I think a lot of people are embarrassed about pro wrestling and I don't think anybody needs to be," Punk said. "My goal is to make this shit cool again."

And for a little while, he really did.

But WWE's creative efforts after his return seemingly did their best to squash Punk's goal as quickly as humanly possible. A title-versus-title match between Punk and Cena headlined *SummerSlam* in August, but neither man left the Staples Center with the belt. Punk defeated Cena to be crowned the undisputed WWE champion, but was attacked moments later by a returning Kevin Nash. With Punk laid out, Alberto Del Rio ran down to the ring to cash in his Money in the Bank contract and become the new title-holder.

One could argue the attack and subsequent loss was a vehicle to garner sympathy for a newly-turned babyface, since the money - as they say - is in the chase. Conversely, one could argue that Punk didn't need sympathy at this juncture but instead a rocket strapped to his back. Plus, the whole "money in the chase" argument took a significant hit the week after *SummerSlam* when Punk lost to Cena in a No. 1 Contender match on *Raw* after another appearance by the Artist Formerly Known as Diesel. This took Punk out of the WWE title picture entirely and spun him into a completely different feud. It's the sort of thing that makes you wonder if Punk's push in June and July was merely circumstantial as opposed to being part of a grander plan.

Alberto Del Rio was clearly the guy WWE wanted in the main event, as "El Patron" won both the Royal Rumble *and* Money in the Bank matches in 2011. So even though Punk's pipe bomb promo itself was not a surprise to the company, the reaction to it certainly might have been, given how quickly Punk's title reign ended. Normally, catching lightning in a bottle would be something to celebrate. Sometimes in WWE, though, when it's not part of the plan, it doesn't feel like it's welcome at all.

"There really is a bit of a strange resentment," Chris Jericho said in 2020 regarding wrestlers 'getting over' on their own. "If Vince [McMahon] doesn't think of it, it's not valid."

Now, Punk did go on to win the WWE championship at *Survivor*

Series in November of 2011 and would hold the title for 434 consecutive days - longer than any man in the previous quarter-century, so it's not like WWE buried him. However, he didn't have the same momentum in November that he did in July or August and if that wasn't intentional on the part of the WWE, then it most certainly qualified as egregious creative malpractice.

Consider this: starting with Del Rio at *SummerSlam*, Punk was pinned at four consecutive pay-per-view events before finally winning the WWE title at *Survivor Series*. Booking the hottest act in the industry to lose four pay-per-view matches in a row would seem to indicate the company didn't *want* the hottest act in the industry to *remain* the hottest act in the industry.

The most significant - and unnecessary - of Punk's string of losses came at *Night of Champions* in September. The match WWE had seemingly hoped for was CM Punk versus Kevin Nash. I'm not sure that was *exactly* the dream match fans were fantasy-booking in August of 2011, but it was certainly unexpected and that's often a positive in pro wrestling. It also gave us a quality back-and-forth promo between two of the all-time great talkers that ended with Nash and Punk separated by security guards, a couple of whom bore a striking resemblance to then-independent wrestlers Eli Drake and Scorpio Sky.

The crux of the story was that Nash allegedly received a text message from fellow Kliq member and newly-christened Chief Operating Officer, Triple H, at *SummerSlam*, instructing him to attack the winner of the match between Punk and Cena, which Nash then did. Triple H denied knowing anything about such a message. Punk had difficulty believing this. As the great philosopher Henry David Thoreau once said, "Some circumstantial evidence is quite strong, as when you find a trout in your milk." Well, HDT never considered HHH when he said such things because Triple H was telling the truth! Though Nash would later claim to have sent the text to himself (odd), John Laurinaitis was *supposed* to be revealed as the man behind it all, as the storyline intended to unfold with "Johnny Ace" undermining Triple H and staging a coup d'etat to seize control of the WWE for himself. For better or worse, that part of the plan never really materialized and by the end of August, the proposed match between Nash and Punk simply turned into a no-disqualification match between Punk and Triple H.

Within the confines of the "WWE Universe," a match between Punk and The Game *at some point* was obvious. Certainly, the guy Punk called Vince McMahon's "doofus son-in-law" on national television would be motivated to get into the ring with him. In reality - to a large extent, anyway - the move from Nash to Triple H came because Nash couldn't pass his physical… which kind of makes you wonder what Creative was thinking by booking the company's most popular wrestler of the moment into a feud with a fifty-two-year-old semi-retired wrestler who had yet to complete a medical examination. Nevertheless, what happened next would signal the beginning of the end of CM Punk's WWE career.

In a match marred by run-ins from The Miz, R-Truth, and Kevin Nash, Triple H pinned CM Punk to formally put an end to WWE's version of "The Summer of Punk." Punk was strong in defeat, to those for whom that means something. It took three Pedigrees to put him down, with no referee present for the first and Punk kicking out of the second. But in the end, Punk lost and Triple H won.

Two-and-a-half years later, Punk would walk out of the WWE, for real and for good. In a private airing of grievances with Vince McMahon and Triple H, Punk - when faced with the prospect of a *WrestleMania* match with The Game in 2014 - confessed, "All due respect, I do not need to wrestle you; you need to wrestle me. I do not want to wrestle you. I seriously resent you for not putting me over three years ago when you should have."

Two months after losing to Triple H at *Night of Champions 2011*, CM Punk defeated Alberto Del Rio to win the WWE Championship at

Survivor Series. He held that title for the next 433 days, at the time making him the longest-reigning champion of the Modern Era. But he never let go of that three-month period between *SummerSlam* and *Survivor Series* where, in his eyes, the WWE intentionally held him down.

* WHAT COULD HAVE HAPPENED *

A match between CM Punk and Triple H was always inevitable. It *had* to happen. But September 2011 was *way* too early, and the proposed *WrestleMania XXX* match in April of 2014 was *way* too late. And, obviously, it goes without saying but I'll say it anyway: CM Punk *had* to win.

I don't think it's an overstatement to say the relationship - or lack thereof - between CM Punk and Triple H is likely the most consequential of the post-Attitude Era. It was an integral element of Punk walking away from the industry and for some time very well may have been essential to his return; though the advent and success of AEW made a reconciliation with WWE significantly less necessary for CM Punk to be welcomed back to the squared circle. But before we try to tackle that mess, let's revisit Punk's original return in 2011.

Punk's title heist needed much longer to breathe than just eight days. The longer he was off television, the more "real" the story would have felt. An even better scenario would be if Punk really did take the belt to New Japan and Ring of Honor like he said he would. What if Punk showed up at ROH's *Death Before Dishonor* at the Manhattan Center in New York the night before WWE's *Night of Champions* pay-per-view? Or if he defended the *real* WWE championship at an NJPW event? In the end, all the buzz would be about the WWE champion - and that's what should have mattered most to WWE.

Punk did actually make a surprise appearance at an All-American

Wrestling show in July of 2011, but it would have been fun to make that his gimmick for a few months: showing up unannounced at different promotions as the "real" world champion. He could have made headlines by crashing Pro Wrestling Guerrilla's annual *Battle of Los Angeles* in August and melting the internet with his return to Ring of Honor at *Death Before Dishonor* in September. He could have toured Japan in October and early November, putting together a brief program with someone like former ECW champion Masato Tanaka at NJPW's *Destruction* and *Power Struggle* before returning stateside in time for a roof-blowing run-in at *Survivor Series*.

What would have been happening in the Punk-less WWE during this time? A lot of "C-M-Punk" chants, for starters. Beyond that, though, the night after *Money in the Bank*, Mr. McMahon would have declared the WWE championship "vacant" and announced the tournament to crown a new title-holder. Instead of cramming it all into two weeks, this time around the angle would stretch all the way through *SummerSlam*. Qualifying matches would have taken place in the two weeks after *Money in the Bank*, with the round of sixteen beginning on August 1 and the quarterfinals scheduled for the week of August 8 - just in time for the go-home episodes of *Raw* and *Smackdown*. The semifinals and finals of the tournament would then take place at the *SummerSlam* pay-per-view.

Instead of threatening to fire John Cena for insubordination, a more realistic approach for Mr. McMahon might have been suspending Cena from all future championship contention. In McMahon's mind, clearly the WWE title hadn't meant enough to Cena. If he had valued the championship as much as McMahon thought he should, Cena would have done anything and everything to keep it. Since he didn't, McMahon would make sure it was never an issue again. In a way, it would have made McMahon an even bigger heel - he would have understood Cena's monetary value to the company, so he wouldn't have fired him; instead, he would have merely exploited his services for profit while ensuring Cena would never rise above a certain level again.

Of course, that plan could also backfire since a significant portion of the WWE fan base was not particularly fond of Cena's seemingly constant presence in the championship scene. Those (very) vocal folks occasionally had a point - in the real timeline, Cena lost to Punk at both *Money in the Bank* and *SummerSlam* but still somehow found himself as the No. 1 contender the week after both matches. Losses rarely seemed to affect Cena's championship opportunities, which may help inform why he became so polarizing to fans.

Cena's championship ban likely would not have lasted long, but it would have gotten us at least through *SummerSlam*. A good dance partner for Cena at that event might have been Alberto Del Rio. Del Rio was clearly a chosen one based on his resume in 2011 alone. Not only that, when Punk was about to escape *Money in the Bank* with the championship, Del Rio answered Mr. McMahon's call. In the eyes of the Chairman, Del Rio was willing to do for the company what Cena wasn't. Now, Del Rio would have almost certainly been included in the tournament to crown a new WWE champion; however, a loss in the quarterfinals as a result of some Cena shenanigans - "Cenanigans," if you weel – would have set the two up for a singles match at *SummerSlam*, which Cena would have won.

Also at *SummerSlam*, Rey Mysterio would defeat Dolph Ziggler and The Miz would defeat Kofi Kingston, setting up a Rey versus Miz finale for the vacant WWE championship. Just like in the real timeline, Rey would win that match to claim the WWE title, and just like in the real timeline, his reign would be short-lived. This time, though, Alberto Del Rio would be the reason why. As Rey was celebrating his victory, Del Rio's music would hit and he would cash in his Money in the Bank contract for a shot at the title. Now in his third match of the night, Mysterio would be out of gas and Del Rio would become the new WWE champion.

In the real timeline, CM Punk did a July media tour with outlets that included GQ, ESPN, and Jimmy Kimmel Live. In the new timeline, Punk would snag his share of headlines during the week preceding

SummerSlam, forcing the theoretical WWE Board of Directors to address - and take action on - his "situation."

The above development is what would bring Triple H into the story. Hunter would interrupt Mr. McMahon in the ring the following night on *Raw* and share the news of the Board's dissatisfaction with McMahon's decision-making of late. He would tell McMahon that the Board lifted John Cena's championship ban, declaring it bad for business. The Board would have also been extremely dismayed with the media coverage over the last month and fans hijacking the show with chants for a former employee who McMahon failed to re-sign. All of this would lead to the bombshell announcement - just as it did in reality (or the kayfabe version of reality, I suppose) - that the Board had placed Triple H in charge of the WWE's day-to-day operations and relieved Mr. McMahon of his duties as Chairman.

Since Rey Mysterio suffered an injury shortly after *SummerSlam* and would be out of action for nearly a year, John Cena would return to the title scene and have a back-and-forth rivalry with Del Rio for the next several months. Cena would win the title back at *Night of Champions*, while Del Rio would snag it for himself at *Hell in a Cell* and successfully defend at *Vengeance*, just as it all went down in reality.

Meanwhile, Triple H would do his best to right the ship and play the role of babyface general manager, though it would become increasingly more difficult as the CM Punk World Tour 2011 got underway. Punk would taunt the WWE and its Chief Operating Officer in his pop-up promos, all while Triple H would be the one forced to face the weekly fan backlash over a performer who "doesn't work here anymore," which would've gotten old in a hurry for The Game - especially after Punk defended the WWE championship in Japan in November. That would have been an incident that required a public address, wherein Triple H could go all in with "CM Punk is no longer a WWE employee, he's in possession of stolen property, WWE is actively pursuing its legal options, et cetera, et cetera."

CM Punk would make his first appearance on WWE programming since July at the November *Survivor Series* pay-per-view. Since he wouldn't have a WWE contract in the storyline, Punk would make his return in the same manner he made his exit months before: through the crowd. After an Alberto Del Rio title defense against Kofi Kingston, perhaps, Punk would shock the Madison Square Garden audience by sliding into the ring to hit a Go To Sleep on Del Rio. Before Triple H and security could get to him, Punk would grab a microphone and head up through the fans again, informing Hunter from the concourse level that if he wanted his belt back, he'd have to take it from Punk's cold, dead hands... but if his guy wanted to try, Punk's calendar had an open spot on December 18 (the date of the upcoming *TLC* pay-per-view). Triple H would be livid... but the *TLC* pay-per-view would be sold in a heartbeat.

Punk, being both untrusting and business-savvy, would want some assurances before showing up again in enemy territory. Since he wouldn't have a WWE contract in the storyline, he could use his Twitter account to publicly communicate his demands and negotiate with Triple H, a wild exercise in working an angle over the still relatively new social media platform. The end result would be a Tables, Ladders, and Chairs match for the undisputed WWE championship. If Punk won, he would get a new WWE contract with all his required provisions included, in addition to his full reign as champion being recognized by the company. If Del Rio won, Punk would surrender his title and never be seen in WWE again. Punk would be sure to add the stipulation that any WWE interference in the match would result in Punk being declared the winner. The Board would be so hellbent on stopping Punk from showing up with the belt in other companies that they would agree to all the demands, much to Triple H's displeasure.

One demand in particular should have been the commissioning of a new WWE championship belt. Back in reality, after The Rock defeated Punk for the WWE championship in 2013, he got to reveal a new, classier championship belt on the February 18 episode of *Raw*, declaring, "The WWE championship title should never look like a toy." This should have been Punk's moment. Hardcore fans hated John Cena's spinner belt and it would have been a massive babyface move for Punk - an old-school soul and supposed voice of the fans - to trash the Cena-era belt and debut a new one that preferably did not spin.

Nevertheless, Punk's victory over Del Rio at *TLC* would have concluded a groundbreaking storyline that successfully combined three of the elements that wrestling fans love most about the art form: reality, suspense, and surprise. And with Punk officially back in the fold, his program with Triple H could officially begin. The program would have shades of the Austin versus McMahon dynamic more than a decade earlier, but with the added benefit that Hunter could step into the ring and give Punk a high-quality thirty-minute match at the end.

Their ill-fated working relationship would function well enough for the first handful of weeks after *TLC*, but things would start to turn south as the *Royal Rumble* approached in January of 2012. Triple H would position "The Big Red Machine" Kane as the No. 1 contender for Punk's title. Punk would argue that Kane had done nothing to earn the opportunity but was put there just to try to get Punk beat up - not to mention another example of Triple H looking out for his Attitude Era buddies at the expense of young talent.[111] Triple H would contend that he made the matches and Punk wrestled them, a pro wrestling way of saying, "Shut up and dribble."

After getting past Kane at the *Rumble*, Triple H would book Punk to defend his title again in the Elimination Chamber at February's pay-per-view of the same title. The match would have been slated to

---

[111] CM Punk was never short on grievances.

include The Miz, Chris Jericho, R-Truth, Dolph Ziggler, and Kofi Kingston as challengers; however, Kingston would be attacked shortly before the match was scheduled to take place. With Miz, Jericho, Truth, and Ziggler in their pods, Punk - who not-so-surprisingly was forced to start the match in the ring - would await one of the cage doors to slide open for what had seemingly become a five-man match. Then, Triple H's music would hit. In need of a sixth man and with no other options, The Game would have ditched his suit and tie for the night in favor of his boots and trunks.

Punk's reaction would be one of indignation. Was Triple H responsible for Kofi's absence? Why did he even have his wrestling gear with him? Was this his plan all along? Was he the one who kept inviting Michael Cole to *WrestleMania*? We would need answers to all of these questions.

Triple H would attempt to explain his presence to the champion: of course he wasn't responsible for Kofi's attack; every wrestler knows to bring their gear to the arena, no matter what; the company advertised a six-man Elimination Chamber match and with such short notice, this was the only way to deliver on that promise; and of course not, no one knew how Cole continued to slip past security but a full-scale investigation needed to be launched.

No fists would fly while Punk and Triple H were alone in the ring together at *Elimination Chamber*, but the arguing would become more and more heated. Just when things appeared ready to become physical, the next combatant would be released from his pod, and the match would actually get underway. At some point during the match, Triple H would have the opportunity to cost Punk the championship... and he would try to do it. Punk would narrowly avoid the loss but the gloves would be off from this point forward - no more attempting to control their disdain for one another.

Punk would then call out Triple H the following night on *Raw*. Punk would tell Triple H that if he wanted a shot at the title, all he had to do was ask. Instead, Triple H schemed and conspired to try to take down Punk because he knew that man-to-man, he couldn't beat Punk. But what ate at Triple H most, Punk would say, was the fact that he was thirteen-time world champion with a Hall of Fame resume and a multi-decade career but never came close to the levels Punk reached in the last eight months.

Triple H would confirm his resentment for the champion. That was no secret. But The Game would claim it wasn't an issue of jealousy but rather, one of respect. In Triple H's eyes, Punk didn't deserve the spotlight he was handed. Hunter would cut right to the heart of the matter, calling Punk an undersized malcontent whose most notable accomplishment in the WWE was quitting. Punk wouldn't have lasted a month with the locker room sharks of the Attitude Era, Triple H might claim. He would apologize that Kofi had to get caught in the crossfire, though - it *was* all part of the plan. And that plan was going to come to completion at the biggest show of the year.

"At *WrestleMania*, I'm going to fix the Board's mistake," Triple H would tell Punk. "I'm going to take the WWE championship… and I'm going to end your career."

That's where the CM Punk versus Triple H match *should* have happened: *WrestleMania XXVIII*… and Punk would have had to win.

In addition to resolving a massive misstep, this rebooking would also allow their opponents in the real timeline to face each other in the revised one. Despite working in the same company for close to two decades, Chris Jericho and The Undertaker only faced each other in singles competitions three times. Few would complain about a *WrestleMania* program between the two.

We would lose out on the Punk versus Jericho feud, which was good but replaceable, as well as the "End of an Era" Hell in a Cell match between Triple H and The Undertaker. The latter was an outstanding match... but was it necessary? What era did that match end? Was it the Attitude Era? Because I feel like that ended at least a decade earlier. Was it the era of Triple H and The Undertaker as in-ring competitors? Spoiler alert, they both performed on the next *six* *WrestleMania* cards and even fought against each other again in a singles match at *Super Show-Down* in Melbourne, Australia in October of 2018, and in a tag match (with respective partners Shawn Michaels and Kane) at *Crown Jewel* a month later in Saudi Arabia. Not exactly the end of any era, if you ask me. But then again, the match between The Rock and John Cena was billed as "Once in a Lifetime" and they ended up main-eventing two straight *WrestleMania*s, so truth in advertising isn't exactly a strong suit of the WWE. Regardless, The Undertaker and Triple H fought at three different *WrestleManias*, which is at least one too many. I would happily sacrifice their final face-off - great as it was - for a more satisfying conclusion to this CM Punk storyline.

Of course, the multi-million dollar question is: would this revised timeline change anything about CM Punk's eventual departure from WWE? It would certainly improve the chances of at least a more amicable breakup, that's for sure. But to gauge that, we'd have to spin Punk's record-setting title reign forward a little bit more. After his triumph over Triple H at *WrestleMania XXVIII*, what *should* have happened next?

* WHAT WOULD HAVE HAPPENED NEXT *

CM Punk's actual reign as WWE champion lasted 434 days, from *Survivor Series* in November 2011 through *Royal Rumble* in January 2013. During that time, Punk engaged in some quality feuds. Among the most notable were his summer program with Daniel Bryan, the rekindling of his rivalry with John Cena, an autumn kerfuffle with Ryback - which coincided with the debut of The Shield - and a championship showdown with The Rock.

There was nothing terribly wrong creatively with any of those storylines; however, one of Punk's key grievances upon reflecting on his WWE career was that the company gave him the title, but still didn't view him as "the guy" and the data confirms that. In his thirteen-pay-per-view run with the title, Punk appeared in the main event slot just five times. He and Alberto Del Rio headlined *TLC* in December 2011, the month after Punk took the title off Del Rio at *Survivor Series*. Punk didn't close another major show until the following September *nine months later* at *Night of Champions*. Though he did main-event four of the final five events of his reign, it's difficult to claim the run was given the gravitas it deserved.

The final match on the card does carry with it significant weight and speaks to how the company views a performer. Steve Austin's match went on last at ten pay-per-views in 1998 alone. During Triple H's "Reign of Terror" in 2003-04, he headlined six straight *Raw* or dual-branded pay-per-views and then two of the next three. Of the 22 pay-per-view events between October 2009 and July 2011, John Cena headlined fifteen of them. Cena also closed six straight shows while Punk was WWE champion from *Elimination Chamber* in February 2012 through *Money in the Bank* in July. And when WWE was doing its best to make fans hate the company's top babyface in 2015-16, Roman Reigns was in the main event of eight out of ten pay-per-view events. Compare those numbers against Punk's 5-for-13 mark - or 5-for-14, if you count *Survivor Series 2011* where the WWE championship match between Punk and Del Rio was the semi-main event and followed by The Rock and John Cena in tag team action against The Miz and R-Truth to close the show - and it should become clearer why Punk had a chip on his shoulder about going on last. World champions traditionally close the show; when Punk consistently didn't, it's not hard to see why Punk felt disrespected.

Fortunately, this gripe could have been largely remedied simply by changing the match order on the card. John Cena's feud with John Laurinaitis and his cronies didn't need to go on last. Or at all. But certainly not last, especially with a CM Punk versus Daniel Bryan match on the card - a rivalry that Punk wanted to evolve into the "Bret and Shawn" of their generation. Why did a predictably subpar ambulance match between Cena and Kane that led nowhere main-event *Elimination Chamber*, while Punk's championship defense inside the pay-per-view's title structure open the show? There is no benefit of hindsight necessary to know that was just lousy ordering.

Punk's greatest unachieved goal from his time in WWE was to main-event *WrestleMania*. While it seems unlikely that accomplishing that would have kept Punk in the company after his contract expired in the summer of 2014, it likely would have kept the two parties at least on speaking terms for a future comeback.

Fixing this issue wouldn't have been quite as easy as flipping a few matches here and there, *but* it wouldn't have been too difficult to correct either. After Punk lost the WWE championship to The Rock at the 2013 *Royal Rumble*, perhaps Punk could have pulled a Becky Lynch and entered the Rumble match at No. 30. Lynch filled in for an injured Lana, while Punk would have done the injuring himself, perhaps taking out entrant No. 29, Sin Cara. Punk would then win the Rumble by eliminating Cena; however, the legitimacy of Punk's win would have to be called into question since he wasn't a true entrant into the match. Punk and Cena would then go on to settle the matter at *Elimination Chamber* in February.

That match could go in a couple different directions. Punk could beat Cena, go on to *WrestleMania* and defeat The Rock to win his belt back in the night's final match. In this scenario, Cena would slide into the spot Punk took on in reality, facing The Undertaker at *WrestleMania XXIX*, giving the pair an actual *'Mania* match instead of the three-minute filler they ended up having at *WrestleMania 34* in 2018. A different route would have Cena beat Punk at *Elimination Chamber* to add himself to the main event and make it a triple threat among Cena, Punk, and The Rock. There would be some poetic justice in this path, since a key element of Punk's "pipe bomb" promo focused on his anger about The Rock and Cena headlining *WrestleMania* a year in advance. He wouldn't get to spoil that match, but in this timeline he would be able to wreck the rematch. I'd put my money on Cena leaving the Show of Shows with the championship since Rock's run was ending and Cena likely "needed" the win more than Punk. As noted in the build to *WrestleMania XXIX*, 2012 was not a great year for Cena, personally or professionally. A *WrestleMania* redemption arc would have helped reestablish him as the top babyface in the territory. With Punk and Cena both off the table for opponents, The Undertaker could have had a shot at a never-before-seen one-on-one feud with The Celtic Warrior, Sheamus.

Would Punk still have walked out in 2014? Maybe. He was still burnt out and beat up after three years of an intense schedule. But, maybe instead of "walking out," all these changes could have bought enough goodwill to keep him around at least until his contract expired in the summer. That would have meant CM Punk would have been part of *WrestleMania XXX*, and it is fun to consider what that might have looked like.

As Punk himself leaked in 2014, the original plan was for Punk and Triple H to square off at the anniversary show. However, we already took care of that feud and wouldn't need to revisit it again in the new timeline. We also know that *WrestleMania XXX* was all about Daniel Bryan's climb to the top and we wouldn't want to change a thing about that. Even right down to Bryan not even being entered in, let alone winning, the *Royal Rumble* - a situation that resulted in Hall of Famer Mick Foley tweeting, "Does @WWE actually hate their own audience? I've never been so disgusted with a PPV." I think most wrestling fans would agree that Bryan should have won the 2014 Royal Rumble match, but I also think most wrestling fans would agree that the story we ended up getting out of that incredible disappointment might have been worth it in the end.

With that in mind, coupled with the reality that Punk was probably out the door by the end of summer anyway, there would only be so many match options for CM Punk at *WrestleMania XXX*. Given the limited choices, I would have liked to see Punk get in the ring with The Shield - a stable he helped create more than a year earlier.

"I said '[Dean] Ambrose, [Seth] Rollins, Chris Hero (or Kassius Ohno),'" Punk told Colt Cabana in 2014. "Hunter shot down Hero. They wanted Roman Reigns. They came to me and they were like 'what about Leakee?'[112]... It wasn't my hill to die on. I said 'sure' because it made sense to me. Oh, they want their guy in, he's the 'pretty guy,' but that's good because this guy can learn from working under me.[113] The idea was they were supposed to be my group."

The Shield acted as mercenaries for Punk in their early days, "shielding" him from defeat. Punk was already feuding with the group in late 2013 and early 2014 and the story of the trio dispatching of their former boss would have been a good one, hopefully slightly better than The Shield's actual three-minute match against Kane and the New Age Outlaws at *WrestleMania XXX*. The issue would be finding tag partners for Punk. The pairing of Punk with the New Age Outlaws didn't make a ton of sense, nor would a potential teaming of Punk with The Usos. Instead, given that WWE had just launched the *WWE Network* in February and its first live streaming event was *NXT Arrival*, what if Punk solved his mystery teammate conundrum by fighting alongside NXT superstars Sami Zayn and

---

[112] Roman Reigns debuted in WWE Developmental as "Roman Leakee" in August 2010. His name was later shortened to just "Leakee" then revised to "Roman Reigns" just before The Shield debuted in 2012.

[113] I can't prove it, but I have long believed that Punk telling Cabana that he wanted Chris Hero to be his third Shield member instead of Roman Reigns was the catalyst for the WWE fanbase turning on Reigns. Don't get me wrong, WWE did everything in its power to kill Reigns as a babyface, but I refuse to believe the fan backlash would have been quite as pronounced as it was had Punk not called Reigns "their guy" on the *Art of Wrestling*.

Adrian Neville? Marketing-wise, this would put a massive spotlight on NXT as the WWE worked hard to sell those $9.99 Network subscriptions at the time. The match would showcase Zayn and Neville as worthy competitors but not put them in a situation where the inevitable loss to The Shield would harm them; on the contrary, just as John Cena's loss to Kurt Angle in the era of "Ruthless Aggression" legitimized him as a future industry star, the "rub" Zayn and Neville would receive from being hand-picked by Punk and taking The Shield to the brink at *WrestleMania* would follow them around for the rest of their NXT and WWE careers. Punk would go out on his back, but he'd go out on his back helping five younger wrestlers establish themselves on the biggest stage in the business.

Of all the creative missteps in pro wrestling history, the mishandling of CM Punk remains among the most disappointing. From 2011-14, he really was exactly what he claimed to be: the best in the world. It's why his return to professional wrestling with AEW in August of 2021 was so electric.[114] Fans weren't ready for his story to be over seven years earlier, which makes it all the more upsetting to think that with a different match here, a rearranged order there, and a little extra communication and understanding towards the end, maybe it wouldn't have been.

---

[114] I was at the United Center in Chicago for Punk's return on August 20, 2021. If I could borrow a phrase from the incomparable Tony Schiavone, it truly was "one of the most historic nights in the history of our great sport." The video of his return garnered more than 1.1 million views in less than an hour and according to Tony Khan on *Busted Open Radio* the following week, "We learned from ESPN that there was more traffic on their social media posts on CM Punk returning to wrestling and arriving to AEW on *Rampage* then they've had on any post since May. That includes the NBA Finals, the European Championship, and the Summer Olympics." Talk about a needle-mover.

THIRTEEN

FEAR MY NAME

> "You guys boo me anyway. I'm the biggest heel in the company."

April 1, 2012
Hard Rock Stadium ◉ *Miami, Florida*
WWE WrestleMania XXVIII

The Rock defeated John Cena by pinfall (30:35).

* WHAT REALLY HAPPENED *

There are exceptionally few things that the majority of wrestling fans are willing to agree on. As Daniel Bryan once accurately asserted, we are a "fickle" bunch. However, there are at least three pro wrestling truths that we all hold to be self-evident: 1) event-specific set designs are awesome; 2) three hours of *Monday Night Raw* is at least one hour too many; and 3) John Cena should have turned heel.

No performer in the modern television era has enjoyed a run on top like John Cena's nine-year tenure as the WWE's premier babyface from 2005-14. During that time, Cena won the WWE or World Heavyweight championship on fifteen occasions. He spent 1,240 days - combined, more than three full years - as a primary champion, won a pair of Royal Rumble matches, as well as one Money in the Bank contract, and headlined five different *WrestleMania*s.

Cena was the company workhorse before and after his main event days as well, not only wrestling on the regular for fifteen years, but also serving as the WWE's chief ambassador to the outside world through promotions like the "Be A Star" anti-bullying campaign, Susan G. Komen For the Cure breast cancer awareness promotion, and, most significantly, setting the Make-A-Wish Foundation record for wishes granted to children with life-threatening illnesses at more than 650.

And yet, John Cena still fascinatingly became the most polarizing performer in industry history, with (mostly) women and children in attendance chanting, "Let's go, Cena!" while (mostly) men in the arena answered back, "Cena sucks!" ...at every event... for more than a decade...

The uninitiated might have some questions about this. Perhaps no one has summarized the Cena era more eloquently than his heir apparent, Roman Reigns, did in 2021: "[Cena] came out here, the same music, the same entrance, the same run to the ring, the same outfit, the same promo, the same insults... it's the same thing over and over and over – it's like missionary position every single night!" Cena was, shall we say, good but unimaginative?

Beyond the creative rut, though, for many in the audience, Cena was also *exhausting*. He wore jean shorts and highlighter-colored t-shirts. His attempts at humor in promos were either corny or sophomoric with little in between. His offensive arsenal consisted of what the Internet liked to mockingly refer to as the "Five Moves of Doom." And he was constant, both in the main event scene - where many have argued his presence and success came at the expense of building up younger talent - and in everything surrounding it, from merchandise to promotions. There was no denying who the face of WWE was and hardcore fans *hated* it.[115] He was professional wrestling's version of Tim Tebow: a good guy so wholesome it seemed unbelievable, who (literally) wore his beliefs on his chest, won in spite of unconventional athleticism, and dominated the spotlight for as long as he was in the sport.

But it didn't have to be that way. And in 2012, it almost wasn't...

---

[115] I myself shattered two computer screens just typing this paragraph.

because John Cena nearly turned heel.

"We were very close," former WWE writer Kevin Eck told reporter Wade Keller on the PWTorch Livecast in 2017. "We even had Vince [McMahon] sign off on it at one point and Cena was on board to do it."

Cena recorded new theme music and commissioned new ring gear in preparation for the decision. Fans even got a glimpse of his supposed costume design on a 2015 episode of *Total Divas* when Cena emerged for a workout with then-significant other Nikki Bella sporting a maroon and yellow wrestling singlet bearing the phrase "Fear My Name" - a slogan WWE trademarked in late 2011 when the seeds were being planted on television for Cena to turn to the dark side.

"We started making plans for it and then Vince got cold feet," Eck said. "We had just signed a John Cena-exclusive merchandise deal with Wal-Mart and Vince came into a booking meeting one day and said 'God, I know you guys really wanna do this but I just can't do it.'"

McMahon had a point. With the significant – though perhaps not irrelevant – exception of the New World Order, heel turns kill merchandise sales and Cena had been the company's top merchandise seller for years. Not only that, the competition for that spot was rarely close. In 2014, the Wrestling Observer Newsletter reported that Cena's merchandise outsold the entire rest of the company *combined*. So while the art may have suffered as a result of Cena's character stagnation, the business was booming because of Cena's appeal to kids.[116] For that reason alone, it's completely understandable that WWE was resistant to fixing something that

---

[116] Well. Not *all* kids. I have vivid memories of an eight-year-old behind me at a *Smackdown* taping in 2014 discussing, at length, Cena's workrate. I can only assume he's now a Reddit moderator on r/SquaredCircle.

financially was far from broken.

So, Cena never made the turn. Storyline-wise, it seemed like he finally might by early 2012, though. At the time, Cena was in between major story arcs. He had just wrapped up his WWE championship storyline with CM Punk and Alberto Del Rio and had begun to transition into the build for *WrestleMania XVIII* against The Rock. But, with The Rock only appearing on television sporadically due to his filming schedule leading up to the main event match on April 1, 2012, Cena needed a side-story to occupy his time. That side-story turned out to be a feud with a "resurrected" version of The Big Red Machine, Kane.

Kane had ceased to be much of a monster since being unmasked at the hands of Triple H and his Evolution stable in June of 2003. However, after time off late in the summer and fall of 2011, Kane reemerged on the December 12 episode of *Raw* with a new take on an old look and the potential to recapture some of the magic that made him the scariest figure in wrestling in the late 1990s. During the main event match between Mark Henry and John Cena on the go-home show before the *TLC* pay-per-view, Kane's pyro hit, the lights went dark, and the Devil's Favorite Demon made his way down to the ring clad in post-autopsy themed ring gear and a full metallic-looking mask which, after chokeslamming Cena, he removed to reveal a new red mask, much to the excitement of longtime fans.

Over the next several weeks, Kane continued to make Cena his target. As Cena's latest t-shirt read, "Rise Above Hate," Kane urged Cena to instead "Embrace The Hate." Though Kane's show-closing promo on the December 26, 2011 episode of *Raw* fell a bit flat in front of the live crowd in Chicago, the verbiage primed Cena for a heel turn that would ultimately never come:

> You want to know why I assaulted you? Why I chose to make you my victim? It's simple. You have led all of these

people astray. You ask them to rise above hate but that's a fallacy. This world is a dark, dark place. It's okay to hate. Humans are hateful by nature. Deep down, everybody hates. Why rise above it when the natural impulse is to embrace it? To let it consume you. People hate. They hate their bosses, they hate their neighbors, they hate their spouses, they hate their miserable existence. Rise above? That's a fraudulent myth perpetuated by you. Hate is the seed from which we are all born. It drives us. It motivates us. It fuels our impulses. And I know that you feel it, John. You feel it swimming underneath your skin like a thousand insects eating away at you. But once you embrace the hate, you become honest with yourself. You become free. *Free.* What you fail to realize, John, is that with your denial, you grow weaker by the moment. And until you embrace that which you deny, you can never be truly free. But I am going to help you, John. And all of these people are going to help you on your path towards enlightenment. Because right now, the last image that you will see this year, the last thing that you will hear, is each and every one of these people chanting the words which tear your soul apart. 'Cena sucks. Cena sucks. Cena sucks. Cena sucks.'

The feud resulted in one-on-one matches between Cena and Kane at *Royal Rumble* in January and *Elimination Chamber* in February, as well as multiple attacks on Cena ally Zack Ryder - including that time Kane pushed a wheelchair-bound Ryder off the stage.[117] However, Cena never did give in to the darkness. He went on to *WrestleMania* - without malice in his heart - and lost to The Rock.

Cena bounced back with an *Extreme Rules* victory over the returning Brock Lesnar the following month, and staying on the straight-and-narrow path largely worked out for him in the end; he closed out

---

[117] That's what you get for getting over on your own.

nine-of-twelve WWE pay-per-views in 2012 (despite being WWE champion for exactly zero of them), won the *Royal Rumble* in 2013 and got his win and title back against The Rock in a rematch at *WrestleMania XXIX*. Being pro wrestling's resident boy scout had seemingly paid off. But fans have long believed that shouldn't have been Cena's story. So what if it hadn't been? What if Cena had followed Kane's advice and embraced the hate? Cena's legacy would certainly be looked at in a different light, but he may not have been the only one whose fortunes would have been radically altered by such a move.

* WHAT COULD HAVE HAPPENED *

Bray Wyatt gave the world a glimpse of what a John Cena heel turn could have looked like during the wonderfully bizarre "Firefly Funhouse" match between the two men at *WrestleMania 36* in 2020. In one of the dream sequences during the cinematic-style match, Cena donned a black-and-white nWo t-shirt and entered the ring with the mannerisms of "Hollywood" Hulk Hogan, whose heel turn nearly a quarter-century earlier sent shockwaves through the pro wrestling industry. Cena's proposed heel turn wouldn't have had the same magnitude as Hogan's for a host of reasons, but a Cena heel turn still would have been seismic.

How do we know? Because before he became the John Cena we know and love to hate today, from October 2002 to October 2003, John Cena... was a villain! On a Halloween-themed episode of *Smackdown!*, Cena shed his vanilla gimmick, dressed as Vanilla Ice, and performed a freestyle rap in a backstage segment. It went over so well that a new character as the "Doctor of Thuganomics" was born. Cena began coming to the ring wearing hats and jerseys of the host city's rival sports teams and cut rhyming promos on each of his opponents. Among the most famous of those was a February 27, 2003 vignette aimed at budding superstar, Brock Lesnar:

"Brock, I sit here glued to the screen, punching these keys,

Watching everything you do on live internet feeds.
I download at high speed all the files I need
To make your hard drive crash and to make your face bleed.
You can't erase me. I'ma make you taste me.
I'm a virus – I'll kill you the next time you face me.
You jealous; you stole my shot at the brass ring.
Everybody knows I'm the 'Next Big Thing.'
You all bark and no bite. You stole my spotlight.
I'm the Great White Hope; you're the Great White Hype.
If you an animal, then I'm going on safari.
I'm rocking PlayStation 2, you can't figure out Atari.
Look in these eyes, Brock – don't think I won't shoot ya.
I'll leave you worthless, like a nerd with no computer.
Show the world that you can't even walk in my shoes.
Your finisher's the F-5? Well, mine's the F-U."[118]

And that, boys and girls, is why John Cena ceased to be a heel much longer. He was so – as the kids say – savage-AF on the mic that fans couldn't help but cheer him.

Unfortunately, the edge that brought him to superstardom dulled when he traded in the rapper gimmick to become WWE's straight-laced do-gooder. He won his first world championship in 2005 and remained a fixture in the main event scene for the better part of the next decade. By 2012, it was difficult for anyone to deny the act had grown creatively stale. Like Hogan prior to 1996, Cena was generally cast as the conquering babyface champion, which meant he needed a slew of baddies and monsters to topple. However, Cena had run through every heel in the company and there were no new stories left to tell… at least not from the same old "Super Cena," the underdog-who-wasn't, perspective.

Cena had no shortage of heel opportunities throughout the 2010s

---

[118] In the pre-PG Era, Cena's finishing maneuver wasn't called the "Attitude Adjustment;" it was the "F-U" as a play on Lesnar's "F-5."

either. He could have turned at *Survivor Series 2010* by gifting Wade Barrett the WWE championship and joining The Nexus. Instead, Cena took the high road, got storyline-fired, and went over at the expense of an entire troupe of up-and-comers. He had another chance at *Money in the Bank 2011*, when he could have aligned with Mr. McMahon to screw CM Punk out of the WWE championship in Chicago. That heat would have been nuclear. Like, ECW Arena, fear-for-your-life kind of heat. But it didn't happen then either. The next option - and perhaps the one that would have made the most sense for both Cena and the WWE - would have been a heel turn following his *WrestleMania XXVIII* loss to The Rock. Cena could have waited one more year and turned on The Rock at *WrestleMania XXIX*, a la Steve Austin at *WrestleMania X-Seven*; however, there would be significantly less meat on the bone in that scenario with Cena's career as a full-time main-eventer starting to wind down by then. That said, a Cena turn in 2013 after his "rock bottom" 2012 would have been a logical resolution to get the championship off The Rock and advance Cena onto a brand new chapter, even if it would be too little, too late in the eyes of many.

In my opinion, the best time to turn Cena would have been after his first loss to The Rock at *WrestleMania XXVIII* in 2012. Losing to a part-timer after a year of building and smack-talking should have changed Cena. It should have hardened him. It should have made him tap into the "ruthless aggression" that had set him on his trajectory to stardom years earlier. It should have made him realize that Kane was right: he did need to embrace a little hate.

But... the *Raw* after *WrestleMania XXVIII* famously featured the return of Brock Lesnar to the WWE. As Cena delivered his show-closing promo, Lesnar's music hit and the former WWE, UFC, and NCAA champion made his way down to the ring where he laid Cena out with his patented F-5 finishing maneuver.

In the revised timeline, Lesnar still could have returned to attack Cena; however, it would have been a much more savage beatdown putting Cena on the shelf for months *and* - as we know from what really happened - one that fans would have cheered for. The *Raw-after-Mania* crowd is the smarkiest of them all, so leveraging their hatred for Cena would have given him exactly the justification needed to return months later as full-blown, fan-hating heel.

In this revised timeline, Cena then would not be seen again until *SummerSlam* in August when he would return to beatdown WWE champion CM Punk following his successful title defense over, let's say, The Miz. Cena's explanation the next night on *Raw* would have been pretty simple:

> "I gave everything for you people. I showed up to work every day to entertain you. I sweat for you. I bled for you. I did signings, I granted wishes. I gave up movie roles. I sacrificed my personal life to be here for you. And how was I thanked? You booed me out of the building at *WrestleMania* and cheered for the guy who *left* you. Then the next night, I showed up for work and offered my congratulations to the guy you all love, and another guy - *who walked out on you* - came out and beat me within an inch of my life… and you cheered him while he did it.
>
> Now, I come back, do the same thing he did, and you hate me for it. Well, you know what? I'm done. For ten years I gave you everything I had, every single night… but every arena I came to, all I heard was you people chanting 'Cena sucks.' No. I've won thirteen world championships in less than a decade. I've main-evented five *WrestleMania*s. I'm the greatest performer of not just my generation, but any generation. Cena doesn't suck. You suck. The WWE Universe sucks. You chant "Rocky, Rocky" and "C-M-Punk, C-M-Punk" but it's my name you should have been chanting all along. And now that time has passed. From now on, I will make sure you never chant my name. From now on, all you're gonna do is fear it."

And thus would begin John Cena's run as wrestling's biggest bad guy. Cena rationalized never turning heel to Chris Jericho on the WWE Network in 2015 when he admitted, "You guys boo me anyway. I'm the biggest heel in the company." To be honest, this was a pretty accurate assessment. So why did fans always want him to turn then? Because the truth is: we always wanted to cheer him. Don't believe me? Go check out Cena's surprise return at *Money in the Bank 2021* when he got one of the loudest pops in pro wrestling history. Look, fans don't want heel turns so they can cheer a villain; they want interesting, multidimensional characters who evolve over time. That *wasn't* Cena. And that's what we hated most about him.

Conversely, consider what happened when WWE finally decided to turn Roman Reigns. The Big Dog really did have the makings of an all-time great (just as the company thought), but he was improperly cast as a babyface for *years* before finally becoming the uncaring, mafia boss-style "Tribal Chief" in 2020. Reigns was always good in the ring and generally fine on the mic, but fans rejected him because they felt Reigns was being force-fed to them as the guy the company wanted them to like, just like Cena had been. When Reigns was able to lean into his own heelish side, he was launched into a whole new stratosphere. Not only that, but all the vitriol fans felt for the babyface version of Reigns soon turned into respect for the richness of his character, which will ultimately translate into love when he eventually finds his way back to the light side in the future.

That could have been Cena's story, too. I would venture to guess that the John Cena "Fear My Name" promo would be immediately celebrated – [not just because I wrote it, but] because it would have been *real*. The best villains tell the truth, or some twisted version of the truth. Roman Reigns' "Acknowledge Me" catchphrase wasn't just about the power trip of forcing opponents to recognize his superiority in the ring; it was a message to fans that he was always this good and they were wrong to reject him. In a similar vein, Cena's promo would have been just as justified and, as Reigns has proven, he still could have sold boatloads of merchandise while rubbing the fans' noses in it.

Cena should have been universally loved, but he wasn't. He did everything the right way, by the book, with hustle, loyalty, and respect, and a huge portion of fans gave none of that back to him. Now, with his white meat babyface days behind him, he could burn the jorts and glow-in-the-dark shirts to show the WWE Universe a version of himself truly worthy of their disdain.

* WHAT WOULD HAVE HAPPENED NEXT *

Cena's theoretical attack on Punk at *SummerSlam 2012* would have catapulted him right back into the title picture. At *Night of Champions* in September, Cena's ruthless aggression would have gotten him disqualified; however, at *Hell in a Cell* the following month, his newfound brutality would make him a fourteen-time world champion, ending Punk's reign at just under a year. Punk would get a rematch at *Survivor Series* but the night would end with the formation of Cena's version of the nWo... The Shield. In reality, Roman Reigns, Seth Rollins, and Dean Ambrose debuted at *Survivor Series 2012* to protect a heel CM Punk. In the revised timeline, they would be Cena's henchmen of choice.

While one might be tempted to reclaim the "Cenation" - the name given to Cena's legion of fans - for this group, "The Shield" actually works well on a couple of fronts. In its functional meaning, the group would shield Cena in this timeline as it shielded Punk in the real one; however, there would also be a real sports tie-in to be capitalized on as well. The National Football League logo is often referred to as "the shield" because it is, well, a shield. One of the nicknames for basketball's Jerry West is "The Logo" because his silhouette not-so-secretly serves as the National Basketball Association's logo. Cena once had a "Hustle, Loyalty, Respect" t-shirt that featured him using his STFU submission hold in a design based on the old American Wrestling Association logo. This is all to say that Cena's next promotional campaign could have been something along the lines of "I Am The Shield" or "We Are The Shield" in reference to Cena and/or his new faction being the "face" of the WWE. And each of our wallets would have been thirty dollars lighter.

The *Survivor Series* assault on Punk would give the former champion a well-deserved and extended holiday vacation until the *Royal Rumble* in January of 2013. Meanwhile, Cena would have taken up the feud with arguably the hottest babyface on the roster at the time, Ryback. From there, the options would be plentiful - which is a good problem to have.

Scenario 1: Punk could have won the Rumble to set up a title match against Cena at *WrestleMania*. This also would have opened The Rock up for his long-rumored but never acted upon *WrestleMania* match against Brock Lesnar.

Scenario 2: Instead of February's Elimination Chamber match being for the No. 1 contendership to the World Heavyweight championship, it could have been for a WWE title match against Cena. At this juncture of his career, The Rock may not have been terribly interested in the violence involved in such a match, but in our theoretical scenario, he might come out the No. 1 contender, to set up a rematch with Cena at the "Showcase of the Immortals."

Scenario 3: Yet another option would be for Cena to drop the title back to Punk at the *Rumble*, make his way into the Rumble match and win by eliminating The Rock thanks to interference by The Shield. The wrong could be righted by The Rock receiving a title shot against Punk at *Elimination Chamber*, winning that match, and carrying the belt into *WrestleMania* against Cena.

Scenario 4: Cena could be stripped of the WWE title as a result of some gratuitous act of violence. The Rock could defeat CM Punk for the vacant championship at the *Royal Rumble*. Cena could win the Rumble match (with the aid of The Shield) and go on to face (and defeat) The Rock at *WrestleMania*.

Regardless of whichever Choose-Your-Own-Adventure scenario you like best, Cena would be walking out of *WrestleMania* as WWE champion. Cena would continue on as champion - just as he did in reality - until *SummerSlam 2013*. Mirroring reality again, The Shield would also pick up gold over the summer, with Dean Ambrose claiming the United States championship and Seth Rollins and Roman Reigns winning the Tag Team titles, giving all four members of Cena's faction championships. However, tension would begin to build between the group's leader and its workhorses.

Ambrose, Reigns, and Rollins might begin to harbor resentment against the group's leader, feeling Cena was holding them back. The impending Shield schism - and the end of Cena's heel run - would occur at *SummerSlam* when Cena would reject assistance from his henchmen during his championship defense against Daniel Bryansending them to the locker room. Without help from The Shield, Bryan would outclass Cena to win the WWE title. After the match, Cena would acknowledge Bryan as the better man that night, hand him the title belt, and raise Bryan's hand in victory, and give him the ring. But, just as it appeared we were getting a *Return of the Jedi* ending, the hyenas from the end of *The Lion King* would come out to (figuratively) devour their former leader. As Cena saluted the fans atop the entry ramp, Roman Reigns would come out behind him. When Cena turned around to see Reigns blocking his exit, Dean Ambrose would enter from stage left and Seth Rollins would appear stage right. The "Hounds of Justice" would then turn on Cena, triple-powerbombing the ex-champion off the stage.

Before Bryan could intervene, special guest referee and WWE COO Triple H would give him a kick to the stomach and a pedigree, paving the way for Randy Orton to cash in his Money in the Bank contract and pin Bryan for the WWE championship. With that, the Empire will have struck back. It's a roller coaster ride of Disney-owned influences at *SummerSlam*. With Orton as his chosen champion,

Triple H would form The Authority[119] faction and set the stage for Bryan's historic *WrestleMania XXX* run the following spring.

Cena's destruction at the hands of his own creation would sideline him (due to a torn triceps muscle, which he suffered in reality during the summer of 2013) until *Survivor Series* in November when he would return as a fairly predictable mystery partner for The Usos and Rhodes Brothers against The Shield and The Real Americans[120] in a traditional five-on-five *Survivor Series* elimination match. The match would come down to The Shield against Cena, and the Shield would prevail.

At *TLC* in December, Cena would take on all three Shield members in a three-on-one handicap match - a bout CM Punk was booked for in the real timeline. Cena would lose (because three future multi-time world champions should beat one man, always). Punk, meanwhile, would join forces with Daniel Bryan against The Wyatt Family. The Wyatts would also get the win.

A penitent Cena would enter 2014 with a "new year, new me" attitude, committed to reclaiming the WWE championship and becoming the champion fans deserved. He would come up short in the Royal Rumble match, though, and when the opportunity presented itself to win the title at *Elimination Chamber* in February, Bray Wyatt would - as he did in reality - prevent it from happening.

---

[119] Very similar to "The Corporation" and "McMahon-Helmsley Faction" before it, The Authority was the McMahon family's heel, well, authority group. Also very similar to the stables before it, The Authority overstayed its welcome by several years.

[120] Composed of "The All-American American" Jack Swagger and the "Swiss Superman" Cesaro - who, in case it wasn't clear, was Swiss - The Real Americans were a heel tag team who got their heat with topical anti-immigration rhetoric. Fans booed because racism is wrong. Nutjobs booed because they felt their beliefs were being mocked. I myself would prefer to never discuss The Real Americans or the Tea Party Movement ever again.

Wyatt would base his attack on the belief that Cena had not truly served his penance yet for the harm he had caused as champion, setting up their program for *WrestleMania XXX* and getting Cena back on track to mirror the real timeline with a critically-acclaimed United States championship run in 2015.

And while WWE never capitalized on a "bad guy" Cena, DC Comics did see the potential. In the DC Extended Universe, Cena was cast as Peacemaker, a misguided pacifist who explains, "I cherish peace with all of my heart. I don't care how many men, women and children I kill to get it." Cena's performance in 2021's *The Suicide Squad* was so good, it spawned a character-specific HBO Max spinoff series starring the sixteen-time world champ. The dude has every tool in the box… but in the WWE, he wasn't able to use all of them.

Was a heel turn from John Cena essential to cementing his legacy as one of pro wrestling's all-time greats? No. He was certainly already in that category. And there's nothing wrong with being a career good guy either; it's good to be good. But no one – in wrestling or reality – should be the same person today that they were ten years ago. And that was really John Cena's problem – he was never allowed to evolve, leaving fans only to wonder about the side of Cena we never got to see.

FOURTEEN

LET HIM IN

"WWE has no idea how to handle Bray Wyatt."

April 6, 2014
Mercedes-Benz Superdome ◉ *New Orleans, Louisiana*
WWE WrestleMania XXX

John Cena defeated Bray Wyatt by pinfall (22:25).

* WHAT REALLY HAPPENED *

Perhaps no character in the history of professional wrestling has been more creative, compelling, or grossly mishandled than Bray Wyatt.

The grandson of WWE Hall of Famer Blackjack Mulligan and son of five-time WWF Tag Team champion Mike Rotunda - better known around tax season as "Irwin R. Schyster" - Bray Wyatt made his WWE debut as a Rookie on NXT in 2010. His name was not yet Bray Wyatt, however. No, the name given to him by WWE Creative at that time was *Husky Harris*, which should reveal exactly how highly the company viewed this third-generation wrestler.

It was a curious name choice, to say the absolute least. At six-foot-two and two-hundred ninety-five pounds, "husky" may have been a technically accurate adjective, though it is difficult to envision someone being brave enough to say it to the face of the former Florida state champion amateur wrestler and Division I offensive lineman. More significant to the pro wrestling industry, it is challenging to picture such a name headlining a marquee. But it could have been worse. He could have been given "Michael McGillicutty," the name prescribed to fellow NXT-er Joe Hennig, son of "Mr. Perfect" Curt Hennig and grandson of Larry "The Axe" Hennig.[121] While the WWE's desire to trademark gimmick names for monetary gain is understandable, clearly someone in Creative wanted to strongly encourage these young men to find another career.

Nevertheless, in June of 2010, Windham[122] Rotunda became Husky Harris, a fairly bland prospect, but one with good athleticism for his size. He was touted as "an army tank with a Ferrari engine." Participating in Season Two of NXT - back when it was something of a hybrid between reality and game show - Harris put together a 4-4 match record and was eliminated from competition in the season's penultimate episode. Reflecting upon his experience in August of 2010, Harris prophetically said, "People aren't ready to see someone like me yet."

Still, he got the call-up to the WWE in October, debuting alongside McGillicutty on behalf of Wade Barrett's Nexus faction against John Cena at the *Hell in a Cell* pay-per-view on October 4, 2010. His initial stay on the main roster was less than stellar. He did not wrestle a single one-on-one match and he and McGillicutty tallied just one victory as a tag team. The final appearance of Husky Harris on television came on the January 31, 2011 episode of *Monday Night Raw* when, after a tag team loss to Santino Marella and Vladimir Kozlov,

---

[121] He would later be repackaged as "Curtis Axel," combining name elements of both his father and grandfather. Kind of. Still, a massive improvement over Michael McGillicutty.

[122] "Windham" is the surname of Rotunda's uncles, Kendall and Barry, who were also famed wrestlers. Kendall was a five-time NWA Florida Heavyweight champion in Championship Wrestling from Florida, while Barry was heralded as one of the greatest grapplers of his generation, earning fame as both a singles competitor and, most notably, as a member of the iconic Four Horsemen stable alongside Ric Flair, Arn Anderson, and Tully Blanchard in World Championship Wrestling.

Harris was violently punted in the head by Randy Orton.

While this was certainly an unceremonious ending for Husky Harris' brief WWE career, it did serve as something of a genesis moment for Rotunda's next character iteration: Bray Wyatt. Generally speaking, the WWE doesn't want fans to remember failed gimmicks. It's why evil dentist Isaac Yankem, D.D.S. isn't part of the Kane character's backstory, or how many fans never realized that Headshrinker Fatu, The Sultan, and Rikishi were all the same dude. Bray Wyatt is an exception to that philosophy, as his evolution as a character is largely and intentional traceable. Ahead of their match at *WrestleMania 37* in 2021, Wyatt tweeted a photo of Orton's kick to the head of Husky Harris ten years prior with a Joker-attributed caption reading, "Someday someone will break you so badly that you'll become unbreakable." In Wyatt's mind, Orton's assault was the catalyst for Husky Harris to become who, or what, he became.

The Bray Wyatt character came to life in April of 2012. A charismatic, backwoods cult leader, Wyatt drew much of his inspiration from the short-lived WWF creation of Waylon Mercy, portrayed by Dan Spivey - a former tag team partner of Mike Rotunda in the mid-1980s. Waylon Mercy was a vicious sociopath disguised as a southern gentleman and based in large part on Robert DeNiro's Max Cady character from the 1991 Martin Scorsese film, *Cape Fear*. Mercy debuted, interestingly enough, against a seventeen-year-old Jeff Hardy[123] in June of 1995, but the character would only last until September, as Spivey was forced into retirement due to nagging injuries from a hard-hitting career in the ring. Spivey met with Windham Rotunda while the latter was repackaging himself post-Husky Harris and gave his blessing to reincarnate elements of

---

[123] Hardy famously lied about his age to get work in the WWF as an enhancement talent. Hardy debuted against Razor Ramon in 1994 at the age of sixteen and went on to enjoy a lengthy career as one of the biggest stars of the last quarter-century.

Waylon Mercy to create Bray Wyatt.

Bray Wyatt officially debuted on Florida Championship Wrestling television on April 22, 2012. Standing in the ring with Eli Cottonwood - a River Falls, Wis. native and former Saint John's University of Minnesota basketball standout during his previous life as Kipp Christianson - Bray Wyatt delivered his first sermon. Wearing white pants and a Hawaiian shirt just like Waylon Mercy had seventeen years earlier, Wyatt declared, "I am the nagging conscience of a world that has thrown itself away to moral monsters. I am everywhere, man. I am everything."

As Aiden English made his way to the ring for what would be a very brief match, Wyatt paid homage to Mercy again, shaking hands with the official and then his opponent before dominating English in a ninety-eight second squash.

"I've been around this industry enough to know when you see somebody that's a true threat," William Regal said on commentary. "We're looking at that man right now."

Wyatt took his act to NXT in July of 2012 and soon founded "The Wyatt Family." After all, one can't be a cult leader without a cult.[124] Luke Harper debuted as his first "son" in November, while Erick Rowan came along as his second in December. The three men captivated NXT audiences until July of the following year when the group made the move to the WWE main roster.

Vignettes from the Wyatt Family Compound began airing on WWE television in late May and on the July 8, 2013 episode of *Monday Night Raw*, the Wyatt Family would make an impactful debut. After Kane scored a pinfall victory over Christian, a Wyatt promo was shown on the TitanTron. It ended with Wyatt lighting a lantern and calmly announcing, "We're here." The lights went out and the group walked

---

[124] You have more fun as a follower, but you make more money as a leader.

to the ring by the light of the lantern. When the lights came back on, Wyatt was sitting in a wooden rocking chair at the bottom of the entry ramp while Harper and Rowan were in the ring to take out Kane.

Kane became Wyatt's first official victim the next month at *SummerSlam* when Wyatt pinned him in a "Ring of Fire" match. Two months later, Wyatt took out Kofi Kingston at *Battleground* in September. By November, the Wyatt Family had its sights set on CM Punk and Daniel Bryan because, as Wyatt stated, "False heroism is a sickness that must be dealt with." This led to a fabulous program with Daniel Bryan wherein Bryan briefly joined the Wyatt Family. Bryan only aligned with the group for about two weeks before turning on Wyatt in a memorable steel cage match on the January 13, 2014 episode of *Raw*. The angle felt rushed, as WWE quickly returned Bryan back to his babyface status thanks in no small part to his "Yes! Yes! Yes!" chant becoming a sensation in mainstream sports. At halftime of the NCAA Division I Men's Basketball game between No. 5 Michigan State and No. 3 Ohio State on January 7, 2014, Spartan football player Travis Jackson led the capacity crowd of more than 15,000 in East Lansing, Mich. in the chant. The video went viral and ended up on ESPN's *SportsCenter*. Daniel Bryan was a babyface again six days later.

Bryan's face-turn on *Raw* generated one of the loudest "Yes!" chants in WWE history and led to a one-on-one matchup with Wyatt at *Royal Rumble 2014*. Wyatt won the match and Bryan went on to headline *WrestleMania* following two months of mea culpa booking, as the company made an egregious error in judgment in leaving him out of the show-closing Royal Rumble match entirely – a decision that significantly marred the pay-per-view.

After defeating Bryan at the *Rumble*, Bray Wyatt's evening was not over. As John Cena was about to defeat Randy Orton to win the WWE World Heavyweight championship, The Wyatt Family caused a distraction which enabled Orton to hit his RKO finisher on Cena for the win. After the match, Wyatt attacked Cena to begin what would be a pivotal program for The Eater of Worlds.

The Wyatt Family continued to torment Cena over the coming weeks. On the January 27, 2014 episode of *Raw*, The Wyatts interjected themselves into an Elimination Chamber qualifying match between Cena, Bryan, and Sheamus against The Shield. The interference meant The Shield lost by disqualification, which led to the long-awaited six-man tag team match between The Shield and The Wyatt Family at the next pay-per-view, which The Wyatts won. Wyatt refocused on Cena after that match, again costing him the WWE title in the main event of *Elimination Chamber*.

The *WrestleMania XXX* feud between Wyatt and Cena was beautifully built around the concept of "legacy" with the pre-match hype video brilliantly employing the Eminem song of the same title as its soundtrack. Cena built his legacy on the pillars of "Hustle, Loyalty, and Respect," which Wyatt called "an era of lies."

"Your heroes, children... they fight only for their own selfish vanity and greed," Wyatt proclaimed.

It was all really excellent storytelling. What wasn't so excellent was the fact that Wyatt lost at *WrestleMania XXX*. *WrestleMania* wasn't the end of the Wyatt versus Cena program. They went on to have matches at the next two pay-per-views with Wyatt winning a steel cage match at *Extreme Rules* and Cena winning the feud-ending Last Man Standing match at *Payback*.

While good should triumph over evil in the end, *WrestleMania* wasn't "the end." The other problem with Wyatt losing was that it began to reveal Wyatt to be a false prophet. Once Wyatt was proven beatable, he lost a huge element of his fear factor. Conversely, had Wyatt defeated "Big Match John" at *WrestleMania*, Wyatt's stock would have shot through the roof with a career-defining victory on the grandest stage.

Instead, Bray Wyatt soon became little more than just another guy. He lost the Money in the Bank match for the WWE championship in June and was pinned by a returning Chris Jericho at *Battleground* in July. He got his win back against Jericho at *SummerSlam* in August and racked up a couple victories against Dean Ambrose, though this feud turned up the cornball factor quite a bit with needless gaga like a hologram and exploding television. The mystique Wyatt possessed coming into 2014 had been replaced with campiness by the end of the year.

Still, Wyatt remained a compelling character, largely because of his abilities on the microphone. Though his promos were often circular and bizarre, he made fans listen even if they couldn't fully track what in the world he was talking about. He even single-handedly built a match against The Undertaker at *WrestleMania 31*, but ended up being fed to The Deadman for his second marquee match loss in as many appearances. The following year, Wyatt was left off the card, but did interrupt a promo from The Rock. This resulted in an impromptu match between The Rock and Wyatt Family member Erick Rowan in which The Rock defeated Rowan in literally six seconds, then John Cena joined him in the ring to dismantle the entire Wyatt Family.

It took a while to recover from that embarrassment, but Wyatt's fortunes finally appeared to be changing by the end of 2016. After feuding earlier in the fall, he and Randy Orton had formed an alliance. The two men were the sole survivors for Team Smackdown in the five-on-five *Survivor Series* match in November. The following month, they defeated Rhyno and Heath Slater for the tag team titles at *Tables, Ladders, and Chairs*. Orton won the *Royal Rumble* in January, making him the No. 1 contender for a title match at *WrestleMania*. Meanwhile, Wyatt won the WWE championship for the first time in his career at *Elimination Chamber* in February. Orton then betrayed Wyatt, setting the Wyatt Compound on fire and desecrating the grave of Sister Abigail,[125] believed to be Wyatt's deceased - or possibly undead - sibling who served as his troubled conscience. These actions were sure to turn up the temperature for the WWE championship match between Orton and Wyatt at *WrestleMania*. Unfortunately, the match failed to deliver. Instead of the brutal collision the story called for, fans got ten-and-a-half minutes of slideshow bugs[126] and prostituted finishes, with Orton defeating Wyatt to win his ninth WWE title.

The result led Luis Paez-Pumar to write in *Rolling Stone* the painful truth fans already began to believe years earlier: "WWE has no idea how to handle Bray Wyatt."

Wyatt got a win back, but not the title, in a hokey "House of Horrors" match against Orton at *Payback* a few weeks later. By *SummerSlam*, Wyatt had moved on to a feud with Finn Bálor and his alter ego, The Demon King. Wyatt came up on the losing end of two straight pay-per-view matches. Ahead of what was supposed to be the third, Wyatt cut a Norman Bates-ish promo in which he "transformed" into Sister Abigail and spoke with a digitally modified voice. Words do not do justice for how bad this was; instead of fear, the segment was met with audible laughter. As one YouTube commenter wrote, "This is why people make fun of me for watching wrestling."

Wyatt and Bálor were supposed to meet at *TLC* in October, but Wyatt was among multiple wrestlers who came down with an illness prior to the show and had to be pulled from competition. According to pro wrestling reporter Ryan Satin, the plan was indeed for Wyatt

---

[125] Wyatt said, "Her touch could save the world, but her kiss burns it to the ground." This added some color to Wyatt's finishing maneuver, named "Sister Abigail" in which he kissed the forehead of his opponent before driving their skull into the mat.

[126] Maggots, worms, and cockroaches were projected onto the ring canvas. I wish I could tell you why. Actually, I just wish it never happened.

to wrestle dressed as Sister Abigail. While it was of course unfortunate that Wyatt's health was not at one-hundred percent, one imagines it was also the silverest of linings that this idea did not come to pass, as the character - and yours truly, who was in attendance at *TLC* that night - may have never recovered.

When Wyatt returned in November, he began a feud with Matt Hardy. While a member of the Impact Wrestling roster two-and-a-half years earlier, Hardy developed the bizarre (in the best way possible) character of "Broken" Matt Hardy, where he mentally snapped during an "I Quit" match with his brother, Jeff. He dyed part of his hair, spoke with a strange accent, and vowed to "delete" his adversaries. A special episode of *Impact* on July 5, 2016 featured "The Final Deletion," a wonderfully outrageous cinematic spectacle filmed on Hardy's property. Impact Wrestling put up a fight for the "Broken" gimmick when the Hardy brothers returned to the WWE in the spring of 2017, but eventually agreed to forfeit the intellectual property ownership. The program with Wyatt led to Hardy becoming "Woken." In March of 2018, the two men engaged in "The Ultimate Deletion" match wherein cinematic action returned to House Hardy and Wyatt was thrown into the Lake of Reincarnation to end their feud. Because how else would one do it?

Wyatt returned at *WrestleMania 34* to actually assist Hardy in winning the André the Giant Memorial Battle Royal, and the two would form a tag team as the "Deleters of Worlds." Though they won the WWE Tag Team titles weeks later in Jeddah, Saudi Arabia, their run as a team was brief, as Hardy was on the shelf due to injuries by July. Hardy, however, has said creative differences between talent and management played a bigger role than his health did in the end of their run.

"I think the reason Bray and I were pulled off TV at that time was [WWE writers] were tired of us suggesting ideas," Hardy told *Busted Open Radio* in 2018. "I think that whole scenario could have been so much more if we were able to get people to listen to our ideas."

This was the last fans would see of Wyatt in his maniacal prophet form. He had not been seen on television in months when strange vignettes began airing in April of 2019. Soon, Wyatt reemerged as the host of a children's program called the "Firefly Fun House." He even wore a nice sweater and everything. The segments featured disturbed puppets, including: Mercy the Buzzard (in reference to Waylon Mercy, the primary inspiration for Bray Wyatt's previous iteration), Abby the Witch (a take on Sister Abigail), Ramblin' Rabbit (a reference to Wyatt's tendencies to ramble in promos), and Huskus the Pig Boy (a shot at Wyatt's first character of Husky Harris). Later on, they even included a devilish character with horns that bore a striking resemblance to the Chairman. Wyatt's persona as a pro wrestling Mr. Rogers was tremendous, but what made the vignettes compelling was the unsettling tone that weaved throughout each promo, letting the audience know that something about this was horribly, horribly wrong.

In his "pilot" episode, Wyatt noted that he "used to be a *very* bad man" but assured the audience that this part of him was dead. He then took a chainsaw to a cardboard cutout of his previous look to symbolically prove it and closed the segment by telling his "fireflies" as he looked into the camera, "I'll always light the way and all you have to do… is let me in…"

Similar segments aired in the weeks that followed. Then, on the May 13, 2019 episode of *Raw,* Wyatt revealed a "secret." There was still darkness inside him, he told the audience. But now he knew how to harness it. Wyatt turned his back to the camera and after a few camera cuts to abandoned toys, a monster out of a horror film appeared in Wyatt's place. The figure wore a long leather jacket, red striped pants, and facial covering that resembled that time The Joker wore his own severed face as a mask.[127] The look was, how you say,

---

[127] The Fiend's mask was actually created by legendary horror makeup artist Tom Savini, who is credited with the special effects and prosthetic work in

"nightmare fuel."

Soon after, Wyatt would explain that his new identity was called "The Fiend" and that he was there "to protect us." Interestingly enough, Wyatt seemingly laid the groundwork for The Fiend character in a 2015 WWE YouTube series called "Superstar Ghost Stories." Wyatt's haunting tale recounted a childhood incident with a creature who, in hindsight, sounds eerily similar to what fans saw debut in 2019.

> "I grew up in south-central Louisiana. Abigail rescued me and my brothers and sisters. She took us to this cabin in the middle of nowhere. It was freedom. But even the greatest freedom comes at a price. She told us, 'Beware of the man in the woods, for he is real and he is The Eater. One day, me and my brothers took our slingshots to go rabbit hunting like we do. We started to hear something strange. At first, we passed it off as a bear. As time passed, the bear - or what we thought was a bear - started to get louder and louder. He let out these sad howls.
>
> My brothers, they started to run. I myself must admit that for a second I was afraid, but I was more intrigued than anything else. I dropped my slingshot and I started moving closer and closer towards the sound. I got so close at one point that the sound started to radiate in my ears and it hurt. That is when I saw it. He was about seven-foot tall walking upright, no pigment in his skin - he was as pale as a pearl. He had thin yellow hairs running all the way down to his knees and he was carrying an alligator with one hand, all the way down the beach line. I prayed, I prayed that he wouldn't see me. I said, 'Abigail, please. Forgive me. Forgive me for not paying attention to you.' And that's when he looked at

---

such films as *Friday the 13th* and *The Texas Chainsaw Massacre 2*.

me. His eyes were yellow like a cat. And still, I stayed frozen in fear. It was just then, he reaches out his hand and in the middle of it was my slingshot. I started to run as fast as my legs could take me. I continued to run for what felt like an eternity.

Finally, the cabin was back in my eyesight. I spring in through the door and I was in a panic. I ran straight to Abby's room and I said, 'Abby, I'm so sorry.' She said, 'Baby Bray, what is wrong?' I said, 'I saw him. I saw the man in the woods. I thought it was a lie but you were telling the truth the whole time. I'm so sorry.' She said, 'Baby, baby, baby. What did he say to you?' 'What? He didn't say anything. Matter of fact, all he did - he looked right at me with his eyes, as if he were staring right through me. And he held out his hand, Abby, and in his hand was my slingshot.' Inside, I was wondering, 'why is she so calm right now?' And she said, 'Baby, don't you understand, Bray? It's his slingshot, too. You *are* the man in the woods.'"

The mind of Bray Wyatt is a fascinating place to visit.

Wyatt's new alter ego appeared in the flesh for the first time on the July 15 episode of *Raw* by attacking Finn Bálor, the man with whom "The Fiend" would make his in-ring debut against at *SummerSlam* the following month. The Fiend dominated the match, ultimately winning with a new finisher, The Mandible Claw. Fans were enthralled, which turned out to be not such a great thing.

Seeing the excitement and intrigue surrounding this new character, WWE decided to hotshot Wyatt into the Universal championship[128] picture right away. This was a poor decision on multiple fronts. First, The Fiend did not strike anyone as a real goal-driven guy, so

---

[128] Of all the ridiculous championship names in all the ridiculous wrestling promotions, this one stands alone.

championship aspirations didn't make a ton of sense. Similar to Batman's greatest adversary or Aaron Rodgers and the Green Bay Packers, "It's not about the money, it's about sending a message." The Fiend existed to heal Bray Wyatt by hurting those who would hurt him. That's his story. It even said so on his gloves! Second, The Fiend was a seemingly unstoppable supernatural force. The moment you put a championship title on him, you have handcuffed your company's top prize and placed an expiration date on your monster's specialness. The only way to successfully book a Fiend championship victory would be to have him win the Universal title and promptly destroy it for being some false idol; but then you'd run into the problem of The Fiend becoming an immediate babyface for having destroyed a title as preposterously named as the "Universal Championship," so… I digress.

After attacking Universal champion Seth Rollins at *Clash of Champions*, a Hell in a Cell match was made for the creatively named *Hell in a Cell* pay-per-view. Dave Meltzer undersold his review when he called this match, "perhaps the worst main event in pro wrestling history where the fault doesn't at all lie in either of the competitors."

This match was a total and complete disaster. Rollins and The Fiend were already behind the eight-ball just due to the circumstances surrounding the match. Rollins was on a babyface run at the time, but in practicality, he should have always been a heel. Despite his exceptional abilities in the ring, there's just something about the guy that makes you want to smack him – which is actually a great quality in a wrestler (provided he's not supposed to be cheered, which he was at the time). Meanwhile, The Fiend was *cool*. He was a bad guy, yes, but in a Freddy Krueger sort of way. Fans wanted to cheer for him. So there was that. Then there was the added complication of the cage match, which should pretty much always be a feud-ender. Cages are for when all other options have been exhausted so two men are forced to enter a cell and only one is allowed to walk out. You're not supposed to *start* a feud in a cage because there's no logical next step for the feud to go.

Then came the psychology of the match itself, which was a train wreck. Not only did the match take place inside a cage - which, though good for television, is a challenge for in-person viewing - but the arena lighting switched to a bright red color to add a "Fiendish" ambiance to the match. This actually made it even harder to see the action, which in hindsight may have been a blessing. Rollins used his curb stomp finisher ELEVEN times and added one Pedigree for good measure ... and The Fiend kicked out at one ELEVEN times and at two on the twelfth pinfall attempt. Rollins also used a chair, a ladder, and a literal metal toolbox against The Fiend to no avail. The end of the match saw Rollins bury The Fiend in weapons and then hit the pile with a sledgehammer, which caused the referee to disqualify him. You may be thinking to yourself, "but I thought cage matches couldn't end in disqualification" and you'd be correct; they don't. You may also be thinking to yourself, "didn't Triple H use sledgehammers in, like, basically every Hell in a Cell match?" and, uh huh, yeah. You might even be wondering, "why did the sledgehammer get Rollins disqualified, but not the chair, ladder, or toolbox?" and yup, that, too.

When paramedics arrived to tend to The Fiend, he got up and slapped the Mandible Claw on Rollins. Then he connected with his Sister Abigail finisher twice, with one coming on the exposed concrete, before locking in one more Mandible Claw as the show closed.

Fans booed the match mercilessly. Chants of "refund" and "A-E-W" echoed throughout the Golden 1 Center. #CancelWWENetwork trended on Twitter. It was a rough night to be World Wrestling Entertainment.

Later that month came a rough night to be a World Wrestling entertainer. While The Fiend defeated Seth Rollins to win the Universal title at *Crown Jewel* in Jeddah, Saudi Arabia, more than 175 WWE performers, production crew members, and employees were stranded on the tarmac after boarding a plane set to return to the

United States after the show. The official reason for the delay was "mechanical issues." However, the Hindustan Times painted a much more concerning picture. Hugo Savinovich asserted the Saudi Arabian government - which negotiated a ten-year partnership with WWE in 2018 - owed the company somewhere between $300 and $500 million for previous shows in the country. The story claimed that when Vince McMahon did not receive his money, he cut the video feed for South Arabia; in retaliation, Saudi Crown Prince Mohammed bin Salman - whom the United States Central Intelligence Agency determined with "high confidence" had ordered the murder of Washington Post journalist Jamal Khashoggi one year earlier - prevented the WWE plane from leaving the country. If that story is true, the WWE had found itself in a hostage situation in a country not exactly celebrated for its embracement of human rights. Complicating matters was the fact that McMahon and several others of high-rank within the WWE chartered private planes and left the country before this incident occurred. One can imagine how well that went over with those left behind. The primary plane carrying most of the talent and staff did return safely to stateside roughly twenty-four hours later, but those on-board were understandably upset, and a significant portion of the WWE fan base remains unsettled to this day by the company's continued relationship with the Saudi Arabian government.

Post-*Crown Jewel*, The Fiend re-engaged with old Wyatt rival Daniel Bryan, headlining matches at *Survivor Series* and *Royal Rumble*, with a short tormenting of The Miz and his family sandwiched in between.

The Fiend's reign of invincibility then inexplicably ended in Riyadh, Saudi Arabia when he was defeated by a fifty-three-year-old Goldberg in less than three minutes. The intent of the outcome was to set up a Goldberg versus Roman Reigns dream match at *WrestleMania 36*; however, this would not happen out of an abundance of caution for Reigns' health as a leukemia survivor amidst the COVID-19 pandemic. The Fiend, on the other hand, immediately moved on to a *WrestleMania* program with John Cena that resulted in the fan favorite "Firefly Fun House" match. Another cinematic-style masterpiece, Wyatt guided Cena through a bizarre, distorted, and occasionally revisionist history of both their careers. The Fiend ultimately got the win, Wyatt's first-ever at *WrestleMania*, six years after his first match at the event.

The Fiend went on to revisit feuds with former Wyatt Family stablemates Braun Strowman and Randy Orton in 2020. His summer program with Strowman included a "Wyatt Swamp Fight," a second Universal title reign (though he would lose the belt in a triple threat match against Strowman and Roman Reigns a week later), and the addition of the Harley Quinn to his Joker in Alexa Bliss. The feud seemingly ended at *TLC* in December when Orton set The Fiend on fire in a "Firefly Inferno Match." The Fiend would not be seen again until *Fastlane* the following March, when his charred body was resurrected, setting up a match between Orton and The Fiend at *WrestleMania 37*. Once again, though, the *'Mania* match was a letdown. A distraction from Alexa Bliss led The Fiend to lose in less than six minutes. Wyatt returned to the Firefly Fun House the night after *WrestleMania* and announced to fans that he felt "reborn" and closed the segment by declaring, "Everything will be fine because he will return!" But return he would not. Wyatt never reemerged and was released from his contract on July 31, 2021, an announcement that stunned the pro wrestling world.

As a talent, Bray Wyatt was undeniable. There's no other way to describe a character that was voted Best Gimmick by the Wrestling Observer Newsletter readership in both 2013 and 2019 for two different sides of the same man. However, the wild inconsistencies in his booking over the years also proved devastating to his credibility as an in-ring competitor. For as compelling as he had been in character, the fact that he received the "Worst Match of the Year" distinction four times in his seven year run in unacceptable... but also not really his fault.[129] Bray Wyatt deserved better, starting way

---

[129] WON readers gave Wyatt "Worst Match of the Year" distinction in 2014

back at *WrestleMania XXX*.

* WHAT COULD HAVE HAPPENED *

Reimagining Bray Wyatt's career is what every fantasy booker dreams of. The complicated part about rebooking Bray Wyatt is that every step of his character's journey informs the next, meaning what we might change in 2014 would ultimately impact what would happen in 2020. The Fiend is basically Bray Wyatt's "Dark Passenger," as Dexter Morgan might say. He's a vehicle of retribution for Wyatt, righting the wrongs of Wyatt's past. In theory, if we fix the wrongs so they never happen to begin with, that would therefore alter the future agenda of The Fiend, assuming The Fiend ever came into being at all. If Wyatt defeated John Cena at *WrestleMania XXX*, would a rematch between the two be necessary at *WrestleMania 36*? Maybe. But we'll get there.

First, let's fix *WrestleMania XXX*. Bray Wyatt should have won. There was a moment in the match where Wyatt presented Cena with a steel chair, knelt down, and begged Cena to swing. This should have been the pivotal point. Cena should have wrestled with the decision to build the drama, but swung over top of Wyatt and tossed the chair outside the ring. When he turned back around, Wyatt should have hit him with the Sister Abigail - for the first time in the match because it needed to be protected and not kicked out of - and pinned Cena for the win. Cena would have resisted the temptation to become the monster Wyatt wanted and it would have cost him the match. So while Wyatt would get the win, he wouldn't succeed in bringing down WWE's White Knight and the feud would

---

(vs. John Cena at *Extreme Rules*), 2017 (vs. Randy Orton at *WrestleMania 33*), 2019 (vs. Seth Rollins at *Hell in a Cell*), and 2020 (vs. Braun Strowman at *The Horror Show at Extreme Rules*). At least *Pro Wrestling Illustrated* gave him (Best) Match of the Year honors for his Last Man Standing loss to Cena at *Payback* in 2014. So there's that.

continue.

In the real timeline, Wyatt did get a win against Cena the next month at *Extreme Rules*. This would be the case in our revised timeline as well. Wyatt won the steel cage match as a result of the lights going out and a child appearing outside the cage door, eerily singing to Cena in a digitally modified voice, "He's Got the Whole World in His Hands," a staple of Wyatt's act at the time. Some have rejected this booking as too campy, but I think it's fine when taking into account the rest of the revised context. The live crowd reacted to it as intended and if Wyatt hadn't lost the first match nor been victimized by bad booking later on in his run, I posit that people would look back on this match and moment more favorably. Plus, the demon child played into the storyline – the John Cena character absolutely catered to children and Wyatt was now corrupting them, forcing Cena to doubt himself, his values, his influence, and his legacy.

Also like in the real timeline, Cena would get the win at *Payback* in a Last Man Standing match because good has to beat evil in the end. The question here though would be: at what cost? Cena would finally vanquish Wyatt, but would need to unleash a level of violence well beyond what he was comfortable with, thus compromising his moral compass. So, yes, he would win the final battle, but would he really have won the war? It would be the old myth of redemptive violence[130] in action, if you will. Wyatt would lose the match but the camera shot of him laughing from his supine position - knowing he finally coaxed the monster out of Cena - would keep Wyatt strong and credible heading into the summer.

---

[130] Redemptive violence theory espouses, in short, that violence saves; force maintains order and war brings about peace. Most level-headed philosophers consider this a myth, despite the concept's pervasiveness.

* WHAT WOULD HAVE HAPPENED NEXT *

Cena would grapple with his actions over the next several months, leveraging his newfound aggression to win the WWE championship at *Money in the Bank* before realizing that wasn't the kind of champion he wanted to be... and then subsequently getting squashed into oblivion by Brock Lesnar (as he did in reality) at *SummerSlam* because he could no longer trust himself after his feud with Wyatt.

Wyatt, meanwhile, would be kept off television until the June 30 episode of *Raw* when he would attack a returning Chris Jericho, setting up a summer program between the two. Just like in the real timeline, the feud would focus on the concept of salvation due to Wyatt taking umbrage with Jericho's "Save Us Y2J" gimmick. After moving past Jericho at *SummerSlam*, Wyatt could "free" his followers, Luke Harper and Erick Rowan, as he did in the real timeline. Wyatt's *Survivor Series* program with Dean Ambrose would not include a hologram or exploding television, but he would spoil Daniel Bryan's return to the ring at the *Royal Rumble*, setting up a *WrestleMania 31* program between the two.

In the real timeline, Wyatt lost to The Undertaker at *WrestleMania 31*. In the revised timeline, there are two other options for The Deadman. The first would be Cena, who defeated Rusev at the event for the U.S. title, effectively ending the Bulgarian Brute's viability for the remainder of his run in the company. The second option would be the dream match on every wrestling fan's wish list: The Undertaker versus Sting. Sting debuted at *Survivor Series* the previous November and battled Triple H in a nonsensical cluster at *WrestleMania 31*. Because The Undertaker's *WrestleMania* win streak ended at the hands of Brock Lesnar the previous year, The Deadman wasn't going to lose again at *WrestleMania 31*. Had he won, Wyatt over The Undertaker here would have made good sense, but with Taker suddenly needing a win, Sting might have been the guy to put him over.

In this scenario, Bryan would get the win against Wyatt at *WrestleMania*, as he would need a big victory to get back into the WWE title picture (even though head trauma would put a stop to that soon after *WrestleMania*). On the other end, Wyatt would have built up enough equity by this point to be able to take the loss and remain a credible threat. Not only that, he would have already had a major singles victory over Bryan at the previous year's *Royal Rumble* and their feud would be reignited in the future when Bryan came out of retirement and Wyatt transformed into The Fiend.

Another potential *WrestleMania* option for Wyatt might have been his pal, Luke Harper. The world finally got to see the sort of performer Harper could be if given the opportunity when he left WWE and joined AEW under his previous alias of Brodie Lee in 2020. Though his life was tragically cut short as a result of idiopathic pulmonary fibrosis in December of 2020, Brodie Lee absolutely proved he belonged at the top of the card. Perhaps instead of simply being released by Wyatt, Harper would rebel against his commander, leading to a match for his freedom at *WrestleMania*. Rowan would be loyal to Wyatt until '*Mania*, when he would betray Bray and assist Harper in victory. The schism would lead to the introduction of Wyatt's new henchman, Braun Strowman, upon his return in August.

Depending on which path we choose, Wyatt would either begin a program with Strowman against Harper and Rowan, or do battle with Sting at *SummerSlam*. Wyatt has long wished for a match against The Stinger, even challenging WCW's franchise player in 2020 to a "Chainsaw Match" during *Halftime Heat* on Super Bowl Sunday. I'm not condoning this particular idea, merely noting that it's a match Wyatt said he'd like to have. It also goes without saying that WWE didn't get much out of Sting, as he only wrestled four matches before a neck injury forced him into (pre-AEW) retirement. In the revised timeline, after a meaningful loss to The Undertaker at *WrestleMania 31*, Sting would be back in the ring against a much younger opponent in Bray Wyatt at *SummerSlam* with Braun Strowman debuting to give

Wyatt an undeserved win. This would also allow WWE to go over on a former WCW talent (which they love) by putting over a younger star (which they don't do enough).

By October, Wyatt's actions would realign with the real timeline for a *Hell in a Cell* match against Roman Reigns, along with the post-main event beatdown of The Undertaker to set up a match at *Survivor Series* with Wyatt and Strowman defeating The Undertaker and Kane. This would appear to be the end of the line for The Phenom… until the *Royal Rumble*. Wyatt would be cleaning house in the Rumble match, looking poised to headline *WrestleMania* when the lights would go out and the bell would toll. When the lights come up, The Undertaker and Wyatt would be alone in the ring. The Deadman would take Wyatt by the throat and chokeslam him over the ropes before turning his head to face the *WrestleMania* sign atop the arena.

At *WrestleMania 32* in Dallas, Texas, Wyatt would cement his status as the "New Face of Fear" by defeating The Undertaker. The next month, he would topple Kane at *Payback* and declare to his Family that their work here was done before disappearing for several months.

In the summer of 2016, the WWE would hold its Draft, where performers would become exclusive to either *Raw* or *Smackdown*. Since none of the Wyatt Family would have been on television in recent months, they would each be conveniently left out of the draft process, free to re-debut on their own terms. This would make more sense than splitting them up via a Draft, as it doesn't seem within their characters to have their whereabouts or alignment dictated to them by brand loyalty. Instead, Wyatt would simply reemerge on *Smackdown* following *SummerSlam* and begin the same feud he did in reality with Randy Orton.

After battling against one another for months, Wyatt and Orton would team up and become Tag Team champions by *TLC* in December. However, seeing Orton for the snake that he was, Harper would try to open Wyatt's eyes to the truth but Wyatt - either through ignorance or arrogance - would refuse to listen, leading to a match between master and apprentice at *Royal Rumble*, which Wyatt would win. Orton, meanwhile, would win the Rumble match to punch his ticket to *WrestleMania*. At the next month's *Elimination Chamber* pay-per-view, Orton and Harper would square off, while Wyatt would win the WWE title to set up a match between him and Orton at '*Mania*, which Wyatt - in this timeline - would win.

Also at *WrestleMania 33* would be the three-way dance WWE never managed to put together on the Show of Shows: Seth Rollins versus Dean Ambrose versus Roman Reigns. These three were always magic in the ring together and, with all due respect to Baron Corbin and Triple H, people would have much rather seen The Shield battling for the Universal title in one match instead of as babyfaces in three separate non-title singles contests. Reigns would prevail and hold the title until dropping it to Samoa Joe at *Extreme Rules*.

After defeating Randy Orton, Wyatt would move on to a feud with AJ Styles… and this is where the wheels would begin to fall off his creepy little wagon. Styles would take the WWE championship at *Money in the Bank* in June and Wyatt would subsequently relocate to the *Raw* brand where he would briefly (and unsuccessfully) engage with Seth Rollins. From there, he would begin his ill-fated feud with Finn Bálor, ultimately leading to a program and partnership with Matt Hardy. Just as in the real timeline, Wyatt and Hardy would battle, then pair up, eventually winning the Tag Team titles before losing them to The B-Team - Bo Dallas and Curtis Axel - at *Extreme Rules 2018*. Hardy would be sidelined shortly thereafter and Wyatt would be decimated by Bálor's "Demon King" alter ego at *SummerSlam*, putting him out of action until the following summer.

Enter The Fiend. Bray Wyatt's inner monster would be unleashed for the first time in-person at *SummerSlam 2019* and would completely squash Bálor - armed with his usually unbeatable Demon King persona - sending him back to NXT. The Fiend's next target would be Seth Rollins at *Hell in a Cell*, though the WWE title would not be involved (Rollins would have dropped that to Braun Strowman at *Night of Champions* the previous month) nor would referees attempt to stop the match. The Fiend would just ravage Rollins. At *Survivor Series* he would demolish The B-Team and at *TLC*, he would dispatch of the Hardy Boyz.

A few things about The Fiend would soon become clear. First, his motivation was vengeance, as his targets would not be random, but deliberate. Bálor embarrassed Bray Wyatt two years in a row. Rollins was a chosen one while Wyatt was cast aside. The B-Team - which consisted of Wyatt's real-life brother, Bo Dallas, and his first WWE tag team partner, Curtis Axel (the Michael McGillicutty to Bray Wyatt's Husky Harris) - left his side when he needed them most early in his career and then seized the opportunity later to take his gold for their own. Matt Hardy abandoned Wyatt only to reunite with his own brother, Jeff. Those "Hurt" and "Heal" inscriptions on his gloves would be true - The Fiend would need to hurt those who hurt Bray in order to heal Bray.

The second hallmark of The Fiend is that no opponent would be the same again after interacting with him. The Fiend wouldn't just be a demon, but a virus, infecting all who fought back against him. Some, like Rollins and Bálor, would turn heel themselves. Others, like the B-Team, would simply disappear.

The Fiend would defeat one of Wyatt's greatest rivals, Daniel Bryanat the *Royal Rumble*, before battling against Roman Reigns at *WrestleMania 36*. This would be the trickiest match to pull off, due to the COVID-19 pandemic and Reigns (justifiably) pulling out of the event due to being immunocompromised after battling leukemia. In theory, since the match between the two would be cinematic, it could have been filmed before the pandemic really got out of control, though that's much easier to put into words than action, especially using hindsight history. If a match with Reigns couldn't happen, the WWE would still have John Cena tucked away in case of emergency for a Firefly Funhouse match on short-notice, especially with the script for Cena and Reigns being fairly interchangeable at that point.

After writing off Reigns (or Cena) for the summer, The Fiend would move on to Braun Strowman with all the campy bells and whistles that feud enjoyed, before Reigns returned to heel out at *SummerSlam* and take the Universal title at *Payback*. This would lead to Wyatt's program with Randy Orton and him being sent back to the underworld extra crispy after the Firefly Inferno match at *TLC*. This would be the death of The Fiend. Bray Wyatt would be the one resurrected, finally free from the grip of his "dark passenger." The purified new version of Wyatt would no longer feel the urge to hurt, but rather an obligation to heal.

Of course, in an artform predicated on simulated violence, healing *instead* of hurting would be a difficult gimmick to pull off with success - which is exactly why the creative mind of Bray Wyatt is the perfect vessel for such a task. Whether settling scores with a truly despicable character like Randy Orton, or confronting those more traditionally heelish than explicitly evil like AJ Styles, or even exploring some gray areas in between with fellow enigmas like Aleister Black, another evolution in the Bray Wyatt character would give more life to one of WWE's most fascinating creations.

The company never did solve its Bray Wyatt conundrum, though. After being released from the WWE in July of 2021, many theorized that the man would be a natural fit to lead – or possibly torment – the Dark Order in AEW. The late Brodie Lee was billed as "The Exalted One;" perhaps Windham Rotunda could come to embody the antithesis of that. Then again, any storyline that might invoke the memory of Brodie Lee could hit too close to home.

One could also imagine a feud with AEW's resident gatekeeper – and Husky Harris' old NXT pro – Cody Rhodes. Wyatt planted the seeds for a feud between the two in 2019, tweeting of Rhodes' influence on Harris: "He was his partner. He trusted him. He was ridiculed in front of the world, for someone else's failed attempt at fame. It destroyed him. And from his ashes a butterfly was born. But the memory remains." That tweet was sent just nine days before AEW's first *ALL OUT* pay-per-view – far from coincidental timing – leading fans to believe that their story may not be fully told yet.

Unlike his cryptic social media posts, though, this much is clear: the artist formerly known as Bray Wyatt still holds all the pieces to become a top-level star. And that reality keeps hope alive for the possibility that perhaps his next reincarnation – wherever and whenever it may be – will be the one that finally defines and cements his legacy.

… WRESTLING REWRITTEN

FIFTEEN

THE "1" IN 21-1

"I wanted to save it for somebody who needed it. I personally didn't think Brock needed it."

April 6, 2014
Mercedes-Benz Superdome ⊙ *New Orleans, Louisiana*
WWE WrestleMania XXX

Brock Lesnar defeated The Undertaker by pinfall (25:12).

* WHAT REALLY HAPPENED *

There are few circumstances in athletics more revered than a streak. In baseball, Joe DiMaggio's 56-game hit streak is an untouchable mark, matched only in veneration by Cal Ripken Jr.'s consecutive game streak of 2,632. In hockey, Wayne Gretzky's 51-game point streak seems unlikely to ever be bested, while Brett Favre's 297 straight starts on the gridiron is the stuff of legend.

Despite being predetermined in nature, professional wrestling has had its share of iconic streaks as well. Bruno Sammartino held onto the World (Wide) Wrestling Federation championship for an incredible 2,803 days - seven years, eight months, and one day - before his shocking defeat at the hands of "The Russian Bear" Ivan Koloff at Madison Square Garden in 1971. André the Giant famously went without being pinned or submitted in a W(W)WF match from 1973-87 before being defeated by Hulk Hogan at *WrestleMania III*. Bill Goldberg's undefeated streak reached 173 before his run was ended through unscrupulous means by Kevin Nash at *Starrcade 1998*.

But the most famous pro wrestling streak of the modern era came to an end on April 6, 2014 at the Mercedes-Benz Superdome in New Orleans, La. when Brock Lesnar left the *WrestleMania XXX* audience in stunned silence by conquering The Undertaker to become the "1" in The Deadman's 21-and-1 record at The Showcase of the Immortals.

"The Streak" officially began with an Undertaker win over Jimmy "Superfly" Snuka at *WrestleMania VII* in 1991. A year later, he defeated Jake "The Snake" Roberts for his second *WrestleMania* victory and his first as a fan favorite.

That was almost the end of it right there. "The Streak" - if one could call it that at the time – came close to snapping in 1993. The Undertaker had petitioned Vince McMahon to square off with Yokozuna, a near six-hundred-pound super heavyweight who debuted with the company the previous October and was quickly becoming the top heel in the WWF. Despite The Undertaker's request, McMahon had other plans at the time. While Yokozuna would leave *WrestleMania IX* with the WWF title, The Undertaker would be put down by a different monster: Giant González.

Billed at eight-feet tall - though in reality he was "only" seven-foot-seven – Jorge "Giant" González had been a third-round selection of the Atlanta Hawks in the 1988 NBA Draft. When injuries quickly derailed his basketball career, Hawks owner Ted Turner offered González a different opportunity to remain on Turner's payroll as a professional wrestler in World Championship Wrestling. González made his WCW debut as "El Gigante" at *Capital Combat* in May of 1990 and spent the next year-and-a-half with the company before taking his talents north to the World Wrestling Federation in 1993.

González made a memorable debut at the 1993 *Royal Rumble* in January. While wearing a full bodysuit - complete with airbrushed muscles and glued-on fur - González sent The Undertaker over the top rope with a giant sized chop to the chest, which, as it turned out, was really the full extent of González's in-ring ability.

Nevertheless, González was cast as the WWF's next monster heel and, as rumor has it, was actually slated to defeat The Undertaker at *WrestleMania IX* before being penciled in for a program with outgoing top babyface, Hulk Hogan. The Hulkster allegedly nixed those plans, but it also wasn't long before the WWF realized González's significant athletic limitations as well. The company still hoped to get some mileage out of González, though, so in lieu of a definitive outcome at *WrestleMania*, González was disqualified for rendering The Undertaker unconscious with a rag soaked in chloroform - an illegal action in wrestling and really most situations in life. Of course, no one told the fans that's what was happening, so to the live audience at Caesars Palace, it all just looked like very slow, uninteresting attempted murder.

While the DQ win over Giant González ended up being the only non-definitive *WrestleMania* outcome on The Deadman's resume, that decision had nothing to do with preserving The Streak because no one in the WWF was even aware that a streak had been building at all until around *WrestleMania X-8* in 2002.

"That was the start of it," The Undertaker told Steve Austin in a 2020 episode of *The Broken Skull Sessions* on WWE Network. "After that, it kind of took on a life of its own and it just kind of magnified each year because the lore and the legacy and the mystique of the whole thing continued to grow year after year. It became almost as important as the main event was."

It wasn't until 2005 that The Streak became a storyline heading into *WrestleMania*. On the March 7, 2005 episode of *Monday Night Raw*, the "Legend Killer" Randy Orton vowed to do what no man had done before: defeat The Undertaker at *WrestleMania*. From that point forward, The Streak became a featured *WrestleMania* attraction. Each year, The Undertaker's win streak appeared in more peril than the year before… and each year, The Deadman would weather the storm to leave *WrestleMania* with his legacy not only intact, but stronger than ever.

That is, until 2014.

It's not that Brock Lesnar was an unworthy adversary. Quite the opposite. As Paul Heyman has been known to say, "Work or shoot, when it comes to Brock Lesnar, the finish is usually the same." In other words, the dude is as legit as they come.

Lesnar was a two-time Big Ten Conference Champion at the University of Minnesota in 1999 and 2000 and won the NCAA Division I Heavyweight title in 2000. When he made his WWE debut in the spring of 2002, he was billed by Heyman as "The Next Big Thing" - and that was the truth. He won the Undisputed title from The Rock at *SummerSlam 2002* just 126 days into his WWE career and – at twenty-five years old – made himself the youngest primary champion in company history to that point.

When Lesnar decided to "put his WWE career on hold" in 2004, he moved on to the National Football League where he earned a preseason look with the Minnesota Vikings despite not having played football since high school, a fact that speaks to the true freakishness of Lesnar's athleticism. Three years later, he joined the Ultimate Fighting Championship (UFC) and on November 15, 2008, he defeated Randy Couture by technical knockout to become the UFC Heavyweight champion, making him the only man in history to win the NCAA, WWE, and UFC Heavyweight titles.

Also among Lesnar's accolades was an unbeaten record against The Undertaker. During Lesnar's initial run in the WWE, he and The Undertaker headlined three pay-per-views together, all for the WWE Heavyweight title. *Unforgiven 2002* ended in a no-contest, while Lesnar came away with wins against The Deadman at both *No Mercy 2002* and *No Mercy 2003*. The chemistry between the two men was clear, which is why WWE actually tried to orchestrate a comeback match for Lesnar against The Undertaker at *WrestleMania XXVII*.

"Lesnar had basically told Vince McMahon that to do the match, [it would be] The Undertaker's streak against the UFC Champion," Dave Meltzer of the Wrestling Observer Newsletter reported.

And so, The Undertaker showed up at UFC 121 in October 2010 to set up the angle.

"I was there to pick a fight," The Deadman recalled for ESPN's Ariel Helwani a decade later in 2020. "There was no personal animosity, really, but it was basically me saying, 'Aright, you left our world. I'm going to come into your world and I'm gonna call you out,' and, you know, that was it."

The attempt was in vain, however. Lesnar ended up losing the UFC title to Cain Velasquez that night, removing any possibility of a "UFC Champion versus The Streak" match. Perhaps more significantly, though, was the fact that UFC President Dana White had no idea such plans between the WWE and his reigning champion were even taking place. Lesnar was negotiating with WWE on his own, which Vince McMahon and The Undertaker did not realize. When McMahon called White to work out the details of the proposed *WrestleMania* bout, White put the kibosh on the whole deal. Without Lesnar on the card, John Cena and The Miz ended up in the main event slot for the pay-per-view while The Undertaker matched up with Triple H in the undercard.

Lesnar did ultimately return to the WWE a year later, though, and after programs with John Cena, Triple H, and CM Punk, rekindling a rivalry with The Undertaker seemed not only inevitable, but natural. The match was made on the February 24, 2014 episode of *Raw* after Paul Heyman insisted the only way that Lesnar would perform at *WrestleMania XXX* was if he had the opportunity to "conquer history." The Undertaker considered that a challenge and put Lesnar through a table before turning to face the *WrestleMania* sign, indicating his intentions.

Given his track record at *WrestleMania* and the fact that The

Deadman had never beaten Lesnar before, The Undertaker came into the Mercedes-Benz Superdome as a *heavy* favorite to win. The Vegas line hit -3000 in The Phenom's favor prior to the event. To put that in context, Daniel Bryan - whose victory in the main event seemed like the surest of sure things, lest the Superdome be burned to the ground - sat at -700 in the Bovada sportsbook. People were *very* confident that The Undertaker was moving on to 22-0.

People were wrong.

At the end of a slow, methodical match that lasted more than twenty-five minutes and saw The Undertaker suffer a severe concussion within the first five, Brock Lesnar kicked out of a Tombstone Piledriver and countered another attempt into an F-5 for the 1-2-3.

"The Streak...is over," Michael Cole uttered in a rare instance of authentic astonishment.

Some fans reacted with outrage, others with visible sadness. But the overwhelming majority of the more than 60,000 fans in attendance at the Mercedes-Benz Superdome that evening were left looking on in stunned silence. WWE does deserve credit for that; regardless of whether ending The Streak was the right decision or not, the result of the match elicited genuine emotion, which is really what this whole pro wrestling game is about. To that end, they succeeded.

But was it the "right" decision? That's a debate that will be argued about for quite some time.

* WHAT COULD HAVE HAPPENED *

Gamblers learned a valuable lesson about trying to predict Vince McMahon that night in New Orleans. The interesting part - or perhaps infuriating part, depending on how much money you lost betting on The Undertaker - is that had the match occurred earlier in the day, the outcome would have been different. The Undertaker had been penciled in to win until about four hours before showtime, when The Chairman made the call to reverse course and end The Streak.

"I showed up thinking I was going over," The Undertaker told CBSSports.com six years after the match. "I found out about 1 p.m. that I wasn't. It is what it is."

McMahon justified the decision on *The Stone Cold Podcast* in 2014 by saying it was time to end The Streak and, based on the talent roster at-hand, Lesnar was the most appropriate man to do it.

"You have to make difficult decisions sometimes," McMahon said. "I think I made the right call at the right time."

At the time, McMahon believed The Deadman's days in the ring were likely behind him after *WrestleMania XXX*. Fair enough. The Undertaker was forty-nine years old and his age was beginning to show. Oh, and he straight-up collapsed after walking through the curtain post-match and had to spend the night in the hospital. It was so serious that McMahon even left his post at *WrestleMania* to ride in the ambulance with him.

"My memory of that day stops at about 3:30 in the afternoon," The Undertaker recalled on *The Bill Simmons Podcast*. "I have no recollection of the match. It was four in the morning before I even knew what my name was."

So that's not great. But then of course, The Undertaker was back on the big stage the very next *WrestleMania* for another match. And the year after that. And the year after that. And the year after that. Not the one after that, but definitely the one *after* that one. The Undertaker actually performed at five more *WrestleMania*s after The Streak ended, and it's not like Mark Calaway just happened to be driving through the area every year... McMahon actively decided to keep bringing him back.

Now, as far as who should have ended The Streak, there's little debate that Brock Lesnar was the most credible opponent *that year* (and, in fairness, maybe any year), but he was not the *only* option.

"I wanted to save [ending The Streak] for somebody who needed it," The Undertaker said in 2020. "I personally didn't think Brock needed it. Brock was 'made,' and beating me - I don't think - was going to elevate Brock that much more."

So, in the words of Vince McMahon himself, "When you look at that talent roster, who was it going to be?"

McMahon's answer to his own rhetorical question was "no one." However, The Deadman did have someone in mind.

"If it was gonna happen, I would have much rather done it for Roman [Reigns]," The Undertaker confessed on *The Broken Skull Sessions*. "It would have meant so much more to Roman."

There was no animosity between Lesnar and The Undertaker. But from the grander view, Roman Reigns was absolutely the right choice… provided he would then take the win and lean all the way into the easiest heel turn in pro wrestling history. Unfortunately, fans got to see how WWE Creative would have handled it in 2017 when Reigns became the second and, to this day, only other man to defeat The Undertaker at *WrestleMania*. On the *Raw* after *WrestleMania 33*, fans berated Reigns as he stood in the ring for a solid eight minutes before he even uttered a word. From chants of "Under-Taker" to "Roman Sucks" to "Go Away" to "F--- You, Roman," Reigns was welcomed with the kind of heat any villain would kill for. When he did finally speak, he only needed five simple words to put the audience's venom over the brink: "This is my yard now." With a smirk on his face, Reigns dropped the mic and made his exit. It was *brilliant*. And yet WWE still refused to let him embrace the bad guy role, so for three more years, Reigns remained cast as a top babyface that fans couldn't stand (which, as a reminder, is a *bad* thing).

If Reigns hadn't been the one to end The Streak, the other viable option was the man The Undertaker squared off with in his first match post-Streak, Bray Wyatt. Fans have fantasy rebooked Wyatt over The Undertaker at *WrestleMania 31* since the day it went down.[131] In reality, Wyatt was dead in the water as soon as that match was made since there was no way The Undertaker was losing at back-to-back *WrestleMania*s. Had The Phenom defeated Lesnar the year prior, though, Wyatt going over at *WrestleMania 31* would have made a lot of sense. And if Wyatt had beaten John Cena at *WrestleMania XXX*, then WWE would have had an unquestioned main event heel right then and there. Back-to-back *WrestleMania* victories over John Cena and The Undertaker? Bray Wyatt would have been a made-man for the rest of his career.

Now, it should be noted that if The Undertaker headed into *WrestleMania* with The Streak still intact against either Reigns or Wyatt, it would have been much less likely to pull off a truly shocking loss, since putting over an up-and-coming superstar would have been, you know, logical. I would contend, however, that whoever beat The Streak would have A) received the massive lifelong recognition of being the one man to finally beat The Undertaker, and B) been Public Enemy No. 1 for a significant period of time as a result of putting The Deadman out of his misery. The shock that came with Lesnar winning was good in the moment, but I do believe that substance outweighs surprise in the long run.

Besides, just because a result might be predictable doesn't necessarily mean it's bad. At *WrestleMania XXX*, we all knew Daniel Bryan was going to win; but knowing that beforehand didn't make seeing it any less satisfying. It was the right ending for that story. On the opposite end of the emotional spectrum, we knew at *WrestleMania XXIV* that it was time for Ric Flair to ride off into the sunset. It was sad to see Shawn Michaels tearfully tell his idol, "I'm sorry, I love you," before driving his foot into the Nature Boy's chin… but it was the beautiful,

---

[131] What a bunch of marks…

heart-wrenching conclusion the story deserved.

It is also possible that the story of The Streak didn't warrant an Undertaker loss at all. The Streak could have lived forever, as many fans - and colleagues of The Undertaker - would have preferred. That option would fly in the face of conventional wrestling wisdom, wherein a departing wrestler goes out on his back. However, The Undertaker resided at a level of veneration and respect that few in the industry could ever dream to achieve, so no one would have blinked had he taken The Streak with him to the proverbial grave.

Then again, Brock Lesnar wasn't necessarily the "wrong" choice. In Mick Foley's 2015 standup comedy special *Cheap Pops*, he explained why that is pretty succinctly: "There's never going to come a moment in time when you look at your television screen at the image of Brock Lesnar and go, '[Gasp!] He's a nice guy!' Because he's not! And that's what makes him the perfect person to end The Streak."

So why then after all these years is The Streak storyline still so controversial to so many? Perhaps it has more to do with what happened - or didn't happen - as a result.

* WHAT WOULD HAVE HAPPENED NEXT *

The most disappointing aspect of The Undertaker's *WrestleMania XXX* loss to Brock Lesnar was not the loss itself, or even the fact that it was Lesnar who ended The Streak. It was that ending The Streak didn't result in a true benefit for anyone.

As The Undertaker accurately asserted, Lesnar never needed The Streak. He was already a main eventer with a Hall of Fame resume. Even though Heyman did successfully work conquering The Streak into every Brock Lesnar promo for basically the rest of their time together, beating The Undertaker had no real bearing on Lesnar's credibility or standing in the WWE. He was already a top guy. He still could have gone on to *SummerSlam*, destroyed John Cena, taken the WWE championship, and we all would have thought, "yeah, that makes sense, he's Brock Lesnar." He didn't need The Streak as a vehicle to get to that point.

The real problem with Lesnar ending The Streak was that the company then failed to leverage his win at *WrestleMania XXX* into creating a new star at *WrestleMania 31* as originally planned. Yes, Roman Reigns shared the main event stage with Lesnar. But he didn't win. And yes, Seth Rollins left *WrestleMania 31* with the WWE title, but he did so by cashing in a Money in the Bank contract late in the match and, more importantly, he didn't pin Lesnar! You know who did end up being the first person to pin Brock Lesnar after Lesnar ended The Streak? Bill. Freaking. Goldberg. Lesnar's first post-Streak pinfall defeat came two-and-a-half years after the fact in an eighty-five-second match against a forty-nine-year-old man who hadn't wrestled in literally twelve years. And aside from that, Lesnar's only other singles loss during that time frame came against The Undertaker - who was fifty years old - at *SummerSlam 2015* when Lesnar gave The Deadman the finger before passing out in the Hell's Gate for a technical submission defeat in a match that probably would have been beloved by fans had it occurred at *WrestleMania XXX*. So that's what WWE chose to do with The Streak's equity: invest in the past. The Streak was *wasted* and that's what made the decision to end it a colossal failure.

If Lesnar *had* to be the "1" in 21-1, then Roman Reigns should have been the one to beat the "1" in 21-1. Instead, Reigns went 1-4 in marquee matches with Lesnar, earning his only victory over The Beast Incarnate at *SummerSlam 2018*, more than four years after Lesnar ended The Streak and nearly two years after Lesnar was pinned for the first time. Seth Rollins' cash in at *WrestleMania 31* was perfectly booked, so if Reigns wasn't going to win the title then, he should have been launched into a program with Lesnar where he could get a career-defining win either at *SummerSlam 2015*, or at *WrestleMania 32* the following spring, before Lesnar went on to revisit prior feuds with old rivals.

If Reigns had gotten to The Undertaker first, Heel Roman would have needed to come out after *WrestleMania 33* in 2017. As previously discussed, the path could not have been clearer, and it would have given a unique backdrop to his brief feud with John Cena later that year. The "Big Dog" wound up as the "top dog" in the end, becoming a five-time world champion and just the ninth Grand Slam title holder in company history, but his route to glory would have been much less painful for all of us had he been the one to end The Streak. Fans still would have hated him, but at least they'd have a storyline reason to boo.

The most interesting option to have ended The Streak is still Bray Wyatt because if Wyatt had won his first two *WrestleMania* matches, his entire legacy would be *vastly* different. Even without the win against Cena at *WrestleMania XXX*, a victory over The Undertaker at *WrestleMania 31* would have been massive for Wyatt and brought a new level of gravitas to his subsequent feuds with the likes of Reigns, Dean Ambrose, and Kane. Not only that, it could have set him up for a world title run heading into *WrestleMania 32*, or even a rematch with The Deadman in Taker's home state of Texas where *'Mania* took place that year. Plus, if The Undertaker continued to hang around as long as he did in reality, perhaps a matchup with The Fiend could have been what finally sent The Phenom into retirement. Regardless, Wyatt would have been fully established as a force to be reckoned with in the WWE.

The end of The Streak will never sit well with some. It was a questionable decision at the time and that decision hasn't aged terribly well since. But if the aftermath had been booked with an eye on the future instead of a grip on the past, perhaps at least some of those who disagreed with the decision at the time could understand why it was made. Instead, we all just feel kind of sad, remembering what was and probably never will be again.

SIXTEEN

THE PHENOMENAL AEW

"When we were pitching ideas to have you guys come in, it was not going to be just the two of you. There was going to be another person, who I would not name."

October 2, 2019
Capital One Arena ⦿ Washington, D.C.
AEW Dynamite

* WHAT REALLY HAPPENED *

The landscape of professional wrestling changed forever when the World Wrestling Federation announced its purchase of World Championship Wrestling on March 24, 2001. When Extreme Championship Wrestling officially closed its doors a few days later on April 4, Vince McMahon's WWF stood tall as the industry's only mainstream television promotion left in the United States.

And it remained that way for quite some time. That's not to say other organizations didn't exist. Ring of Honor and TNA Wrestling were both born out of the ashes of the Monday Night Wars and have even stood the test of time, though neither could be considered legitimate competition to the WWE today.

TNA was close once after scoring national television contracts with Fox Sports Net and Spike TV, but when it tried to go head-to-head against the WWE behemoth in 2010, things went so poorly that the company ended up having to rebrand the following year.

And Ring of Honor certainly had the talent to compete. A significant portion of the WWE roster in the early 2020s spent time with ROH in the 2000s and 2010s, including Cesaro, Daniel Bryan, Seth Rollins,

Kevin Owens, Sami Zayn, Samoa Joe, Adam Cole, Kyle O'Reilly, Roderick Strong, Bobby Fish, Tommaso Ciampa, Damian Priest, Keith Lee, and the Viking Raiders[132]... to name just a few.

By scouting out and stockpiling the world's top independent wrestling talent, WWE was able to maintain its chokehold on mainstream appeal. But around 2017, things began to change. That was the year that Smashing Pumpkins lead singer and longtime pro wrestling fan Billy Corgan purchased the National Wrestling Alliance. It was also the year that former WWE writer Court Bauer announced the revival of his Major League Wrestling enterprise. Moreover, it was the year that Netflix broke into the pro wrestling game, picking up the first two seasons of the groundbreaking Lucha Underground promotion before launching a wildly successful fictional series of its own, *GLOW*.

Perhaps the most significant event of 2017, however, was also the calendar's first one. On January 4, 2017, New Japan Pro Wrestling's *Wrestle Kingdom* at the Tokyo Dome - hailed as "the Japanese equivalent to the Super Bowl" by Hall of Fame commentator Jim Ross - was headlined by Kenny Omega battling Kazuchika Okada for the IWGP Heavyweight title.

Okada entered the match as the heralded defending champion and leader of NJPW's "Chaos" faction, while rising star Kenny Omega headed up the villainous stable of foreigners known as "Bullet Club." Okada came away with the victory in a bout that lasted forty-six minutes and forty-five seconds. It was the longest match ever at a *Wrestle Kingdom*, and one that prompted the Wrestling Observer Newsletter's Dave Meltzer to proclaim, "Kenny Omega and Kazuchika Okada may have put on the greatest match in pro wrestling history." Meltzer, famed for his five-star grading system,

---

[132] I assume the renaming of ROH's "War Machine" came down to either "Viking Raiders" or "Patriot Cowboys." Personally, if I was going to saddle a tag team with a weird combination of pro football mascots, I'd have picked some that had won a game of significance this millennium. Oh well.

awarded the match six stars.

Wrestle Kingdom 11 was critically acclaimed from top to bottom, as the event also put a massive spotlight on the partnership between New Japan Pro Wrestling and Ring of Honor. The talent sharing arrangement led to ROH wrestlers like The Young Bucks, Adam Cole, Kyle O'Reilly, Hangman Page, and Cody Rhodes - who was granted his release from the WWE a year earlier - to perform on an international stage and in front of more than 26,000 fans at one of the world's more iconic sports venues.

A few months later, Ring of Honor set a new attendance record with a crowd of 3,500 fans at Jenkins Arena in Lakeland, Fla. for *Supercard of Honor XI* on April 1. The success of that show prompted a tweet that changed *everything*. On May 16, 2017, Twitter user @TheWWEGuy_[133] asked Dave Meltzer, "Do you think ROH can ever sell out an arena with 10k+ fans?" to which Meltzer bluntly replied, "Not any time soon." It wasn't long before Cody Rhodes chimed in: "I'll take that bet Dave. I already gave them their biggest buyrate...put The Bucks & I on the card & 3-months to promote."

The resulting event became *ALL IN*, organized by Rhodes and The Young Bucks and billed as "The Biggest Independent Wrestling Show Ever." In January of 2018 the announcement came that *ALL IN* would take place on September 1, 2018. In March, the venue for the event was revealed to be the Sears Centre in the shadows of Chicago, Ill. Despite having only one match announced for the show - a singles bout between Rhodes and Nick Aldis for the NWA Worlds Heavyweight championship - tickets to attend the event at the ten-thousand-plus-seat arena went on sale on May 13, 2018... and sold out in just twenty-nine minutes and thirty-six seconds. For the first time since 1993, a professional wrestling event in the United States not affiliated with WWE or WCW would be seen live and in-

---

[133] A name that will live in infamy. God bless you, friend.

person by an audience of more than 10,000 fans.

The final attendance number - which, full disclosure, quite proudly included yours truly - came out to 11,263. After the main event, The Young Bucks - brothers Matt and Nick Jackson - were joined in the ring by Cody Rhodes, Hangman Page, and Kenny Omega. All members of what was at that point a red-hot and babyface Bullet Club, the five men together had become collectively known as "The Elite." Matt Jackson told the still-capacity crowd, "There's a hunger. There's a thirst. You guys want good pro wrestling and good entertainment. What we presented to you in those four hours and fifty-seven minutes was our vision of what we think we can do with pro wrestling."

When the microphone made its way to Rhodes, he addressed the elephant in the room. All five men had expiring contracts and at the end of the year, the members of The Elite were set to become the biggest free agents on the pro wrestling market.

"That big question of what happens next with this group? We are sticking together. Because nobody, no man, no company, no entity, owns pro wrestling. *We* [pointing to the fans] own pro wrestling."

Needless to say, the WWE was interested - not just due to the clear drawing power of The Elite, but also, if we're being honest, to continue to avoid any real competition from other companies. As a result, WWE continually raided independent promotions for top talent. Ring of Honor stars Adam Cole, Kyle O'Reilly, and Bobby Fish defected for the WWE's NXT brand in 2017. In 2018, NXT added indy stars Ricochet, Keith Lee, Matt Riddle, and Punishment Martinez (later to be known as Damian Priest). After the success of *ALL IN*, Triple H - now serving as the WWE's COO, Executive Vice President of Global Talent Strategy Development, and Executive Producer of NXT - made acquiring The Elite in 2019 a paramount priority.

According to Meltzer, Triple H envisioned an invasion angle to begin at the 2019 *Royal Rumble* and culminate in a program payoff at *WrestleMania 35*. "Hangman" Adam Page was reportedly offered "main roster money" to work as a top star in NXT. The Young Bucks were presented with a three-year deal that included significant cash as well as a WWE Network slot for their hit YouTube series, *Being The Elite*. With the genuinely impressive self-awareness that WWE did not have a great track record in handling tag teams, the Bucks were also provided an unprecedented six-month window in which to void their contracts if they were not satisfied with the creative direction the company was giving them. Kenny Omega, fresh off of earning Pro Wrestling Illustrated's vaunted No. 1 spot in the PWI 500, was provided with a "fantastic offer." And while Cody Rhodes' request to leave WWE for the independent circuit in 2016 still flummoxed company management, Rhodes called a potential return to the company "pretty possible" just weeks after *ALL IN*.

The WWE offers for The Elite were all generous, and likely superior to anything Ring of Honor, New Japan, or Impact Wrestling could put together. What WWE did not anticipate, though, was the creation of a brand new territory - and one with the firm financial backing of a bona fide billionaire.

On November 5, 2018, trademarks were filed to create All Elite Wrestling, LLC. Trademarks for AEW, AEW All Out, All Elite Wrestling, Tuesday Night Dynamite, and AEW Double or Nothing were all linked to the address of TIAA Bank Field, home of the NFL's Jacksonville Jaguars, a franchise co-owned by auto parts billionaire Shad Khan and his son - a lifelong wrestling fan - Tony Khan.

When the clock struck midnight Pacific time on January 1, 2019, a new episode of *Being The Elite* dropped on YouTube, breaking the news that The Young Bucks, Cody Rhodes, and Hangman Page had formed All Elite Wrestling and the company's inaugural event would be called *Double or Nothing*, a play off the previous autumn's *ALL IN*. The next day, The Young Bucks and Rhodes officially signed contracts to become Executive Vice Presidents of the new venture, while Tony Khan would serve as company President. The first round of talent signings were announced at a press conference on January 8 and included former Ring of Honor stars Christopher Daniels, Scorpio Sky, Frankie Kazarian, and Hangman Page, as well as independent performers Joey Janela and Dr. Britt Baker, D.M.D., in addition to the surprise signings of former WWE superstars PAC (known in WWE as Adrian Neville) and Chris Jericho.[134] When the company held its ticket release press conference in February for the May *Double or Nothing* pay-per-view, Kenny Omega joined as AEW's fourth EVP, and two more tag teams - The Lucha Brothers and Best Friends - were added to the fold.

Ten days before *Double or Nothing*, AEW and WarnerMedia announced a historic television deal that would bring professional wrestling back to TNT for the first time since the final episode of *WCW Monday Nitro* in March of 2001. The announcement only bolstered the atmosphere for the company's debut event on Memorial Day weekend, which was highlighted by Pro Wrestling Illustrated's Match of the Year - twenty-two minutes of blood, sweat, and tears between brothers Cody and Dustin Rhodes - as well as the unannounced debut of Jon Moxley, better known to WWE fans at the time as former WWE champion and one-third of The Shield, Dean Ambrose. After Chris Jericho defeated Kenny Omega in the main event to become one of two contenders for the AEW World championship, Moxley made his debut, a la Scott Hall, coming

---

[134] Jericho made a surprise appearance at *ALL IN* the previous September. It was shocking not just because Jericho had not appeared on a non-WWE show since joining the company in 1999, but because he was actually in Little Rock, Ark. performing with his band, Fozzy, earlier in the day. He took a private jet to get to Chicago and beat down Kenny Omega later that night. It was later revealed that the man who financed the jet was none other than future AEW President, Tony Khan.

through the shocked and elated crowd at the MGM Grand Garden Arena in Las Vegas, Nev. Moxley laid out Jericho before turning his attention to Omega, with whom he brawled up the entrance ramp before ultimately tossing the "Best Bout Machine" through the stage to close the show.

Double or Nothing proved to be a tremendous success, seeing 11,000 in live attendance and garnering between 98,000 and 113,000 pay-per-view buys, making it the best-selling non-WWE or WCW pay-per-view in pro wrestling history to that point. With anticipation at a fever pitch, AEW announced in July that *Dynamite* - a weekly two-hour live show on TNT - would premiere on Wednesday, October 2. Aiming to pull out all the stops for the program's debut episode, AEW was in search of one more blockbuster move to really put *Dynamite* over the top.

"We were originally going to debut AEW Dynamite at Madison Square Garden," Matt Jackson told "Machine Gun" Karl Anderson and Luke Gallows on *Talk'n Shop* in 2020.

Though the pilot episode ended up at the Capital One Arena in Washington, D.C., AEW still very much wanted to close the show with a big surprise. Gallows and Anderson - tag team partners in five major promotions across the globe since coming together as members of Bullet Club in 2013 - had expiring contracts with the WWE in the summer of 2019, and they weren't the only ones.

"When we were pitching ideas to have you guys come in, it was not going to be just the two of you," Jackson continued. "There was going to be another person, who I would not name. Let's just say he's another Bullet Club member you may not want to talk about."

Spoiler alert: it was AJ Styles.

Pro Wrestling Illustrated's Wrestler of the Decade for the 2010s, "The Phenomenal" AJ Styles had been the hottest free agent on the market three years earlier when he left New Japan Pro Wrestling and the Bullet Club for the bright lights of WWE. A highly-regarded prospect in the dying days of WCW back in 2001, Styles made a name for himself as one of Ring of Honor's first top talents from 2002-04 before becoming the cornerstone of TNA Wrestling for the next ten years. A five-time world champion during his time in TNA, Styles left the company in 2014 for a return to Ring of Honor and a run in NJPW where he became the new leader of the Bullet Club, taking the reins from the stable's founder, Prince Devitt, who was leaving to become Finn Bálor in WWE.

When Styles was back on the market again in January 2016, WWE was ready to pounce. Hours after *Wrestle Kingdom 10* on January 4, wrestling news outlets began reporting that WWE had come to terms with four of NJPW's biggest stars: Shinsuke Nakamura, Karl Anderson, Luke Gallows, and AJ Styles. To account for his departure, the Bullet Club immediately turned on Styles and positioned Kenny Omega as the faction's new leader. Styles debuted to incredible fanfare three weeks later at the *WWE Royal Rumble* and soon went on to become a two-time WWE champion, winning the title for the first time just nine months into his tenure and carrying the championship for more than a full calendar year during his second reign from November 2017 to November 2018.

After reigning five-hundred-and-eleven days as champion, Styles' WWE contract was up in April of 2019 and AEW had big plans for The Phenomenal One if he wanted to jump ship to the fledgling organization.

"At the end of our match [in the main event of the first episode of *Dynamite*], the three of you [Anderson, Gallows, and Styles] were supposed to jump the guardrail, and we were going to have a Bullet Club reunion," Jackson said.

Karl Anderson confirmed the plans to reporter Ryan Satin in 2020.

"'Machine Gun' music is gonna hit. I'm gonna come out. Gallows comes from behind. We walk to the ring. We 'Too Sweet' The Young Bucks and Kenny," Anderson said. "Turn around, everyone's happy... and then we beat the f--- out of them."

A Bullet Club reunion and subsequent implosion would have been a major shot across the bow - which is why WWE worked extremely hard to prevent it from happening. Just months before his forty-second birthday, Styles was presented with a five-year contract that according to Forbes included a seven-figure downside guarantee. Styles wisely accepted what would likely be the final contract of his in-ring career.

After not-so-coincidentally tagging with Triple H on a June house show loop in Japan, Gallows and Anderson landed $700,000 deals, putting the ixnay on AEW's October plans. Of course, those contracts were not exactly iron-clad, as the WWE wound up releasing Gallows and Anderson the following April as post-*WrestleMania* "budget cuts" amidst the COVID-19 pandemic.

Nonetheless, "The Good Brothers," as they were soon to be known, wouldn't be out of work for long. They showed up in Impact Wrestling in July and won the Impact Tag Team titles in November. Eight weeks later, they made their long-awaited AEW debut, coming to the aid of heel champion Kenny Omega and laying out most of the AEW locker room. Though AJ Styles would never join them, he did win in the end.

"The first guy in this conversation [AJ Styles] buzzed us and said, 'I just got too good of an offer [from WWE] and I would have never got that money without you guys' offer. So, I want to thank you,'" Matt Jackson recalled.

Even though WWE's fear-based 2019 spending spree came back to bite them when the company reorganized and began making major quarterly cutdowns under new President and Chief Revenue Officer

Nick Khan (no relation) in 2020,[135] AEW's mere existence forced an increased recognition of performer value in the industry, which was a tremendously positive change. Still, getting the Bullet Club band back together for one more power struggle angle would have been fun.

* WHAT COULD HAVE HAPPENED *

There may be a quality "what if" discussion to be had regarding The Elite choosing WWE instead of forming AEW, but the reality is that as good as those five men are, they would have been just five more signings for WWE. Big signings. Quality signings. But not company-altering signings at the time. Instead, consider that acquiring the services of AJ Styles would have been a true game-changer for AEW, not just because of what Styles offered between the ropes, but what his signing would have represented for the brand new company.

Before we go any further, we might as well address a standard criticism of free agency in pro wrestling. No, it's not the fact that wrestlers are allegedly independent contractors who somehow still sign company-exclusive contracts that typically don't include healthcare coverage. That's a whole different book. What I'm referring to here is the segment of wrestling fans that throws a hissy fit any time a non-WWE entity brings in a former WWE star. This warped argumentation usually ends up painting the incoming talent as, in so many words, a "WWE reject," which is all sorts of wrong on multiple levels. Please bear in mind that both Ric Flair and Steve Austin wound up in the WWF because they were fired by WCW.

Not only that, the WWE is the premiere professional wrestling company on the planet. It would stand to reason then, that in order to be the premiere professional wrestling company on the planet, WWE likely also employs the premiere professional wrestling *talent*

---

[135] WWE released more than one hundred wrestlers from their contracts from April 2020 through the summer of 2021.

on the planet. So, when that talent suddenly becomes available, it would seem to make a good deal of sense for a wrestling company that is not yet on WWE's level to acquire said talent in hopes of improving that company's own fortunes. Consider this: if you and I were to start a professional football league, would the quality of the game be better if our rosters were filled entirely with guys from the top semi-pro leagues around the country... or with a lot of semi-pro guys *plus* a bunch of players with NFL experience sprinkled throughout the league? Furthermore, if an NFL team releases a player from their contract, should we not pursue them for our league because they're an "NFL reject?" One imagines the Tampa Bay Buccaneers feel fairly good about adding Tom Brady to the roster, even after the New England Patriots decided they didn't want him anymore. Things to ponder, Internet Wrestling Community.

That said, I understand where many - misguided though they may be at times - are coming from. Fans want to see companies create new stars. They *don't* want to see a potential new star lose to an incoming ex-WWE performer because it halts the momentum of the prospect and makes the non-WWE company look "less-than" for its "homegrown" talent being fed to a WWE castoff. In the mental health field, we call this Post-Traumatic TNA Booking Syndrome. My wife, a mental health therapist, denies such a malady exists, and though it may not be in the DSM-5 yet, I assure you that PT TNA BS is very real and very pervasive.

In any case, professional wrestling is a star-driven industry and for AEW to actually take significant market share away from the WWE, then they need more established stars. And for the folks who object, I'll even offer a qualifier: AEW needs established stars who *choose* to be in AEW *instead* of WWE.

Former WWE champions Chris Jericho and Jon Moxley are foundational pieces for AEW because they *chose* to be, not because they *had* to be. Moxley in particular had another decade of high-profile matches and big money ahead of him with the WWE but he turned it down to find something more creatively satisfying with AEW. The same goes for fellow free agents Bryan Danielson – whose final match in WWE was for the Universal championship in the main event of *WrestleMania 37* – and Adam Cole (bay bay) – who ended his WWE tenure as the longest-reigning champion in NXT history.[136] Danielson and Cole each made unannounced debuts in AEW at *All Out* in September 2021 after passing on new contracts with the WWE. They both *chose* AEW.

"I'm one of the few people who loved where I worked before and still left," Danielson said in his post-*All Out* press conference.

While many a skittish fan compared AEW's spending spree in 2021 to that of WCW's twenty-five years earlier, the key difference is that when WWF talent was bolting for WCW in the mid-1990s, they did so for fewer dates and guaranteed pay. AEW may have been able to offer competitive salaries and lighter work schedules, too, but what wooed the likes of CM Punk and Bryan Danielson was the company's vision.

"I am a *wrestler*," Danielson told the capacity crowd after his debut at *All Out 2021*. "I never left wrestling; I took wrestling wherever I went. I said 'wrestling' when I wasn't supposed to say 'wrestling' and now I am here to goddamn wrestle!"

We may never see the Monday Night Wars again, but if you're a wrestling fan who didn't love the summer of 2021, I'm not sure you're a wrestling fan.

That's the level of excitement that would have existed two years earlier had AJ Styles jumped ship to the competition. It's why the

---

[136] Cole had been a champion and main event draw everywhere he went and yet when WWE attempted to re-sign him in August of 2021, Dave Meltzer reported that one of the ideas pitched was for Cole to change his name (to avoid confusion with play-by-play man Michael Cole) and become the *manager* for a directionless Keith Lee. If true, it's difficult to imagine a more egregious misuse of top level talent. And *that* is "undisputed."

company also negotiated with the likes of Edge and Randy Orton in 2019 and why more of those such overtures will continue as additional cornerstone contracts expire.[137]

As far as the pursuit of AJ Styles is concerned, AEW came in with a great pitch and plan; it just didn't work out. Had it, though, booking him effectively still would have come with its share of complications. The original plan for *All Out* on August 31, 2019 was for Kenny Omega to take on Jon Moxley in the payoff match from May's *Double or Nothing* brawl between the two. However, Moxley contracted a staph infection a week before the show and had to pull out of the match. Had that match occurred as scheduled, booking Styles into AEW would have been much cleaner. Without Styles in the fold or the match at *All Out*, Moxley ended up being the surprise at the end of *Dynamite*, resurfacing to attack Omega and set up an unsanctioned bout for the *Full Gear* pay-per-view in November.

Instead of waiting until *Full Gear* though, AEW could have given the Omega versus Moxley match away for free on TNT. While normally offering up pay-per-view main events on basic cable would be a no-no, AEW *had* to hit a home run with the *Dynamite*'s debut episode, and the drawing power of that match alone - followed by the invasion by Styles, Gallows, and Anderson - would have absolutely assured it. It also would have closed out that storyline for the moment and pushed off the upcoming program between The Elite and The Inner Circle for a little while longer. Not to mention, Omega defeated Moxley for the AEW title the following December on *Dynamite*.

If Styles would have made the jump to AEW in 2019, it's interesting to consider what his wrestling legacy might have been. Styles will

---

[137] For as proactive as WWE was with Styles, Orton, and Edge, the company was asleep at the wheel with the contracts of Danielson, Cole, and Kevin Owens. Should any of the company's Four Horsewomen – Becky Lynch, Sasha Banks, Bayley, or Charlotte Flair – ever hit the open market, Tony Khan should be backing up a Brink's truck himself.

almost certainly be remembered as an all-time great in WWE since re-signing long-term. Had he left after his first contract, though, WWE might have only been a blip on a career radar that spanned WCW, ROH, TNA, NJPW, WWE, *and then* AEW. He might not be viewed as a "WWE guy" at all, but rather just one of the world's greatest wrestlers, who shined brightly on every stage imaginable.

* WHAT WOULD HAVE HAPPENED NEXT *

What would an AJ Styles run in AEW look like after the planned Bullet Club breakup on *Dynamite*? The table would be set for a six-man tag team match at *Full Gear* featuring Kenny Omega and The Young Bucks versus Styles and The Good Brothers. With the Omega match behind him, Jon Moxley would shift to a one-on-one bout against Inner Circle up-and-comer Sammy Guevara.

In the real timeline, Omega went on to team up with and win the Tag Team titles with Hangman Page. While it would be a bummer to lose their *Revolution* match against The Young Bucks - which Dave Meltzer called the best tag team match he'd ever seen - Omega would have had his hands full with Styles in the revised timeline.

Bash at the Beach in January would lead off with a four-way tag team match for the No. 1 contendership to the AEW Tag Team titles. The Inner Circle's Santana and Ortiz would win the match by pinning Best Friends, but The Good Brothers and The Young Bucks would steal some spotlight by working together and increasingly getting along. They would still fight when they needed to, but they wouldn't be mortal enemies either. The lack of complete disdain would not be well-received by Styles, who would chastise Gallows and Anderson for having a soft spot for their former stablemates.

That would come back to bite him at *Revolution*, when The Good Brothers would turn their backs on Styles in favor of a reunion with Omega. In defense of The Good Brothers, they didn't have a real motivation to carry such vitriol toward their former Bullet Club comrades. Styles was the one who got kicked out in Japan; Gallows and Anderson left quietly for WWE on their own. This new turn would allow Styles to spin out into true singles competition, while giving The Elite a solid five-man foundation for most of the year.

That said, Hangman Page would still be in the family photo for a little while, teaming alongside The Young Bucks at *Revolution* against PAC and the Lucha Brothers before moving on to a feud with Styles and a singles match with the Phenomenal One at *Double or Nothing*. At *Fight for the Fallen* in July, Styles would win a triple threat match against Omega and Page to headline *All Out 2020* against Jon Moxley for the AEW World championship. Moxley would take that match and Styles would move on to new horizons - perhaps a winter program with Pentagón Jr. and Rey Fénix before matching up with Cody Rhodes for the first time ever in early 2021.

Despite spending the first fifteen years of his career outside of the WWE, there remain so many never-before-seen feuds and potential must-see matches between Styles and the AEW roster. From Brian Cage to Sammy Guevara to Jungle Boy to Darby Allin, there would be no shortage of intriguing matchups and storylines for Styles to sink his teeth into. C'est la vie.

Though adding Styles to the roster would have been huge for AEW, *Dynamite* managed to do fine without him. The debut episode of *Dynamite* averaged 1.409 million viewers, making it TNT's best debut in five years. Less than a year later, TV Guide ranked *Dynamite* among the top sixty programs on television, calling it "an electric jolt to mainstream wrestling, which had gotten creatively stagnant over the last few years."

And therein lies the great success of AEW's failed pursuit of Styles, Gallows, and Anderson in 2019. For the first time in nearly two decades, another billionaire-backed organization had come along to push the top dog to get better, both creatively and in the marketplace - and that is great news for professional wrestling as a whole. And who knows, Styles did leave the door open just a crack when addressing his audience on Twitch in 2020 when he said, "As far as AEW is concerned, never say never... right?"

That's the fascinating, frustrating, beautiful thing about professional wrestling. Plans change, pal.

ACKNOWLEDGMENTS

While it is true that I first fell in love on April 20, 1998, I must also confess that I fell in love again on November 11, 2011 – and because of that, this book exists. November 11, 2011 was the day I first went out on a date with the girl who would become my wife, best friend, and, as fate would have it, book editor. Holly has also been my proud plus-one at countless WWE, NXT, AEW, Ring of Honor, House of Hardcore, and even Great Lakes Championship Wrestling events over the years. She is the Hawk to my Animal, even if she doesn't entirely understand or appreciate the reference.

I would also like to thank my dad, Brent, for staying up late to watch WCW with me and taking me to my first real live wrestling show; my mom, Jan, for always selling when I bring up Mike "The Bull" Gueke; and my brother, Zachary – known in backyard wrestling circles as the ironically named "Little Zack" – for helping me perfect my form on suplexes, powerbombs, and swinging neckbreakers, in addition to tagging along to so many pay-per-views, television tapings, and house shows throughout his youth.

Thank you to Julian, who confirmed for me that all the cool kids indeed did watch wrestling in the 90s; John, Shelby, Dan, and Emily for their constant encouragement and support; my sister, Meghan, for offering feedback (and occasionally confusion) on this book as a non-fan; Sahel Miah for designing my killer cover art; the fine folks at Cagematch.net and The Smackdown Hotel for their exceptional database work that proved to be an immense help in researching for this publication; and every individual who has ever set foot inside the squared circle, or offered their creativity for the entertainment of pro wrestling fans. Thank you.

ABOUT THE AUTHOR

BJ Pickard is a veteran athletics administrator and executive in the sports industry, as well as a lifelong fan of professional wrestling. A graduate of the University of Wisconsin-Eau Claire (B.A.) and University of Washington (M.Ed.), his career has included stops with the Philadelphia 76ers, Arena Football League, and Minnesota Intercollegiate Athletic Conference. In 2018, Pickard was recognized by the College Sports Information Directors of America (CoSIDA) as the recipient of the Best in Nation award for Event Coverage at the record-setting Saint John's University versus University of St. Thomas college football game at Target Field in St. Paul, Minn.

WORKS CITED

In researching the incredible history of this wild artform, I relied a great deal on the outstanding prior work put forth by numerous other authors, reporters, podcasters, and content producers, including most prominently the source material listed below.

Barrasso, Justin. "Pro wrestling's Wolfpac discuss Undertaker in WCW and Their Legacy." Sports Illustrated, 23 April 2015, https://www.si.com/extra-mustard/2015/04/23/wwe-wcw-wolfpac-kevin-nash-scott-hall.

Barrasso, Justin. "Q&A: Steve Corino on leaving ROH for NXT and training WWE's first China-born talent." Sports Illustrated, 11 August 2017, https://www.si.com/extra-mustard/2017/08/11/wwe-steve-corino-nxt-roh.

Barrasso, Justin. "Week in Wrestling: Jimmy Hart on the art of theme songs; Trish Stratus." Sports Illustrated, 11 May 2016, https://www.si.com/extra-mustard/2016/05/11/trish-stratus-jimmy-hart-wwe-new-japan-kazuchika-okada.

Bentley, Ross. "A Former WWE Creative Writer Finally Explained How Hornswoggle Became The Anonymous Raw GM." Yahoo! News, 13 May 2016, https://www.yahoo.com/news/former-wwe-creative-writer-finally-220052413.html.

"The Big Bang." 83 Weeks, created by Conrad Thompson and Eric Bischoff, episode 157, 29 March 2021.

"The Bionic Redneck Gimmick And Other Assorted Tales." The Steve Austin Show Unleashed, created by Steve Austin, 28 May 2017.

Bischoff, Eric. Controversy Creates Cash. Pocket Books, a division of Simon & Schuster, 2006.

CAGEMATCH: The Internet Wrestling Database, https://www.cagematch.net/.

Campbell, Brian. "The Undertaker was set to beat Brock Lesnar at WrestleMania 30 until Vince McMahon changed it." CBSSports.com, 8 June 2020, https://www.cbssports.com/wwe/news/the-undertaker-was-set-to-beat-brock-lesnar-at-wrestlemania-30-until-vince-mcmahon-changed-it/.

Cheap Pops. Written by Mick Foley, WWE Network, 2015.

"CM Punk." The B.S. Report, created by Bill Simmons, 27 July 2011.

"CM Punk." The Art of Wrestling, created by Colt Cabana, episode 226, November 2014.

"Daniel Bryan." Journey to WrestleMania, created by World Wrestling Entertainment, WWE Network, 8 April 2014.

"The Deep...Dive with Rich Fann." PWTorch Dailycast, created by Rich Fann, 26 October 2019.

Dunn, Kevin, director. Stone Cold Steve Austin: The Bottom Line on the Most Popular Superstar of All Time. WWE Network, 2011.

Eck, Kevin. "Q&A with Christopher Daniels." Baltimore Sun, 29 January 2009, https://www.baltimoresun.com/bs-mtblog-2009-01-qa_with_christopher_daniels_1-story.html.

"Edge Pt 2." Talk is Jericho, created by Chris Jericho, 25 December 2013.

Eisner, Jason, director. "The Montreal Screwjob." Dark Side of the Ring, created by Evan Husney and Jason Eisner, season 1, episode 2, Vice Studios Canada, 17 April 2019.

"Eric Bischoff shoots on Hulk Hogan's creative control." After 83 Weeks with Christy Olson, created by Christy Olson, 31 December 2019.

Evans, Guy. NITRO: The Incredible Rise and Inevitable Collapse of Ted Turner's WCW. WCWNitroBook.com, 2018.

"The Failed Relaunch of WCW." WWE Untold, created by World Wrestling Entertainment, season 2, episode 3, WWE Network, 26 May 2019.

Foley, Mick. Have A Nice Day! A Tale of Blood and Sweatsocks. HarperCollins, 1999.

"Goldberg's Streak." WWE Untold, created by World Wrestling Entertainment, season 3, episode 8, WWE Network, 13 December 2020.

Gordon, Jeremy. "Is Everything Wrestling?" The New York Times, 27 May 2016, https://www.nytimes.com/2016/05/27/magazine/is-everything-wrestling.html.

Hart, Bret. Hitman: My Real Life in the Cartoon World of Wrestling. Random House Canada, 2007.

"He Lied to Us!" My World, created by Conrad Thompson and Jeff Jarrett, episode 9, 29 June 2021.

Huffman, Booker T., and Andrew W. Wright. Booker T: My Rise To Wrestling Royalty. Medallion Press, Inc., 2015.

"Invasion PPV (July 2001)." Something To Wrestle With Bruce Prichard, created by Conrad Thompson and Bruce Prichard, episode 111, 20 July 2018.

Jericho, Chris. A Lion's Tale: Around the World in Spandex. New York, Grand Central Publishing, 2007.

"John Cena." Live! With Chris Jericho, created by Chris Jericho, season 1, episode 2, WWE Network, 6 April 2015.

Johnson, Mike. "TNA News and Notes." PWInsider, 6 July 2015, https://www.pwinsider.com/article/94917/tna-news-and-notes.html?p=1.

Kaplan, Don. "Injured Wrestling Star Could Be Out Cold." The New York Post, 25 November 1999, https://nypost.com/1999/11/25/injured-wrestling-star-could-be-out-cold/.

Keller, Wade. "Interview Friday with Kevin Nash." Pro Wrestling Torch, March 2012, https://www.pwtorch.com/artman2/publish/WWE_News_3/article_59453.shtml#.YK6ecZNKjfA.

"Kevin Nash." The Ross Report, created by Jim Ross, episode 162, 22 March 2017.

Konuwa, Alfred. "WWE Criticized For Cutting Hundreds Of Staff Despite Having Over $500 Million In Cash Reserves." Forbes, 16 April 2020, https://www.forbes.com/sites/alfredkonuwa/2020/04/16/wwe-criticized-for-cutting-hundreds-of-staff-despite-having-over-500-million-in-cash-reserves/?sh=78c37bf4119e.

Laboon, Jeff. "Big Bang: The untold story of the WCW pay-per-view that almost happened." WWE.com, 19 February 2016, https://www.wwe.com/article/big-bang-untold-story-wcw-pay-view-almost-happened.

"Life After Wartime." The Monday Night War, created by World Wrestling Entertainment, season 1, episode 20, WWE Network, 13 January 2015.

Linder, Zach. "The complex history of WWE's era of unification." WWE.com, 10 September 2012, https://www.wwe.com/classics/era-of-unification/page-5.

Linder, Zach. "Raw is WCW: The most awkward match ever." WWE.com, 1 July 2013, https://www.wwe.com/classics/raw-is-wcw-the-most-awkward-match-ever.

"#LoveToKnow." Something to Wrestle With Bruce Prichard, created by Conrad Thompson and Bruce Prichard, episode 22, 7 December 2017.

Marvez, Alex. "NFL alum Monty Brown's ring career turns on a heel." South Florida Sun-Sentinel, 16 July 2004, https://www.sun-sentinel.com/news/fl-xpm-2004-07-16-0407140731-story.html.

Melok, Bobby. "Remembering the WCW/ECW Invasion." WWE.com, 13 July 2012, https://www.wwe.com/classics/wcw-ecw-invasion.

Meltzer, Dave. Wrestling Observer Newsletter, 17 November 1997.

Oestriecher, Blake. "WWE Is Breaking The Bank To Re-Sign Its Top Stars." Forbes, 5 October 2019, https://www.forbes.com/sites/blakeoestriecher/2019/10/05/wwe-is-breaking-the-bank-to-re-sign-its-top-stars/?sh=6e0ff2b83d5c.

Paez-Pumar, Luis. "7 'WrestleMania 33' Takeaways: What Comes Next for WWE Superstars." Rolling Stone, 3 April 2017, https://www.rollingstone.com/culture/culture-sports/7-wrestlemania-33-takeaways-what-comes-next-for-wwe-superstars-193863/.

"Paul Heyman." MMA Hour, created by Ariel Helwani, 10 August 2010.

"Rikishi." Something to Wrestle With Bruce Prichard, created by Conrad Thompson and Bruce Prichard, episode 123, 2018.

Satin, Ryan. "Karl Anderson and Doc Gallows Open Up About Talks With All Elite Wrestling." The Sportster, 17 July 2020, https://www.thesportster.com/wrestling/karl-anderson-and-doc-gallows-open-up-about-talks-with-all-elite-wrestling/.

Shoemaker, David. "How to Make a Monster." Grantland, 25 October 2012, http://grantland.com/features/the-beginner-guide-ryback-wwe-superstar-headlining-hell-cell/.

"Shoot Interview with Konnan, Part Two." Created by RF Video, RF Video, 2010.

Spike TV. "Total Nonstop Action (TNA) Wrestling and Spike TV Announce New Multi-Year Deal." 4 October 2007.

"Starrcade 1997." 83 Weeks, created by Conrad Thompson and Eric Bischoff, episode 33, 11 December 2018.

"Starrcade 1998." What Happened When, created by Conrad Thompson and Tony Schiavone, episode 206, 23 December 2020.

"Sting's 1997 in WCW." 83 Weeks, created by Conrad Thompson and Eric Bischoff, episode 103, 31 March 2020.

Storm, Lance. "WrestleMania X-Seven." StormWrestling.com, 5 March 2011, http://www.stormwrestling.com/030511.html.

"Survivor Series 2002." Something to Wrestle With Bruce Prichard, created by Conrad Thompson and Bruce Prichard, episode 74, 7 December 2017.

Thomas, Andrew. "Exclusive Interview with The Alpha Male." TNAWrestling.com, 18 June 2004.

"TNA Impact goes to Monday Nights." 83 Weeks, created by Conrad Thompson and Eric Bischoff, episode 108, 5 May 2020.

"The Undertaker." The Broken Skull Sessions, created by Steve Austin, season 1, episode 1, WWE Network, 22 November 2020.

"The Undertaker clears the air on infamous Brock Lesnar exchange at UFC 121." ESPN MMA, created by Ariel Helwani, ESPN, 13 May 2020.

"Vince McMahon." The Stone Cold Podcast, created by Steve Austin, WWE Network, 1 December 2014.

"The War Begins." The Monday Night War, created by World Wrestling Entertainment, season 1, episode 1, WWE Network, 22 August 2014.

"WCW Top Live Gates." OSW Review, http://oswreview.com/history/wcw-top-live-gates/.

"World Championship Wrestling Talent Database Contract Summary." U.S. District Court Northern District of Georgia, January 2003, https://www.scribd.com/doc/282738951/WCW-Talent-Contract-Database.

World Wrestling Entertainment. "WWE NXT Debuts on SyFy." WWE.com, 16 February 2010.

World Wrestling Entertainment. "WWE® Reports Strong Third Quarter 2020 Results." 29

October 2020, https://corporate.wwe.com/~/media/Files/W/WWE/press-releases/2020/3q20-earnings-pr.pdf.

"WWE Invasion." *83 Weeks*, created by Conrad Thompson and Eric Bischoff, episode 65, 23 July 2019.

"WWE WrestleMania XIX." *Something to Wrestle With Bruce Prichard*, created by Conrad Thompson and Bruce Prichard, episode 92, 16 March 2018.

"The Young Bucks w/ Matt & Nick Jackson." *Talk'n Shop*, created by Karl Anderson and Luke Gallows, episode 24, Patreon, 6 September 2020.

INDEX

1-2-3 Kid. *See* Waltman, Sean
3Live Kru, 123, 198
Abyss, 187-188, 194
The Acolytes, 79, 91, 94
  APA, 153-154, 159, 162
Adams, Brian, 122, 127, 144, 152
  Crush, 39
Aldis, Nick, 325
  Magnus, 218
Ali, Mustafa, 179
The Alliance, 140-143
Allin, Darby, 337
Amazing Red, 131, 217
Ambrose, Dean. *See* Moxley, Jon
Amell, Stephen, 176
America's Most Wanted, 123, 198
American Wolves, 220
Anderson, Arn, 135, 286
Anderson, Karl, 329-330, 335, 337
Anderson, Randy, 46
Andrade, 235
André the Giant, 159, 293, 311
Angle, Kurt, 35, 102-105, 136, 140-142, 145, 147-148, 150-152, 154-155, 157-159, 161-162, 169, 172, 175, 185, 194, 203-204, 216, 218-219, 267
APA. *See* Acolytes
Archer, Lance, 6, 193
  Hoyt, Lance, 198
Aries, Austin, 202, 211, 217-218
Arquette, David, 178
Asuka, 235
A-Train, 164
Austin, Steve "Stone Cold", 11, 15-17, 19-20, 24-25, 28, 30, 32-35, 67, 73, 77-78, 80, 83-86, 88-90, 93-94, 97-107, 119, 131-132, 136, 140-142, 145-151, 153-159, 161-162, 164, 167, 169, 172, 243, 259, 263, 276, 313, 332
Awesome, Mike, 120-121, 126, 128, 138-139, 144, 150-151, 156, 158
Axel, Curtis, 286, *See* Hennig, Joe
Bagwell, Marcus "Buff", 122, 135-136, 149, 156
Baker, Dr. Britt, 328
Bálor, Finn, 235, 240, 292, 296, 306-307, 330
Banks, Sasha, 335
Barrett, Wade, 176, 225-226, 230-231, 234, 236, 238-240, 276, 286

Bastien, Red, 4
Batista, Dave, 171, 175
Bayley, 335
Bearer, Paul, 22, 73-74, 77-78, 81-82, 87, 93-94
Belair, Bianca, 235
Benoit, Chris, 35, 68, 103, 108, 145, 147-150, 169
Best Friends, 328
Beyond the Mat (1999), 4
Big Boss Man, 80-82, 84
Big E, 180
Big Show, 94-95, 139, 142, 148-149, 153-159, 164, 242
  The Giant, 39, 49, 65, 94
Bigelow, Bam Bam, 59, 120, 121, 126, 128, 159
Bischoff, Eric, 2, 15-16, 23, 27, 30, 38, 43-44, 48, 55, 58, 60, 79, 110-113, 116-123, 127, 129-132, 152-153, 155, 157-161, 167-168, 185, 205, 207-214, 221-222
Black, Aleister, 235, 308
Black, PJ. *See* Gabriel, Justin
Blanchard, Tully, 286
Blayze, Alundra. *See* Madusa
Bliss, Alexa, 300
Blitzkrieg, 125
Bockwinkel, Nick, 4
Boogie Knights, 122
Booker T, 68, 119, 128, 132, 135-137, 140-142, 145, 147-148, 152, 167, 172-180
Borash, Jeremy, 188
Borne, Matt, 143
Bourne, Evan, 236
Brandi, Tom, 31
Breezango, 122
Briscoe, Jay, 131
Briscoe, Mark, 131
British Bulldog, 14, 19-20, 24, 33
The Brood, 35, 80-82
The Brothers of Destruction, 5, 31, 147, 149-151, 154, 158, 161-162
Brown, Bob, 137
Brown, D'Lo, 34, 187
Brown, Monty, 183, 185, 188-189, 191-198, 200, 202-204
  Cor Von, Marcus, 192
Bryan, Daniel. See Danielson, Bryan
B-Team, 306-307

Bullet Club, 324, 326, 329-332, 336
Bully Ray, 34, 211, 219
Burke, Elijah, 192
Burks, Antonio. *See* Porter, Montel Vontavious
Cabana, Colt, 131, 245, 247, 266
Cactus Jack. *See* Foley, Mick
Cage, Brian, 120, 337
Calaway, Mark. *See* The Undertaker
Callihan, Sami, 216
Callis, Don, 79, 90-91, 93-94, 118-119
   Cyrus, 118
   The Jackyl, 79, 90-91
Callous, Mark. *See* The Undertaker
Carter, Dixie, 200, 205-206, 210-212, 219
Cena, John, 71, 107, 163, 226-233, 236-237, 243, 246-252, 255-257, 259, 262-265, 267, 269-283, 285-286, 289-291, 299-303, 307-308, 315, 319-320, 322
Cesaro, 235, 282
Charles, Rudy, 188-190, 194-195
Christian, 80, 108, 145, 147, 149, 151, 157, 159, 185, 191-192, 203, 288
Chyna, 21, 126, 130, 149, 199
Ciampa, Tommaso, 216, 324
Clark, Bryan, 122, 127, 144, 152
CM Punk, 107, 131-132, 192, 212, 223, 226, 232, 236, 239, 241-267, 272, 276-277, 279, 280, 282, 289, 315, 334
Cole, Adam, 216, 324-326, 334-335
Cole, Michael, 2, 80, 81, 82, 173, 227, 232, 243, 260, 316, 334
Cor Von, Marcus. *See* Brown, Monty
Corino, Steve, 121, 126-127, 131
Cornette, Jim, 24
The Corporate Ministry. *See* Ministry of Darkness
The Corporation, 84, 93, 98
The Corre, 232, 239
Cottonwood, Eli, 288
Credible, Justin, 139
Cross, Nikki, 235
Crush. *See* Adams, Brian
The Crusher, 4
Cyrus. *See* Callis, Don
Dallas, Bo, 306-307
Daniels, Christopher, 87, 124, 131-132, 176, 197, 200, 203, 214, 218, 328
Danielson, Bryan, 131, 215-218, 220, 222-223, 334-335
   Bryan, Daniel, 181, 215, 222, 226, 229, 233, 235-236, 262, 264-265, 269, 281-282, 289, 299, 303, 307, 316, 319, 323
Dark Order, 308
Dark Side of the Ring, 25
Darkchild, 4
Dawn Marie, 151, 156
Del Rio, Alberto, 248, 251-253, 256-259, 263, 272
Devine, Johnny, 198
D-Generation X, 18, 21, 29-31, 100, 103, 199
DiBiase, Ted, 88-89
Diesel. *See* Nash, Kevin
Dillon, James J., 42, 46
The Disciple, 2
Disco Inferno, 59, 122
Doll, Steve, 37
Douglas, Shane, 120-121
Dragunov, Ilja, 235
Drake, Eli, 252
Dreamer, Tommy, 138, 150, 151-152, 157, 161-162, 192
Drozdov, Darren, 34
Dude Love. *See* Foley, Mick
Dudley Boyz, 135, 139-140, 142, 145, 149-154, 157, 159, 162
   Team 3D, 185, 219
Dudley, D-Von, 219
Dunne, Pete, 235
Edge, 35, 80, 108, 141, 145, 147, 149-151, 154, 157, 161-162, 229-230, 335
El Santo, 124
Elias, 127
The Elite, 176, 326, 335, 337
English, Aiden, 288
Evans, Jack, 125
Evolution, 171, 178
Faarooq. *See* Simmons, Ron
Farmer, Jeff, 40, 52
Fatu. *See* Rikishi
Feinstein, Rob, 131
Fénix, 337
Ferrara, Ed, 110
The Fiend. *See* Wyatt, Bray
The Filthy Animals, 123, 126
Fish, Bobby, 324, 326
Flair, Charlotte, 335
Flair, Ric, 5, 14, 23, 40, 107, 117, 119, 129, 155-158, 161-162, 168, 170-171, 173-174, 177-179, 207, 210, 214, 219, 222, 286, 319, 332
The Flock, 52
Foley, Mick, 4, 32-33, 61, 76, 88, 90, 100-101, 110, 129, 214, 265, 320
   Cactus Jack, 32, 90, 110, 129
   Dude Love, 32, 33, 90

Mankind, 21, 30, 32, 35, 76, 90, 110
Fortune, Chad, 56
The Four Horsemen, 286
Francine, 151
Funk, Terry, 4
Gabriel, Justin, 226, 232, 234, 236-237, 239, 240
  Black, PJ, 240
Gadaski, George "Scrap Iron", 4-5
Gagne, Verne, 15
Gagnon, Jim, 3
Gallows, Luke, 226, 247, 329-331, 335-337
Gangrel, 80
Gargano, Johnny, 216
Generation Me. *See* The Young Bucks
The Giant. *See* Big Show
Giant González, 312
GLOW (2017), 324
Goldberg, Bill, 2-3, 25, 47, 50-71, 107, 117-120, 127-129, 132, 142, 158-159, 161-162, 172, 175, 179, 216, 239, 299, 311, 321
Goldust, 20, 282
  Rhodes, Dustin, 328
The Good Brothers, 331, 336
Gordon, Flip, 176
Grand Master Sexay, 101
Gueke, Mike "The Bull", 4
Guerrera, Juventud, 2, 124-127
Guerrero, Chavo Jr., 124, 148-149
Guerrero, Eddie, 11, 35, 68, 104, 108, 123, 131, 147
Guevara, Sammy, 336-337
Gunn, Billy, 139, 198-200
  The Outlaw, 198-199
Hall, Scott, 16, 18, 23, 25, 37-40, 42, 47-48, 50, 59, 61, 66-68, 79, 119, 142, 160, 187, 196, 199, 208, 214, 328
  Razor Ramon, 16, 23, 37-38, 114, 287
Hannibal, 4, 100
The Hardy Boyz, 135, 142, 145, 154-155, 157, 162, 220, 307
Hardy, Jeff, 108, 147-149, 151-153, 187, 191, 203, 207, 218-219, 287, 293, 307
Hardy, Matt, 147, 149-150, 293, 306-307
Harper, Luke. *See* Lee, Brodie
Harris, Chris, 123
Harris, Husky. *See* Wyatt, Bray
The Hart Dynasty, 234, 236
The Hart Foundation, 14, 19, 24
Hart, Bret, 2, 13-36, 39, 43, 45, 48-49, 51-52, 63, 71, 207, 221, 227, 264
Hart, Owen, 11, 14, 19-20, 24, 33, 35, 97, 106
Hart, Stu, 13
Hayashi, Kaz, 124, 148
The Headshrinkers, 101
Hebner, Earl, 23, 25
Heels (2021), 177
Heenan, Bobby "The Brain", 4, 60
Helms, Shane, 124, 126-127
  Helms, Gregory, 144, 148, 156
Hennig, Curt, 14, 42, 286
  Mr. Perfect, 159, 161, 286
Hennig, Joe, 285
  Axel, Curtis, 231, 306-307
  McGillicutty, Michael, 285-286
Hennig, Larry, 4, 286
Henry, Mark, 34, 236, 272
Hero, Chris, 266
Heyman, Paul, 112, 117, 131, 135, 139, 150, 160, 212-220, 222-223, 244, 314-315, 320
Hodge, Danny, 110
Hogan, Hulk, 2-3, 8, 10, 16, 37, 39-40, 42-52, 57, 59-62, 65, 67, 70-71, 79, 118-119, 128-129, 142, 160-162, 164, 205-214, 219, 221-222, 244, 249, 274-275, 311, 313
Holly, Bob "Hardcore", 139, 149
Holly, Crash, 147
Holly, Molly, 125, 147, 157
Hollywood Blonds, 155
Homicide, 131
Hornswoggle, 228
Hudson, Scott, 118-119, 135
The Inner Circle, 335-336
Irwin R. Schyster. *See* Rotunda, Mike
Ivory, 157
Jackson, Ezekiel, 232, 236
The Jackyl. *See* Callis, Don
Jacqueline, 157
James, B.G.. *See* Road Dogg
James, Mickie, 126
  Laree, Alexis, 126, 130-131
Janela, Joey, 328
Jannetty, Marty, 14
Jarrett, Jeff, 32-35, 120-121, 130, 143, 183-184, 186-188, 190-193, 195-196, 198, 201, 203, 214
Jarrett, Jerry, 9, 183
Jazz, 126, 130, 157, 159, 162
Jericho, Chris, 2, 12, 35, 64-65, 67-68, 70, 108, 123, 137-140, 142, 148-151, 153-162, 167, 169, 179, 229-230, 251, 260-261, 278, 291, 303, 328-329, 333
Jindrak, Mark, 122, 126, 128, 139, 144,

149, 162
Jungle Boy, 337
Kane, 22, 28, 30-31, 73-75, 77-78, 81, 87, 104-105, 138-140, 142, 152, 159, 170-171, 236, 259, 262, 264, 266, 272-274, 276, 287-289, 305, 322
Yankem, Isaac D.D.S, 287
Kanyon, Chris, 120, 126-127, 139, 144, 148-149, 151
Kazarian, Frankie, 176, 200, 214, 217, 328
Keibler, Stacy, 126, 156
Kendrick, Brian, 131, 216
Khan, Nick, 332
Khan, Tony, 327-328, 335
Kid Kash, 198
Kid Romeo, 119, 124, 126-127
Kidman, Billy, 123-124, 127, 132, 144, 148-149, 152-153, 156-157, 161-162
Killings, Ron, 123, 186-187, 199
R-Truth, 123, 243, 253, 260, 263
Kingston, Kofi, 179-182, 233, 242, 256, 258, 260, 289
The Kliq, 17-18, 21, 252
Knight, Dennis. *See* Mideon
Koloff, Ivan, 311
Konnan, 123-124, 191
Kowalski, Killer, 4-5
Kozlov, Vladimir, 236, 286
KroniK, 122-123, 126, 154, 156, 158, 161
La Parka, 127
L.A. Park, 124
Lana, 264
Laree, Alexis. *See* James, Mickie
Lashley, Bobby, 212
Laurinaitis, John, 112, 245, 248, 252, 263
Lawler, Jerry, 81, 118, 226, 243, 248
Layfield, John "Bradshaw", 79, 91, 139
Lee, Brodie, 11, 304
Harper, Luke, 289, 303-306
Lee, Keith, 324, 326, 334
Legion of Doom, 20
LeRoux, Lash, 124
Lesnar, Brock, 69, 107, 132, 163, 168, 174, 177, 213, 223, 244, 273-274, 276, 280, 303, 311-312, 314-321
Lethal, Jay, 217
Li, Xia, 235
Lita, 147, 149, 151, 154, 156-157, 159, 162
London, Paul, 131
Low Ki, 131
Lucha Brothers, 328, 337

Luger, Lex, 16, 39-41, 49, 51, 61, 122
Lynch, Becky, 181, 235, 264, 335
Lynn, Jerry, 147
Mabel, 39, 79
Viscera, 79, 94
Madusa, 23, 126
Magnus. *See* Aldis, Nick
Malenko, Dean, 35
Malone, Karl, 53
Mankind. *See* Foley, Mick
Mannibal, 4, 100
Marella, Santino, 236, 286
The Mauler, 37
McDevitt, Jerry, 114
McGillicutty, Michael. *See* Hennig, Joe
McIntyre, Drew, 235-236
McMahon, Linda, 9, 85
McMahon, Shane, 84, 88, 115-116, 133-134, 139, 142-143, 146-147, 150, 152
McMahon, Stephanie, 82-83, 88, 95, 139, 168, 220
McMahon, Vince, 8-9, 14-15, 21-24, 26-27, 30, 32, 76, 78, 81, 85, 87, 91, 94-95, 98, 100, 114-115, 131-133, 135, 139-141, 143, 145-147, 150, 152-153, 159, 161, 164, 168, 171, 178, 180, 184, 206, 212, 220-221, 225, 227-228, 244-246, 251, 253, 271, 299, 312, 314-316, 318, 323
Mr. McMahon, 30, 32, 80-82, 84-86, 92-93, 106, 146, 180, 228, 246, 248-249, 255-256, 257, 259, 276
McMahon, Vince Sr., 180
Meltzer, Dave, 22, 47, 125, 127, 297, 315, 324-325, 327, 336
Mercy, Waylon. *See* Spivey, Dan
Michaels, Shawn, 10-11, 13-15, 17-25, 27-32, 35, 51, 75, 107, 163, 169, 179, 207, 216, 262, 264, 319
Midajah, 126
Mideon, 79, 94
Knight, Dennis, 78, 79
Miller, Ernest, 126, 128
Millionaire's Club, 134
Ministry of Darkness, 73, 79-80, 83-84, 90-95
Corporate Ministry, 84, 86, 88
Miss Elizabeth, 60
The Miz, 215, 232, 234, 236-237, 243, 249-250, 253, 256, 260, 263, 277, 299, 315
Monsoon, Gorilla, 15
Moose, 193
Morrison, John, 236
Motor City Machine Guns, 216

Moxley, Jon, 193, 216, 328-329, 333, 335-337
  Ambrose, Dean, 266, 279, 281, 291, 303, 306, 322, 328
Mr. Perfect. *See* Hennig, Curt
Mulligan, Blackjack, 285
Murphy, Buddy, 235
Mysterio, Rey Jr., 123-125, 127, 132, 159, 161-162, 175, 242, 249-250, 256, 257
Nakamura, Shinsuke, 235, 330
Nash, Kevin, 2, 16, 18, 23, 38-39, 40, 42, 48, 50, 55, 57-69, 79, 92, 118-119, 129, 142, 160, 172, 179, 188, 196, 199, 208, 214, 251, 252-253, 311
  Diesel, 16, 23, 38, 58, 114, 251
  Natural Born Thrillers, 119, 122, 126, 144, 148, 153-154
Neidhart, Jim "The Anvil", 14, 19-20, 24, 33
Neidhart, Natalya, 235
Neville, Adrian. *See* PAC
New Age Outlaws, 199-200, 266
The New Breed, 192
New World Order (nWo), 18, 39-43, 48-49, 57-58, 61-62, 67, 79, 138, 160, 271, 279
  nWo 2000, 62
  Wolfpac, 50, 58, 62
The Nexus, 215, 229-234, 236-240, 242, 276, 286
Noble, Jamie, 124, 148
O'Haire, Sean, 122-123, 127, 135, 139, 144, 148-149, 158, 162
O'Neil, Titus, 238
O'Reilly, Kyle, 324-326
Okada, Kazuchika, 10, 47, 324
Okerlund, Gene, 38
Omega, Kenny, 10, 47, 176, 324, 326-331, 335-337
Ortiz, 336
Orton, Randy, 57, 75, 163, 169, 171, 175, 179, 225, 230-232, 242, 281, 287, 289, 291-292, 300-301, 305-306, 308, 313, 335
Otunga, David, 226, 236-237, 239
The Outlaw. *See* Gunn, Billy
The Outsiders, 39, 49, 51, 52, 67, 124, 161-162
Owens, Kevin, 107, 235, 324, 335
PAC, 328, 337
  Neville, Adrian, 176, 267, 328
Page, Adam "Hangman", 325-328, 336-337
Page, Diamond Dallas, 49, 53, 57, 63-65, 67, 118-119, 127, 129, 134, 138, 140, 142, 148-153, 156-158, 161-162, 164, 188, 196, 198
Paige, 11
Palumbo, Chuck, 122-123, 127, 135, 139, 144, 148-149
Patrick, Nick, 45
Patterson, Pat, 4
Pentagón Jr., 337
Pillman, Brian, 11, 19-20, 155
Piper, Roddy "Rowdy", 2
Poffo, Angelo, 4
Poffo, Lanny, 163
Porter, Montel Vontavious
  Burks, Antonio, 187
Prichard, Bruce, 82, 87, 100, 171, 173, 174-175, 177
Priest, Damian, 324, 326
  Punishment Martinez, 326
Prince Devitt. *See* Finn Bálor
The Prophecy, 87
Psychosis, 124, 127
Punishment Martinez. *See* Priest, Damian
Race, Harley, 4, 174
Raven, 2, 52, 56, 139, 147, 150-153, 156, 187, 200-201
Razor Ramon. *See* Hall, Scott
The Real Americans, 282
Regal, William, 35, 149, 154-156, 159, 288
Reigns, Roman, 223, 263, 266, 278-279, 281, 299-300, 305-307, 318, 321-322
Rhodes, Cody, 176, 236, 282, 325-328, 337
  Stardust, 176
Rhodes, Dustin. *See* Goldust
Rhodes, Dusty, 4, 121, 138
Rhyno, 139-140, 147-148, 150-152, 156-157, 203, 291
Richards, Stevie, 150
Ricochet, 216, 326
Riddle, Matt, 326
Rikishi, 101-102, 105, 108, 287
  Fatu, 101, 287
  Sultan, 287
  The Sultan, 101
Ripley, Rhea, 235
Road Dogg, 123, 187, 198
  James, B.G., 199-200
Robbie E, 217
Roberts, Jake, 88-89, 93-94, 312
Roberts, Justin, 215, 226
The Rock, 11, 30, 32, 35, 61, 67, 77, 93, 98-101, 103-105, 110, 119, 135, 137,

141-142, 145-146, 152-155, 157-158, 160-162, 164, 167-168, 172, 180, 243-244, 246, 258, 262-265, 269, 272-274, 276, 280, 291, 314
Rock 'n' Roll Express, 33
The Rockers, 14
Rodman, Dennis, 53
Rogers, Buddy, 180
Rollins, Seth, 240, 242, 266, 279, 281, 297, 298, 301, 306-307, 321, 323
Roode, Bobby, 196, 198, 203, 211, 214, 218-219
Ross, Jim, 62, 77, 83, 88, 91, 134-135, 211-212
Rotunda, Mike, 285
Schyster, Irwin R., 285
Rowan, Erick, 288-289, 291, 303-304
R-Truth. *See* Killings, Ron
Rude, Rick, 21, 24
Rusev, 303
Russo, Vince, 35, 88, 110, 116, 178, 184, 194, 211
Ryback, 238-239, 262, 280
Sheffield, Skip, 230, 236, 238-239
Ryder, Bob, 183-184
Ryder, Zack, 273
Sabin, Chris, 211
Sabu, 186, 192
Sammartino, Bruno, 181, 311
Samoa Joe, 5, 131, 194, 197, 202-203, 214, 217, 241, 306, 324
Samu, 101
Sandman, 157, 192
Santana, 336
Sapolsky, Gabe, 131, 215-216
Saturn, Perry, 36, 134
Savage, Randy, 2, 16, 39, 42, 50-52, 68, 163-164
Savio Vega, 88
Saxton, Byron, 180
Schiavone, Tony, 37, 110, 118-119
Scorpio Sky, 176, 252, 328
Scotty 2 Hotty, 101
Severn, Dan, 186
Shamrock, Ken, 20, 29, 82-83, 199
Shamrock, Ryan, 83
Sheamus, 228, 230, 234, 236-238, 265, 290
Sheffield, Skip. *See* Ryback
Shelley, Alex, 202
The Shield, 262, 266-267, 279-282, 290, 306, 328
Sid, 19, 69, 71
Simmons, Ron, 32, 174
Faarooq, 79, 91, 139

Skipper, Elix, 119, 124, 126, 127
Slater, Heath, 69, 226, 229, 232, 234, 236-237, 239, 291
Snuka, Jimmy "Superfly", 312
Spanky. *See* Kendrick, Brian
Spivey, Dan, 287
Mercy, Waylon, 287-288, 294
Stamp, Dennis, 4
Stasiak, Shawn, 122, 126, 128, 133, 139, 143
Steiner, Scott, 51, 61, 70-71, 119, 127, 129, 132, 149-152, 154, 156-159, 161-162, 171, 178-179, 204, 214
Stevens, Ray, 4
Sting, 5, 37, 39-52, 59, 65, 68-69, 87, 117, 119-120, 127-129, 132, 137-138, 142, 164, 185, 203, 210, 212, 214, 219, 303, 304
Storm, James, 123, 203, 211, 214, 218-219
Storm, Lance, 108, 120-121, 126, 128, 133-134, 138-139, 144, 149-154, 157-159, 161
Storm, Toni, 235
Straight Edge Society, 242
Stratus, Trish, 151, 154, 157, 161-162
Striker, Matt, 192, 226
Strong, Roderick, 324
Strowman, Braun, 300-301, 304-305, 307-308
Styles, AJ, 124, 131-132, 187, 194, 197-199, 203, 207, 214, 217-218, 221-222, 235, 306, 308, 329, 330-332, 335-338
Styles, Joey, 118
The Sultan. *See* Rikishi
Sunny, 19
Super Crazy, 124, 127
Swagger, Jack, 282
Swann, Rich, 216
Syxx. *See* Waltman, Sean
Tajiri, Yoshihiro, 124, 127, 150-151, 153, 158, 161
Tanaka, Masato, 255
Tarver, Michael, 226, 236, 238
Taylor, Chuck, 216
Tazz, 139, 151, 157
Team 3D. *See* Dudley Boyz
Tenay, Mike, 119
Test, 141
The Crow (1994), 41
The Fiend. *See* Wyatt, Bray
Thomas, Andrew, 190, 195-196
Thorn, Kevin, 192
Too Cool, 108

Tozawa, Akira, 216
Triple H, 18, 21, 30, 35, 88, 90, 99-100, 102-103, 105, 107, 138, 147-150, 158-159, 161-162, 167-175, 178-180, 191, 241, 249-250, 252-254, 257-263, 265, 272, 281, 298, 303, 306, 315, 326, 327, 331
    Hunter Hearst Helmsley, 21, 33, 174
Trytan, 197
Turner, Ted, 9, 15, 38, 114-115, 312
Two Dudes with Attitudes, 179
Tyson, Mike, 98
The Ultimate Warrior, 10, 89, 239
The Undertaker, 10, 15, 19-20, 22, 25, 28-31, 73-95, 107, 134-135, 140, 142, 152, 157, 159, 164, 169, 171, 236, 261-262, 264-265, 291, 303-305, 311-322
    Calaway, Mark, 92, 317
    Callous, Mark, 10
The Usos, 101, 236, 282
Vachon, Mad Dog, 4
Vader, 29, 138, 174
Vampiro, 87
Van Dam, Rob, 35, 108, 121, 126, 128, 132, 138, 142, 150-153, 155, 157, 159, 161-162, 169-170, 192, 214, 217, 219, 239
Venis, Val, 34
Vick, Katie, 171
Viking Raiders, 324
    War Machine, 324
Viscera. *See* Mabel
Waltman, Sean, 18, 35, 42, 197, 199, 208, 214
    1-2-3 Kid, 197
    Syxx, 197
    X-Pac, 34, 149, 151, 154, 157-158, 197
War Machine. *See* Viking Raiders
Watts, Bill, 4, 15, 174
Williams, Doug, 217
Wilson, Torrie, 126, 156
Windham, Barry, 286
Windham, Kendall, 286
Women's Revolution, 9, 125, 130
Woods, Xavier, 180
Wrestling with Shadows (1998), 25
Wright, Alex, 122
The Wyatt Family, 282, 288-290, 305
Wyatt, Bray, 75, 231, 274, 282, 285, 287-294, 296-297, 300-308, 319, 322
    The Fiend, 75, 294-301, 304, 306-308, 322

Harris, Husky, 231, 285-287, 294
X-Pac. *See* Waltman, Sean
Yang, Jimmy "Wang", 124, 148
Yankem, Isaac D.D.S.. *See* Kane
Yeaton, Mark, 147, 226
Yokozuna, 312
The Young Bucks, 10, 176, 325-328, 331, 336-337
    Jackson, Matt, 120, 326, 329, 331
    Jackson, Nick, 326
Young, Darren, 226, 230, 236-238
Young, Eric, 196, 217
Zayn, Sami, 266-267, 324
Zbyszko, Larry, 37, 43, 48
Ziggler, Dolph, 236, 256, 260

Printed in Great Britain
by Amazon